MONTH-BY-MONTH GARDENING

ARIZONA, NEVADA & NEW MEXICO

Brimming with creative inspiration, how-to projects, and useful information to enrich your everyday life, Quarto Knows is a favorite destination for those pursuing their interests and passions. Visit our site and dig deeper with our books into your area of interest: Quarto Creates, Quarto Cooks, Quarto Homes, Quarto Lives, Quarto Drives, Quarto Explores, Quarto Gifts, or Quarto Kids.

First Published in 2016 by Cool Springs Press, an imprint of The Quarto Group,
100 Cummings Center, Suite 265-D, Beverly, MA 01915, USA.
T (978) 282-9590 F (978) 283-2742
QuartoKnows.com

Cool Springs Press titles are also available at discount for retail, wholesale, promotional, and bulk purchase. For details, contact the Special Sales Manager by email at specialsales@quarto.com or by mail at The Quarto Group, Attn: Special Sales Manager, 100 Cummings Center, Suite 265-D, Beverly, MA 01915, USA.

ISBN: 978-1-59186-670-1

Library of Congress Cataloging-in-Publication Data

Names: Soule, Jacqueline A., author.
Title: Arizona, Nevada & New Mexico month-by-month gardening / Jacqueline Soule.
Other titles: Arizona, Nevada and New Mexico month by month gardening
Description: Minneapolis, MN : Cool Springs Press, 2016. | Includes index.
Identifiers: LCCN 2016019824 | ISBN 9781591866701 (sc)
Subjects: LCSH: Gardening--Arizona. | Gardening--Nevada. | Gardening--New Mexico.
Classification: LCC SB453.2.A6 S68 2016 | DDC 635.09791--dc23
LC record available at https://lccn.loc.gov/2016019824

Acquiring Editor: Bryan Trandem
Project Manager: Alyssa Bluhm
Art Director: Brad Springer
Layout: Danielle Smith-Boldt

MONTH-BY-MONTH GARDENING

ARIZONA, NEVADA & NEW MEXICO

What to Do Each Month to Have a Beautiful Garden All Year

JACQUELINE A. SOULE

Dedication

For Paul.

Acknowledgments

It takes a great deal of effort to craft a book of this scope. Massive research had to be done to ensure accuracy for all the special little nooks and crannies of climate across our extensive region. Research included books and databases, as well as helpful comments from an array of gardening friends in various USDA zones.

I want to thank the many people who contributed with their knowledge, plus the ones who stood on the sidelines and cheered me on. I need to acknowledge the folks who helped me become a better photographer, but especially the people who helped me become a better writer. In alphabetic order by first name: Ann McCormick, Billie Brownell, Chad Borseth, Claire Splan, Cynthia Baker, Denise Schreiber, Dennis Swartzell, Edith Isidoro-Mills, Ellen Zachos, Helen Stone, Jack Kelly, Jennifer Bartley, Jo Ellen Meyers Sharp, John Bagnasco, Joyce Rychener, Justine Hernandez, Ken Coppola, Kirk Ryan Brown, Koibeatu Kat, Louise Clarke, Mark Dimmitt, Mark Turner, Mary-Kate Mackey, Matt Johnson, Nan Sterman, Nicholas Staddon, Pat Stone, Paul Meyer, Peter Gierlach, Randy Schultz, Sally Ferguson, Scott Aiken, Steve Biggs, and Sylvia Gordon. Musical inspiration was provided by Eddie Rhoades, Fish & the Guppies, John O'Conner of Eko, and Ken Rhoads.

I wish to thank so many members of the Garden Writers Association (GWA), starting with the judges in 1986, who thought my garden writing was worthy of an award and got me started down this path as a career instead of a hobby. Thanks go out to current GWA members, many of whom helped with advice, clarification, and tidbits of knowledge gleaned from their gardens across the Southwest. What a wonderful corner of the world we live in—with awesome sunsets too.

Kinja and Shira did their share of helping, but this book would not be possible without the love, support, and endless patience of my beloved Paul.

Contents

Introduction

Welcome to growing a garden in one of the most fascinating and diverse places on earth. First, there is the geographic region itself, with strongly up-thrusting mountains, windswept plateaus, and canyons and valleys that reach down into the dawn of earth's prehistory. We have elevations ranging from below sea level in Nevada to some of the tallest peaks in the lower 48 states, such as the snow-capped San Francisco Peaks near Flagstaff, Arizona, and the Sangre de Cristo Range in New Mexico. Along with this expansive geography in the Southwest comes vast climate variation—as much change as you could see in a journey from the tip of Florida to the mountains of Maine.

Our strongly up-thrusting mountains lead to wide differences in precipitation. Rainfall averages vary from 0.5 to 50 inches in a year, depending on location. Precipitation varies *wildly* as well, from drought to snow, sleet, hail, torrential monsoon downpours, and, all too seldom, gentle soaking rains.

Two things that are the same across the Southwest are our low average humidity and our alkaline soils. Both of these provide the major challenge to gardeners who, like so many of you reading this, have moved here from "back East," as we say. The solution is *not* to simply put more water on your plants. Southwestern gardening requires some new practices and new habits for the transplanted gardener.

Despite the challenges, the Southwest is a wonderful place to garden. Wherever you live here, there is a vast palate of native and drought-adapted plants that will thrive in your soil and climate—many of them yielding yummy edibles. Wonderfully, in most of our area you can get outdoors and relax in your garden almost all year long.

This book is crafted to help you enjoy your garden by eliminating the gardening guesswork. Knowing the when and how of gardening in our unique area will help you become a successful Southwestern gardener. With this guide to help, your gardening efforts should become more rewarding—saving you time and money—while making gardening an immensely enjoyable and vastly rewarding hobby.

BUILDING YOUR OUTDOORS LIVINGSCAPE

Across the Southwest, we average 300 sunny days per year. With all that sun, our outdoor spaces can easily become additional living areas, adding entire rooms to our home. A patio off the kitchen can become a breakfast nook, while a cozy garden swing in a shady area can be the reading room. A big back porch with an outdoor ceiling fan can be the perfect spot for relaxing with friends and family during summer evenings.

Whether you have lived in your home for a long time or just moved in, it is useful to evaluate your space and how you use it. Using outdoor areas calls for some planning of space use prior to putting in new plants and installing pathways.

PLANT WITH A PLAN

I have visited any number of gardens where owners tell me, "I wish I had planned this better." You can get away with spontaneously planting annuals and even smaller perennials, but larger plants and garden structures need planning. Trees, shrubs, large succulents, raised bed vegetable gardens, irrigation, lighting, fire pits, plant arbors, greenhouses, and paths all require planning prior to spending time and money.

A site plan allows you to better map out features you wish to add to the landscape.

Some things are fairly obvious. You don't want prickly things too close to pathways. Often used plants, such as herbs and vegetables, should be easily accessible for care and harvest. Put the grilling area close to the kitchen. Plan for easy storage of gardening tools. Don't forget to check your views from inside the house while you are at it. There are so many lovely vistas to be treasured in the Southwest, it is a shame to block them with an inadvertent planting.

MICROCLIMATES

A microclimate is a localized area where the climate differs from the surrounding area. In gardening, the term generally refers to small areas in the yard where plants will experience conditions different from the rest of the yard.

No matter where you live, you can use microclimates within your yard to help plants survive either heat or cold. For example, Las Vegas is considered too hot for violets to survive the summer. Try planting them on the cool, shady north side of the house, where the cooler microclimate there will help them survive.

KEEP RECORDS

A garden journal is a very helpful tool. Keeping records about both your plants and your gardening practices helps you in two ways. First, it makes it very easy to keep track of your successes and triumphs and repeat them. Second, it helps you note any failures or mistakes and avoid repeating them. Additionally, certain vegetables need to be rotated to a different patch of garden soil each year. Record keeping helps you keep track as the years go by.

START WITH YOUR SOIL

Perhaps the biggest challenge awaiting any gardener in our three states is the soil itself. Most urban or suburban yards begin as a patch of land scraped down or back-filled and then compacted so the building site is firm and level. Newer constructions may have a slope to the yard to aid in drainage, but all too often a poor grade allows rain to run over the patio.

Throughout this book you'll find tips for building better soil. Be warned: this is not a one-and-done action. Improving your soil is a constant, ongoing process. Not only are our base soils alkaline; in most cases our tap water is alkaline, too. Although you may attain the perfect pH in your garden, because tap water is alkaline it will gradually shift the soil back towards alkaline, meaning you have to amend the garden again. Planting only natives is not necessarily the solution. Many native plants, including succulents, prefer a soil that is not excessively alkaline.

Along with our alkaline soils, the Southwest has a problem common in all areas of low rainfall: *caliche*. Caliche is a form of sedimentary rock—a hardened deposit or layer of calcium carbonate that forms beneath the soil. This calcium carbonate cements together other materials, including gravel, sand, clay, and silt. Caliche is generally light colored and forms in layers anywhere from a few inches to a few feet thick; multiple layers can exist in a single location. Also called hardpan or calcrete, *caliche* is a Spanish word based on the Latin *calx*, meaning lime.

Caliche forms when minerals are leached from the upper layer of the soil and accumulate in layers below the surface, often called caliche beds. Plants also contribute to the formation of caliche. As the roots take up water, they leave behind the dissolved calcium carbonate, which hardens into caliche.

Caliche causes three problems for the gardener. First, an impermeable caliche layer prevents water from draining properly, leading to waterlogged soils, which drown roots. Second, caliche beds prevent plant roots from growing deeply into the soil, which means the roots have a limited supply of nutrients, water, and space, preventing the roots from developing normally. Large trees may not adequately form anchoring roots and can be easily toppled by a heavy wind. Third, caliche beds, even ten feet down, will still cause the soil above them to be alkaline. Alkaline soil, along with the calcium carbonate from the caliche, can block plants from taking up nutrients from the soil, especially iron. Throughout this book, dealing with the Southwest's alkaline and caliche-laden soils is discussed.

One aspect of soil to consider is the life in the soil. Soils are teaming with all manner of microscopic

Caliche forms in layers a few inches to a few feet thick, and multiple layers can exist in a single location.

life forms: bacteria, algae, fungi, animals, and even tiny mosses. Sunbaked and barren-looking desert soil is alive too; although it might be dormant, a chance rain shower can activate all the microscopic forms of life that abound on our planet.

PLANT

There is more to planting in the Southwest than digging a hole and plunking in your plant. Our soils are notoriously lacking in the organic matter (also called *humus*) needed for garden plants to thrive. Organic matter is needed everywhere but in your most heavily amended beds.

Time of planting is key. Mother's Day in Phoenix may look like an ideal time to plant a rose bush, but it will be 100°F within two weeks; meanwhile in Santa Fe it is a great time to plant container roses. The opposite also applies; Thanksgiving in

HERE'S HOW

TO DETERMINE SOIL TEXTURE

Soil is more than just dirt. It has texture. Soil textures are classified based on three main components: sand, clay, and loam. Good soil for plants will also include organic matter, such as decaying leaves and old twigs. This provides nutrients for the plants, helps aerate the soil, helps our Southwestern soils be more acidic (which plants prefer), and provides substrate for all the soil microbes that help plants grow in ways we are just beginning to understand.

- **Clay soils** easily become waterlogged, drowning the roots of plants. Clay soils are highly alkaline, which few plants tolerate. Add compost to acidify the soil and some coarse sand to promote drainage and air retention in the soil. Some gardeners have also found success adding the smaller grade of pea gravel. Don't simply add sand: clay plus sand is called mortar (left).
- **Sandy soils** will drain quickly, the water quickly sinking below the level that plant roots can reach. Plants will dry out rapidly. Add compost to sandy soil to improve the water-holding capacity of the soil (right).
- **Loamy soils** are just right. Southwest soils are very rarely loamy; it is what we are trying to turn our garden soils into (center).

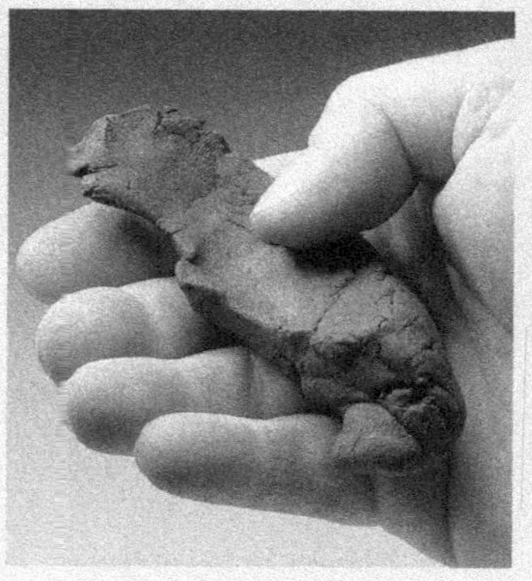

Santa Fe is not the time to plant mums, but it is in Phoenix. We live in a land of contrasts.

Recommended species and cultivars will vary with the zone you live in. Your cooperative extension service is paid for with your tax dollars, so do seek their advice.

Planting a blend of plants of various heights can create private nooks where you can sit and enjoy your outdoor space.

CARE

Plants are living things. Lopping off plant material willy-nilly can lead to unintended consequences—at best, an unsightly plant; at worst, a mesquite tree that drips sap onto your car for the rest of its life. Proper techniques for careful pruning and shaping your plants to grow to their best potential are discussed throughout the book.

A large part of plant care is nurturing the underground half of the plant we can't see. This is done with the invaluable help of mulch.

WATER

Face it, water is an issue throughout the West, not just in our three states. Your local government may be urging you to *xeriscape* your yard. A xeriscape is not a "zero-scape"! A xeriscape can be truly lovely, and is easy to do following the seven principles of xeriscaping described in Here's How to Understand Xeriscaping.

HERE'S HOW

MULCH HELPS THE LANDSCAPE

Mulch serves many purposes, including:

- Reduces soil moisture evaporation
- Ensures a more even soil moisture supply
- Reduces or prevents weed growth
- Insulates soil from extreme temperatures
- Prevents soil from splashing on plants and structures
- Reduces fruit and vegetable rots
- Reduces soil crusting
- Reduces soil erosion
- Reduces soil compaction
- Protects plants from freezing
- Improves neatness of the garden and landscape

Organically based mulches, such as cedar bark, wood chips, palo verde or pine needles, or wheat or sorghum straw, are all preferred over inorganic rock mulches, which trap and hold in excessive heat.

Xeriscape principles include an oasis zone where you can site a burbling fountain.

Every living thing needs water. Even if all your plants are low-water, drought-adapted native plants, your landscape will have a greater plant density than a similarly sized area in the wild, and hence greater water needs. Furthermore, the windows and walls of you home reflect light and heat in a manner generally not experienced by plants in the wild.

Irrigating your garden while conserving water is easy once you learn the needs of the specific plants you are growing. Passive rainwater harvesting with berms and basins (plant wells) can also tremendously reduce the need for added irrigation.

FERTILIZE

According to the older agriculture text books, there are nineteen elements (often called minerals) that plants need for growth and maintenance. In recent years, they found that there are eight additional elements needed in trace amounts for most plants to thrive.

HERE'S HOW

TO UNDERSTAND XERISCAPING

There are seven basic xeriscape principles. Even if you don't plan on xeriscaping your yard, these are all excellent gardening practices for the Southwest.

1. **Plan your design.** Design your garden so the area you use most is an oasis area. Plant heavy water users, such as lawn and roses, in the oasis zone where you can easily enjoy them.
2. **Select adapted plants.** Look for plants suitable for the climate in your yard.
3. **Improve your soil.** When you add organic material to the soil, it holds water better and thus plants can live with less applied water.
4. **Use proper watering techniques.** Train your plants to be tough. Water deeply and less often so that plants develop good water-seeking roots. They will also develop good anchoring roots at the same time.
5. **Use mulch.** Mulch is a soil covering that reduces evaporation, limits weed growth, keeps summer soils cool, and keeps winter soils from freezing. The best mulch is free—the dropped leaves and other plant debris from healthy plants.
6. **Limit lawn area.** A single grass plant can use *gallons* of water on a summer day. Limit your lawn area to a space that will be actively used for recreation and enjoyment.
7. **Use proper maintenance.** Keep pruning to a minimum, and do it at the right time of year. Avoid topiary shearing at all times.

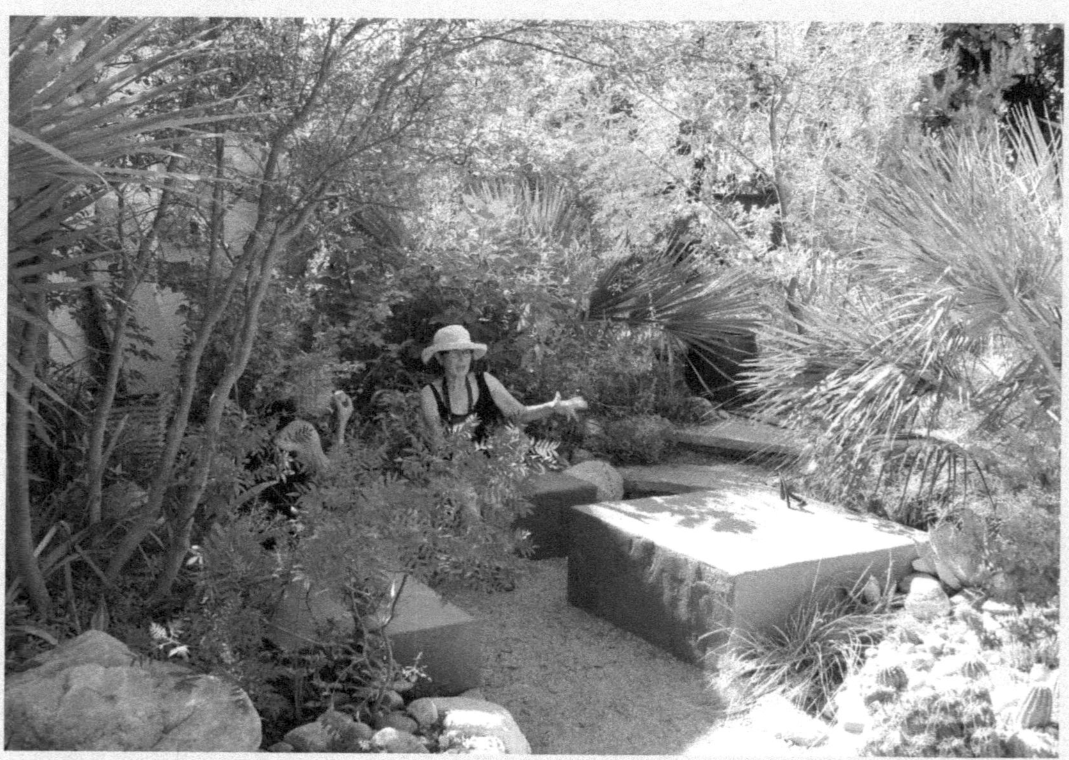

Throughout this book, you are urged to add compost to your gardens. Compost is decomposed plant materials containing some of those trace minerals needed. Compost holds these minerals in a matrix that is more readily available for roots to absorb. Compost is good, and so is store-bought fertilizer. Together, they can help your garden thrive.

PROBLEM-SOLVE

If you grow it, they will come: pests from all five kingdoms of life—bacteria, fungi, algae, plants, and animals—all are waiting in the wings to enjoy the fruits of your labor. In most cases your care or *culture* of plants will prevent problems from getting out of hand.

Throughout the book, I discuss integrated pest management (IPM) practices for control of garden pests. As a gardener, you may hear horror tales of the pests that attack your garden, but in fact, 99 percent of the estimated thirty million species of insects on earth are not garden pests. We just have to guard against the "one-percenters." Lucky for us, a substantial number of the 99-percenters like to eat those one-percenters.

Part of educating ourselves about pests is not freaking out when encountering an individual insect or even 88 individual insects. They may not be pest species, and even if they are, the harm may be tolerable.

If pest species do get out of hand, there are a number of IPM products that target the one-percenters specifically and don't harm other insects.

Female hummingbirds eat numerous insects to get the protein they need when nesting and feeding their young.

Your local botanical garden or arboretum is a valuable resource for classes, demonstration areas, and mature examples of the plants that will grow in your region.

You can find insecticidal products labeled "natural" or "organic." Carefully read the label—many of them are made from plants, and hence they are indeed natural. That doesn't mean they should be used freely. Most of these are toxic to many forms of life, including humans. When opting for a pest control product, look for IPM products that narrowly target the one-percenters.

LEARNING MORE

Use the Resources at the back of this book. There are a growing number of companies based in the West that understand our unique region and conditions. Sometimes you don't have to go far afield to get the information you need. Local botanical gardens, arboreta, and various demonstration gardens are hidden all over our region. A local nursery or garden center may have a demonstration garden. Garden clubs are still out there and their members can be amazingly helpful.

You may not need to leave your armchair to get the information you need. Since my last book for Cool Springs Press, the cooperative extension services in all three of our states have vastly improved their websites and search engines. All offer an array of printable publications on gardening in our region.

HOW TO USE THIS BOOK

Our three states have USDA Cold Hardiness Zones ranging from 10b down to 4a, totaling 14 categories. Rather than tediously referring to these zones throughout the book, I divide your gardening tasks primarily into lower and upper elevations.

Lower elevations—USDA Zones 10b to 8a—includes Alamogordo, Kingman, Las Cruces, Las Vegas, Parker, Phoenix, Safford, Tucson, Wilcox, and Yuma. Some of these cities routinely experience moderate winter freezes, while others rarely do.

Upper elevations—USDA Zones 7a to 4a—include Carson City, Elko, Ely, Fallon, Flagstaff, Gallup, Holbrook, Prescott, Reno, Santa Fe, Sedona, Show Low, Taos, Window Rock, and Winnemucca. These areas always freeze in winter, and often experience below-zero weather.

There is always an exception, and here it is: USDA Zone 7b, which includes the cities of Albuquerque, Socorro, and Tonopah. In general, gardeners in 7b should consider themselves an upper elevation. The exception occurs when you experience an unusual season, such as a warm spring—then you can do lower-elevation tasks. Every so often I will mention this specifically to remind you. One factor you can't fudge in 7b is the chill hours certain fruit trees need. You will need to select fruit trees with fewer required chill hours.

In each month, this book covers the action subheadings of Plan, Plant, Care, Water, Fertilize, and Problem-Solve for each of the eight categories of plants: Annuals & Bulbs; Edibles (including vegetables, herbs, fruit and nut trees and shrubs); Lawns; Perennials; Roses; Shrubs; Trees; and Vines, Groundcovers & Ornamental Grasses.

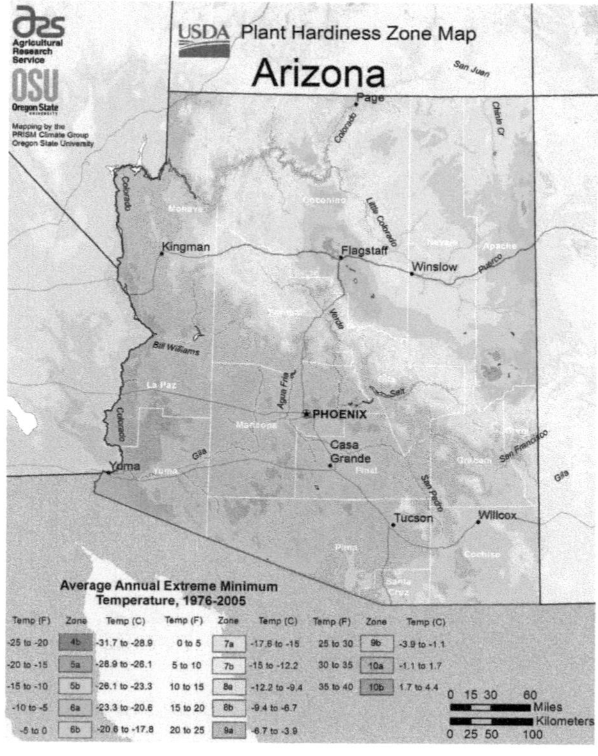

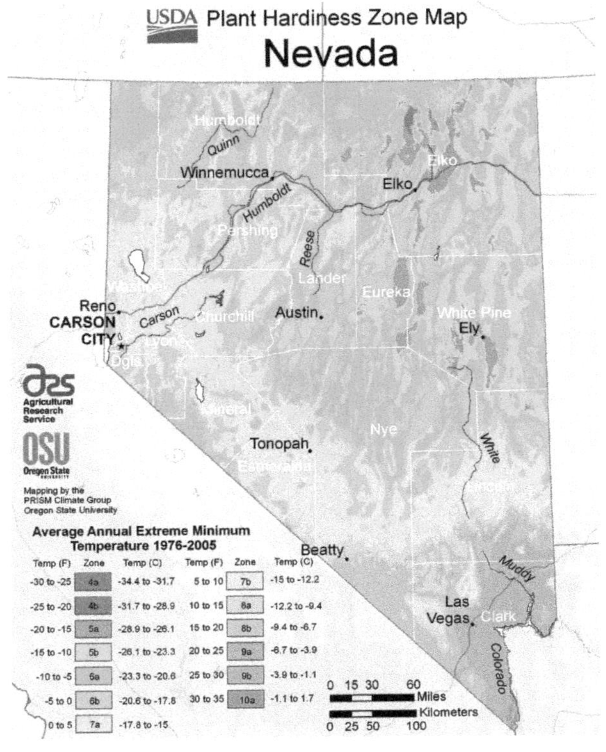
USDA Plant Hardiness Zone Map
Nevada
Humboldt
Quinn
Winnemucca
Elko
Humboldt
Pershing
Reese
Lander
Eureka
Reno
CARSON CITY
Carson
Churchill
Austin
White Pine
Ely
Lyon
Dgls
Agricultural Research Service
OSU
Oregon State
Mapping by the PRISM Climate Group Oregon State University
Tonopah
Nye
White
Average Annual Extreme Minimum Temperature 1976-2005
Temp (F) Zone Temp (C) Temp (F) Zone Temp (C)
-30 to -25 4a -34.4 to -31.7 5 to 10 7b -15 to -12.2
-25 to -20 4b -31.7 to -28.9 10 to 15 8a -12.2 to -9.4
-20 to -15 5a -28.9 to -26.1 15 to 20 8b -9.4 to -6.7
-15 to -10 5b -26.1 to -23.3 20 to 25 9a -6.7 to -3.9
-10 to -5 6a -23.3 to -20.6 25 to 30 9b -3.9 to -1.1
-5 to 0 6b -20.6 to -17.8 30 to 35 10a -1.1 to 1.7
0 to 5 7a -17.8 to -15
Beatty
Muddy
Las Vegas
Clark
Colorado
0 15 30 60 Miles
Kilometers 0 25 50 100

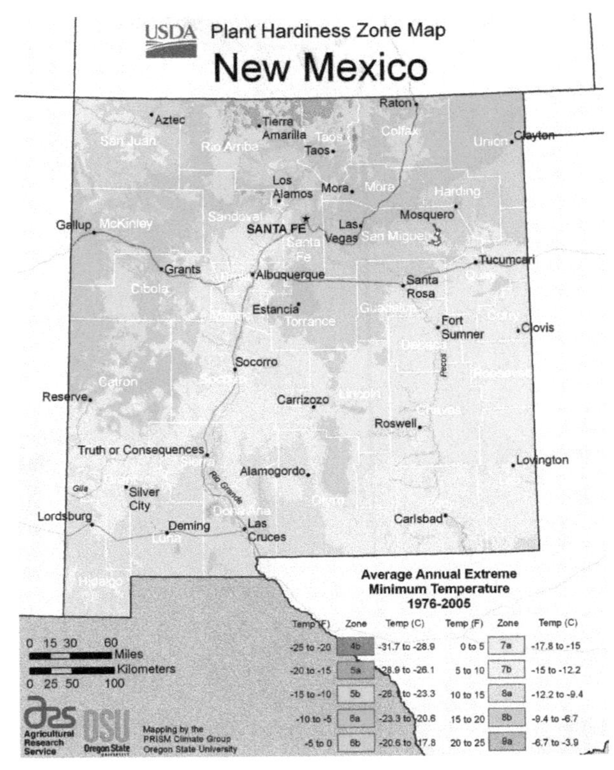
USDA Plant Hardiness Zone Map
New Mexico
Raton
Aztec
Tierra Amarilla
San Juan
Rio Arriba
Taos
Colfax
Union
Clayton
Los Alamos
Mora
Harding
Mosquero
Gallup
McKinley
Sandoval
SANTA FE
Las Vegas
San Miguel
Santa Fe
Tucumcari
Grants
Albuquerque
Santa Rosa
Cibola
Estancia
Torrance
Fort Sumner
Clovis
Socorro
Pecos
Catron
Reserve
Carrizozo
Lincoln
Roswell
Truth or Consequences
Lovington
Alamogordo
Rio Grande
Gila
Silver City
Lordsburg
Deming
Las Cruces
Carlsbad
Luna
Hidalgo
Average Annual Extreme Minimum Temperature 1976-2005
Temp (F) Zone Temp (C) Temp (F) Zone Temp (C)
-25 to -20 4b -31.7 to -28.9 0 to 5 7a -17.8 to -15
-20 to -15 5a -28.9 to -26.1 5 to 10 7b -15 to -12.2
-15 to -10 5b -26.1 to -23.3 10 to 15 8a -12.2 to -9.4
-10 to -5 6a -23.3 to -20.6 15 to 20 8b -9.4 to -6.7
-5 to 0 6b -20.6 to -17.8 20 to 25 9a -6.7 to -3.9
0 15 30 60 Miles
Kilometers
0 25 50 100
Agricultural Research Service
OSU
Oregon State
Mapping by the PRISM Climate Group Oregon State University

January

January is the start of the calendar year, the time when many of us make New Year's resolutions to improve our lives in various ways. One resolution I do hope you'll make and keep is to start or continue to keep a garden journal to help track your gardening practices and ultimately become a better gardener.

If you made a New Year's resolution to get in shape, you can't beat gardening to help with that goal. Weeding, raking, planting, pruning, and generally taking care of a garden helps strengthen and tone the muscles in your abdomen, back, legs, shoulders, arms, and hands. As with any exercise program, start slow and easy at first and stay hydrated. Simply getting out and moving around will help oxygenate your blood and help you feel energetic enough to do yet more tomorrow.

While January is the start of a calendar year, it's not necessarily the start of a garden year. The winter season is continuing and spring is a distant dream. If you live in USDA Zones 6, 5, or 4, then spring is a *far* distant dream. That said, there are a number of gardening activities you can do this month no matter which zone you live in.

Any time is a good time to work on your soil. Even with snow on the ground, go ahead and sprinkle used coffee grounds in planting beds or under trees and shrubs. You can work on composting, especially if you have access to goat, rabbit, or chicken manures. (Due to weed seed issues, avoid using horse manure in the Southwest.) Any manure needs to be well aged before adding it to the garden, and composting it now will get the aging process started.

Indoor gardening activities are not lacking. You can plan and prepare for the gardening year ahead: peruse catalogs (online and print); order seeds, bulbs, and plants; sharpen gardening tools, plus clean and oil all your garden implements. It is great to start the New Year with a clean slate.

PLAN

Revel in the planning process, especially if it's too cold to get out into the garden. January is the month for seed catalogs to appear in the mailbox, so now is a perfect time to plan the garden year ahead. Consider adding a pollinator patch of annual and perennial flowers, decide to try some new flavors of vegetables—perhaps some of the heirloom varieties now being widely offered. If you have a seed library in your area, they are worth a visit. If you resolved to be a better gardener, consider starting to compost if you don't already (see Here's How to Compost in the Southwest).

ANNUALS & BULBS

In warmer areas of the lower elevations, you can add cool-season annuals, such as calendula or pansy, to the garden, but be ready to protect them in case of a hard freeze.

Check post-Christmas sales for amaryllis bulbs. Often greatly reduced in price, you can still get them to bloom indoors this winter. They can be planted outdoors afterwards in zones 10 and 9.

EDIBLES

Begin planning the spring garden by looking through catalogs for vegetable seed and any fruit and nut trees or shrubs you may want to add.

In all areas, the key to success for the vegetable garden is to sow seed indoors so you can plant outdoors as soon as temperatures are optimal. In low elevations, beat the heat with a spring crop of tomato-family plants (including peppers and eggplant). Count back from the official last frost date in your area and get ready for indoor sowing: six weeks for cool-season crops, such as kale, fennel, and broccoli; and eight weeks for warm-season vegetables that bear fruit, such as cucumber, melon, pepper, squash, and tomato.

■ *As you peruse your catalogs, plan for varying bloom times, and keep in mind the mature sizes of plants.*

■ *A clear edge to your lawn will make it easier to care for.*

LAWNS

If you have problems mowing where the lawn runs up next to trees, walkways, or other landscape elements, consider adding a mower strip—a decorative border of brick or pavers set flush with the ground and surrounding your lawn. A mower strip also reduces the chance of mower damage to lawn irrigation systems.

Or consider eliminating lawns entirely. A number of Southwest cities offer rebates to homeowners who eliminate lawns. You'll save money on water, have far fewer garden chores, and have less equipment cluttering your life (mower, edger, fertilizer spreader). January is generally a slow time for landscape designers, thus they'll be available to help plan your new yard.

PERENNIALS

Perennials are fun to grow, and for little effort they add needed dimension to your landscape design. Perennials are also easy to move around—if you decide you really don't like how they look, dig them up and move them. Some gardeners move perennials the way other folks rearrange their closets. January is a great month to walk around and decide where you'd like to add some perennials.

ROSES

Add roses to your planning palette. Roses are often relegated to rose beds, but can be easily grown throughout the landscape—especially the durable heirlooms and miniature roses. Order roses now so that they will arrive in time for spring planting in your area. Upper elevations can consider the charming and durable Southwest native Woods' rose (*Rosa woodsii*).

SHRUBS

A landscape of only tall trees and low perennials lacks interest and mid-level layers. Shrubs provide that. If you like hummingbirds or butterflies, plan on adding some shrubs to help draw them into your yard.

TREES

Late in January, it will be time to celebrate Tu B'Shvat, also called "the Birthday of the Trees." This holiday is an old one, dating back around 3,000 years, and is said to have started the first year the Jews came back to Israel after their slavery in Egypt. If you think of the Holy Land and its climate, you'll realize January is indeed the best time to plant trees, especially in that corner of the globe. January is a pretty good time of year to plant trees in *this* corner of the globe as well, at least in the lower elevations. Consider adding these Biblical trees to your landscape: carob or St. John's Bread (*Ceratonia siliqua*), date palm (*Phoenix dactylifera*), Aleppo pine (*Pinus halepensis*), as well as olive, fig, pomegranate, frankincense, myrrh, bay laurel, mulberry, peach, almond, apricot, and citrus.

In upper elevations you will need to wait to plant outdoors, but you could consider dwarf trees for indoors. Fig, pomegranate, and citrus all come in dwarf varieties and are known to bear fruit indoors. Bay laurel makes a lovely houseplant, looking somewhat like a ficus tree, but with leaves you can harvest, dry, and cook with.

VINES, GROUNDCOVERS & ORNAMENTAL GRASSES

Was your yard too hot to enjoy last summer? A vine-covered ramada or arbor, planted with winter-deciduous vines, such as edible grapes, hops, or queen's wreath, is an excellent solution. Landscape contractors generally experience a slow time of year now and may offer a good price on installation.

PLANT

Should a plant hole be only as large as the pot or larger? In a nonscientific study carried out in my different Southwest yards over the years, the answer is: dig a really wide hole and amply amend the soil. No matter what soil you have—sand, clay, rocky, or caliche-laden—soil amending helps. In my experience, every species—even natives and succulents—will establish more rapidly and grow faster when planted in soil that's been amended with up to 50 percent organic matter (compost). This is especially true for nursery-grown plants that have been pampered pets all their life. (See October, Here's How to Dig a Hundred-Dollar Hole.)

ANNUALS & BULBS

In warmer areas of the lower elevations, you can plant seedlings of winter annuals outdoors, including calendula, pansy, clarkia, snapdragon,

Plan now for shade in summer with a ramada and deciduous vine or climbing shrub or rose, such as the Tombstone rose.

HERE'S HOW

TO COMPOST IN THE SOUTHWEST

Unlike humid areas, there are three components to successfully create compost in the Southwest: green, brown, and blue. Green ingredients are materials high in nitrogen, such as banana peels and melon rinds. Brown materials are high in carbon, such as shredded newspaper or sawdust. Brown can also be a shovel full of soil from your yard. It will contain the microorganisms required to do the actual composting. Blue represents the water. Water is essential in the Southwest to keep everything moist so the microorganisms can break down the brown and green materials.

GREEN MATERIALS

- Citrus and melon rinds
- Coffee grounds and tea bags
- Non-invasive grass clippings
- Vegetable kitchen scraps

BROWN MATERIALS

- Shredded paper—junk mail, newspaper, paper towels, etc.
- Dried leaves, palo verde, pine needles, etc.
- Sawdust or wood chips
- Wheat or sorghum straw

BLUE MATERIALS

- Water—keep your compost enclosed and moist

AVOID THESE!

- Animal products such as meat, dairy, eggshells, and bacon grease
- Bermudagrass in any form (grass clippings, hay, horse manure)
- Eggshells
- Weeds gone to seed

Grass clippings (green)

Kitchen scraps (green)

Leaves (brown)

Shredded newspaper (brown)

COMPOST CONTAINER

You will need a fully enclosed space. Open compost heaps and compost piles fail in the Southwest, because our air lacks humidity, causing materials to quickly dry out and stop decomposing. There are numerous fully enclosed compost bin options on the market. If they have air vents, make sure the vents are screened to keep out insect pests. You can build your own bin with cinder blocks, using five-gallon buckets with lids; or simply dig a hole in the ground and compost in it. Just keep the compost covered to prevent evaporation.

COMPOST CREATION

Add green and brown components in layers, as if you were making a giant lasagna. Add ample moisture, and keep the pile "cooking" by turning the compost with a shovel once a week. This helps mix the components and add necessary oxygen. Add more green and brown in equal portions anytime, and blue as needed. One month before you are going to harvest the compost, stop adding any new material, but continue to keep it moist.

Select a container that can hold in the moisture required for the composting microbes to do their work.

and Johnny-jump-ups. Nasturtium is marginal, but can be coddled in containers. If a hard frost is predicted, you may have to protect all annuals, especially newly planted ones.

Throughout the lower elevations, if you did not plant bulbs in autumn, get them in the ground now. Early bulbs such as narcissus may begin to show themselves after mid-month.

EDIBLES

In zones 10 to 8, winter vegetables can be planted from seedlings. Crops tolerant of mild frosts include beets, bok choy, carrots, chard, collard greens, green onions (including I'itoi onions and scallions), leaf lettuce, mustard greens, radish, European spinach, and turnips.

In warmer areas of the lower elevations, you can plant seedlings of winter herbs, including calendula, borage, German chamomile, and cold-tolerant perennial herbs, such as horehound.

Upper elevations can start seed for the vegetable garden indoors six to eight weeks before the last frost day in your area.

LAWNS

Do not plant lawn grass this month.

PERENNIALS

In the upper elevations, it may be too cold to plant outdoors, but a number of perennials can be started from seed indoors, such as penstemon, columbine, and blanket flower (*Gaillardia*). Unlike annual or vegetable seeds, perennials can be fussy about growing conditions. Carefully read and follow seed package directions.

In lower elevations, the earlier you plant spring-blooming perennials, the better. Most spring-bloomers are more cold tolerant than summer and autumn bloomers, but be ready to protect young transplants in case of hard freezes.

In the lowest elevations, transplant seedlings or container-grown natives such as desert marigold (*Baileya*), penstemon, and globe mallow (*Sphaeralcea*). Smaller succulents such as desert milkweed (*Asclepias subulata*) and hedgehog cacti

HERE'S HOW

TO START SEEDS INDOORS

If you want to grow varieties that will thrive in the Southwest, you generally need to order seeds and grow your own transplants. If you are just starting out gardening, wait until you have more experience caring for plants before investing in light benches and other accessories in a big way. If you wish to try, here are some tips.

Necessary Supplies	Optional Supplies
Seed-starting mix	Heat mat
Seedling trays	Grow lights
Clear plastic covers	Light bench

You can purchase kits that have seedling flats and covers that fit, or get creative with clear take-out salad boxes or even cut-open soda bottles covered with plastic wrap. Fill the tray with pre-moistened seed-starting mix, *not* potting soil. This lightweight mix is sterile and specially formulated to encourage easy, problem-free germination. Plant seeds according to their package instructions. Water seeds carefully so as not to wash them away. A heat mat can aid in faster germination and growth.

1 *Fill tray with seed-sprouting mix and plant seeds according to package instructions.*

2 *Cover seeds until they sprout.*

Keep the seeds covered with plastic until they sprout, then move to a brightly lit area or hang grow lights 2 inches above the tops of the seedlings. As the plants grow, move the lights up so that they're no more than 2 inches above the plants. Keep the seedling mix moist, but not soggy. Damping off (which looks like rotting or wilting of new seedlings) is a problem when seeds stay too wet and cold while germinating. When plants have 8 to 12 true leaves, transplant to a 4-inch pot with regular potting soil.

PLANTING TRANSPLANTS OUTDOORS

Plant transplants outside according to the spacing the fully grown plants will need. Plant so that the soil line of the hole and the soil line of the transplant are exactly the same. Before planting any transplants outside, prepare them by hardening them off (see March).

are used as perennials in the landscape and should be planted only after the last frost day in your area.

ROSES

In lower elevations you can plant roses. In zones 10 to 8, it is mild enough to plant roses now through March—the sooner the better so they can become well established before our scorching summers. If bare-root roses are available, plant them now. For best success, dig the hole before you buy the plant.

In upper elevations, it is better to wait until the official last frost day or later to plant your rose bushes, even in containers. Information formulated back East does not take into account our low

HERE'S HOW

TO PLANT BARE-ROOT PLANTS

1. **Prepare the hole.** Dig the hole only as deep as the roots of the plant, generally about 18 inches. The hole should be two to three times as large as the size of the specimen you are planting. The soil removed will need amending before replacing. Depending on the soil's texture, add compost alone (for sandy soil) or compost and sand (for clay soil). Mix in 50 percent compost with the soil from your hole. Remove any large rocks.
2. **Place the plant.** Set the plant so it will be at the same level it was growing previously. Look for the change in color on its stem that indicates the previous soil line. This might be barely above the roots, but it's *not* the knobby lump partway up the stem; that's the graft union.

   Spread the roots out in the planting hole; you may have to make a mound so the plant will stand up as you arrange its roots. Use the amended soil you prepared when you dug the hole. Make sure roots do not circle around in the hole—dig a wider hole if you need to.
3. **Refill the hole.** Using the amended soil you prepared when you dug the hole, bury your bare root halfway. Stop and firm the soil in around the roots. Water the soil to help drive out any air pockets. Now is the time you may have to re-level the plant. Once all is well, finish filling the hole.
4. **Make a basin.** Form a circular berm of soil around the plant. Make it wide enough that it will be at the edges of the plant's canopy. This is also called a plant well or plant basin, and it should be at the same depth as the surrounding soil; the berm is the raised part.

   Water again to finish settling the soil. Finish by filling the plant basin with an organic mulch to help shield the roots from excess cold and heat. It also reduces the weeds. Do not mound mulch against the trunk or stem.

humidity and drying winds—both sure killers of tender, newly planted roses.

SHRUBS

In upper elevations, now is *not* the time to plant shrubs, even if the ground is not frozen. This month can bring strong winds, temperature fluctuations, and other challenges.

In lower elevations, plant a wide variety of shrubs this month and next. Spring-flowering natives include brittle bush (*Encelia*) and goldeneye (*Bahiopsis parishii*, also sold as *Viguiera parishii* and *V. deltoidea*). Summer-flowering natives such as turpentine bush (*Ericameria laricifolia*) and San Marcos hibiscus (*Gossypium harknessii*) are better planted when it's warmer, in March and April.

Large succulents used as shrubs in the landscape, such as agave, yucca and cacti, should be planted only after all chance of frost is past.

TREES

All elevations can plant living Christmas trees this month. First, acclimatize the plant to cooler temperatures. A week or so in an unheated garage or on a protected porch offers the plant a chance to switch from house mode to winter mode before being exposed to the additional stress of cold winds while trying to root itself. Second, do not "kill with kindness." Avoid overwatering a newly planted tree in this cold month when not much water is needed.

In areas of frozen soil, hopefully you planned ahead and dug the hole back in November. If not, you can still acclimatize (harden off) your tree and move it to a porch or protected area of the yard. Mound blankets or cold-thwarting mulch around the pot to help roots survive.

In lower elevations, plant deciduous trees that offer shade in summer but let the sun passively heat your home in winter. Deciduous trees that also offer summer flowers, such as desert willow (*Chilopsis linearis*) and Texas or Mexican olive (*Cordia boissieri*), are delightful.

VINES, GROUNDCOVERS & ORNAMENTAL GRASSES

In upper elevations, this is not the month to plant this category of plants.

Herbs grown close to the kitchen door make it easier to use them.

In lower elevations, evergreen vines such as lilac vine (*Hardenbergia violacea*) are just starting to bloom and are found in nurseries now. Wait until next month to plant most other vines. Plant lawn-replacing, low-water groundcovers, such as creeping germander (*Teucrium chamaedrys* 'Prostratum'), dalea (*Dalea*), or iceplant. It is not ideal to plant ornamental grasses until next month.

CARE

As tempting as it is to tidy up, gardeners in lower elevations should not remove any frost-damaged material until after the last frost day in your area. Even if it's dead, dead branches help shelter and protect the still living branches lower on the plant, as well as the roots, from any subsequent frost. This is especially true for tropicals such as bougainvillea and citrus.

ANNUALS & BULBS

If you are growing annuals from seed, they often come up too thickly. With a sharp pair of garden scissors, snip off the excess plants. Such thinning helps the remaining plants grow more rapidly. You could simply pull some of the seedlings to thin them, but that will disturb the soil around the roots of the plants you are keeping, and you may lose more than you wish.

Don't forget to deadhead (remove) spent blooms, especially on calendula, carnation, and dianthus.

EDIBLES

In zone 10, young deciduous fruit and nut trees, including apple, apricot, plum, and jujube, require their training pruning this month. The topic is extensive, but the idea is that you are shaping them for fruit production for years to come. Avoid pruning fruiting plants with tropical genes, such as citrus, guava, Natal plum, and mesquite. When in doubt, do not prune if it has leaves on it. In all other zones, avoid pruning edibles this month.

In lower elevations, if you have planted vegetable seeds, see the notes on thinning seedlings under Annuals.

Herbs you are overwintering indoors should have their pots turned a quarter turn each week so all foliage receives an even amount of light.

LAWNS

Overseeded lawns should not be mowed too closely this cold month. Overall grass height should be 2 to 3 inches.

If you have snow or ice, avoid walking on your lawn. Soil compaction due to foot traffic can lead to a number of problems later. Avoid using deicing salts too near your lawn. Consider nonsalt alternatives, such as sand or kitty litter.

You can deadhead using your fingers to snap off spent blooms, or use clippers.

Clean or replace the air filter at the beginning of every season.

Most lawnmowers have a dipstick as part of the oil cap. Remove the dipstick and look at the oil on the end, which should be clear to light brown. If it is darker, you'll need to change the oil. Consult your owner's manual about how to change oil, and the correct weight and type of oil for your mower. Recycle the used oil at an engine repair shop or auto parts store.

If you have no other lawn care to do, service your mower. The five critical care items for mowers: sharpen the blade, clean or change the air filter, change the oil (once per season), clean or change the spark plug (once per season), and oil all moving parts, such as wheel hubs and wire cables. If you neglected to before the end of last season, empty the gas tank and clean the undercarriage.

PERENNIALS

In zones 10 and 9, you can start dividing summer- and fall-blooming perennials, such as garlic chives, yarrow, Mexican hat (*Ratibida*), black-eyed Susan (*Rudbeckia*), coreopsis, and gaillardia. In all other zones, wait until the last frost date in your area.

ROSES

Roses may bloom once or many times per year. It is important to know which they are before you prune. For the one-and-done roses, including many hybrids and climbers such as the Lady Banks, do *not* prune them now.

If your roses bloom many times throughout the year—especially the case with heirlooms, miniatures, and landscape roses—prune prior to their new spring growth. In zones 10 and 9, this is the month to give established roses their rejuvenation pruning. (See February, Here's How to Prune Roses.) All other zones wait until later in the year.

SHRUBS & TREES

In all elevations, mature shrubs and trees should not be pruned this month in the Southwest.

VINES, GROUNDCOVERS & ORNAMENTAL GRASSES

In zone 10, ornamental grasses need their annual rejuvenation pruning prior to starting spring growth. (See Here's How to Prune Ornamental Grasses in February.)

No other pruning of plants in this category is required this month at any elevation.

Lavender does not require constant deadheading, one of its numerous charms.

WATER

Think your plants are not doing anything in the dead of winter? As long as they are alive, they need water. Even the upper elevations may need to irrigate in winter, especially if a snow cover is lacking and the soil is not frozen.

Water when the soil is dry below 1 inch for annuals, 2 to 3 inches for perennials, and 3 to 4 inches for shrubs and trees. I advocate digging test holes until you get used to your plants, your soil, and the microclimates in your yard. Avoid overwatering in winter, when cool soils and slow growth could lead to drowned plants.

If you are new to gardening in our region and like to be very organized, keep a calendar just for watering notes. Note which bed you watered, how much, when, plus relevant weather notes (windy, rain). Over time, a clear picture of how often you have to water each plant will emerge.

Plants overwintering indoors can easily dry out with forced air from the furnace and need special monitoring.

In lower elevations, maintain the irrigation system by taking off the end cap and flushing the system. Check the filter and clean out debris.

Use a trowel to dig down into the soil, under any mulch, to test soil moisture. If it's dry several inches down, it's time to water.

ANNUALS & BULBS

Outdoor annuals will generally need water once a week to at least 6 inches deep. If you don't get rain, you will need to water them. Seedlings need to be closely monitored; they may need water every day until they have 8 to 12 true leaves. After that you can gradually taper off watering.

Bulbs need slightly damp, not soaking wet, soil. Depending on rainfall, they will need water every 10 to 21 days. In lower elevations, early spring bulbs will be breaking dormancy after mid-month and will need more frequent water—as often as every four to eight days.

EDIBLES

Vegetable gardens in the lower elevations need watering every three to seven days. How often depends on if it's raised bed or in-ground, local weather, and the maturity of the crops.

Soil drying in winter has been linked to poor fruit-set in tree and shrub fruits in the rose family (apple, apricot, peaches, quince). Water non-drought-adapted fruiting plants every 14 to 21 days if soils are not frozen. Water drought-adapted fruiting trees and shrubs, such as jujube, mesquite, goji berry, and Russian olive, every 30 to 60 days in winter. Loquat blooms this month and should get a deep soak to 3 feet deep once it begins to bloom.

Herbs will need water in amounts that depend on their growth form. Most herbs require well-drained soil, so avoid overwatering them. Herbs you are overwintering indoors get less light than outdoors and thus need little water.

LAWNS

Overseeded lawns need water every 7 to 14 days. Make sure the water penetrates to two feet deep. This encourages a deep root system that will not dry out quickly once summer heat arrives. If it rains, avoid overwatering your lawn, since too much water can cause problems. A straw-colored Bermudagrass lawn is alive and will need water once every 14 to 21 days.

Perennial beds can be watered with a soaker hose left in place in any nonfreezing month.

PERENNIALS

Perennials will need water as often as a lawn, about every 10 to 21 days depending on species and exposure.

Many succulent perennials are winter dormant and need no water this month.

ROSES

If it remains dry, lower-elevation roses will need water every 10 to 21 days. In the upper elevations remove a patch of mulch and dig down 2 inches. If the soil is moist (or frozen), they don't need water.

SHRUBS & TREES

In all elevations, established shrubs and trees with leaves (or needles) will need at least one good watering in January.

Lower-elevation shrubs and trees, even if dormant, need water once in January.

Upper elevation trees can face soil drying issues, especially in areas with repeated freezes and thaws, as often seen in zones 7 and 6. Water early in the month and avoid watering if there is a January thaw with buds breaking open (generally seen around the third week of the month). The subsequent freeze will be harder on trees watered during a January thaw.

VINES, GROUNDCOVERS & ORNAMENTAL GRASSES

In areas of nonfrozen soils, vines, groundcovers, and ornamentals grasses need watering every 14 to 21 days.

FERTILIZE

If it's growing outdoors, it doesn't need fertilizer this month.

ANNUALS & BULBS

Annuals you are overwintering indoors should be fertilized minimally. Too much fertilizer will encourage them to etiolate (grow spindly).

Bulbs, such as amaryllis or other bulbs actively growing in soil indoors, can be fertilized with a general-purpose fertilizer at half strength.

EDIBLES

Plants outdoors do not need fertilizer this month. Herbs and other edibles overwintering indoors should be fertilized minimally this month.

LAWNS

Do not fertilize a dormant lawn that's not overseeded. If you have an overseeded lawn that is turning yellow, the issue is most commonly overwatering. If this isn't the problem, apply a fertilizer specifically formulated for winter lawns.

PERENNIALS

January is not the month to encourage growth in perennials. Do not fertilize succulents that you are overwintering indoors.

ROSES

Roses growing outdoors do not need fertilizer this month. Roses growing indoors need occasional fertilizing. I prefer slow-release granular fertilizer mixed into potting soil. If I receive a gift rose and see no added fertilizer in the mix, I'll use bloom fertilizer at half-strength once a month.

SHRUBS, TREES, VINES, GROUNDCOVERS & ORNAMENTAL GRASSES

January is *not* the time to fertilize these plants, no matter how warm it is. Frost could still occur in all areas, and you don't want to stimulate new growth.

PROBLEM-SOLVE

Be on the lookout for places where four-legged wildlife large and small—rabbits, rodents, javelina, deer, or elk—have made holes in your animal proofing.

Plants overwintering indoors are susceptible to six- and eight-legged pests. Watch for and treat all common houseplant pests, including fungus gnat, spider mite, scale, and mealybug.

Fungus gnats are a clear indicator that your potting soil is remaining overly moist. Step one is culture: water less. If you still have issues, I have successfully treated fungus gnats by adding a half-inch deep layer of diatomaceous earth on top of the soil. This kills the adults as they emerge seeking mates. There are also a number of poisons you can buy to treat the larvae down in the soil. Avoid using these if you have pets that might munch on your plants.

ANNUALS & BULBS

Those in lower elevations may see aphids on outdoor plants. A strong jet of water can blast them off the plant, or you may need to use insecticidal soap. Repeat as needed.

EDIBLES

Tender branches of fruit trees are often browsed by deer and elk in winter. Nurseries offer a number of herbivore deterrents, including a hot pepper spray. You will need to reapply it after precipitation. In time, these animals will learn to avoid your yard.

LAWNS

There are few lawn pests during this cold month. In areas of snow and ice, avoid using deicing salts near lawns; you will see the damage after the thaw.

PERENNIALS

In the upper elevations, check the protective mulch over perennials. Winds in our region can be

To catch whiteflies and other flying insects, use yellow sticky traps—small pieces of yellow cardboard coated with a sticky substance.

Sap-sucking aphids appreciate tender new growth.

HERE'S HOW

TO PROTECT LANDSCAPES FROM WILDLIFE

The Southwest has its own share of hungry, plant-eating wildlife, including meadow mice, ground squirrels, pack rats, squirrels, gophers, cottontails, jackrabbits, porcupine, javelina, deer, antelope, and elk. While no plant is completely herbivore proof, there are many species and varieties that these critters are highly unlikely to browse. Select aromatic plants—those with oils in their stems and leaves. These release a scent when bent or crushed, and such scents, often pleasant to the gardener, are generally distasteful to herbivores. Culinary herbs, such as sage, thyme, rosemary, and garlic chives, are great choices for herbivore resistance, plus you can use them in cooking. Yarrow, echinacea, agastache or hummingbird mint, tansy, horseradish, lavender, and beebalm are other examples of strongly scented plants that deter herbivores.

A number of native plants appear to be herbivore proof, including cinquefoil (*Potentilla*), datura, and sumac (*Rhus*). Some plants are rarely bothered, including hellebore, heliotrope, lantana, yucca, most ornamental grasses, and the charming annual forget-me-not.

Don't overlook spring bulbs when choosing plants for deer resistance. Autumn crocus, Siberian squill, daffodil, bearded iris, hyacinths, and muscari offer bright color and delightful fragrance and are rarely browsed by deer. On the other hand, rabbits and javelina devour all bulbs as far as I can tell.

Very destructive to a garden, cottontails can squeeze through a chain-link fence.

Ground squirrels dig burrows throughout the garden, eating both plant roots and gnawing bark off trees and shrubs.

incredible, and you may have to lay some chicken wire over the bed to hold the mulch down (pin it in place with landscape staples).

ROSES

In lower elevations, as roses break dormancy, aphids may appear to suck sap. A strong jet of water often solves the problem, or you may need to use insecticidal soap.

SHRUBS

In lower elevations, aphids may appear on shrubs gearing up to bloom, since tender flower stalks are rich in sweet sap. Blast them off with a jet of water from the hose, or use insecticidal soap.

TREES

While leaves are off trees, look for borer entry and exit holes on trunk and branches. Control borers later in the year, when it's warm and they are active.

VINES, GROUNDCOVERS & ORNAMENTAL GRASSES

Other than hungry herbivores, there are few pests this month on these plants.

February

Spring is nigh! Towards the end of the month, Arizona, Nevada, and New Mexico will start to experience either a "land" spring or a "sea" spring. When we have a sea spring, the winds off the Pacific bring us ample rain and moderate temperatures. This type of spring is gentle and often long lasting. If we have a land spring, air masses sweep down across the land from the Arctic tundra, bringing a tumultuous spring and a headlong rush into a generally blistering summer.

While many folks pray for the return of warm weather, I revel in a cold winter. The longer the cold, the fewer the garden pests in summer. Not just insect pests. Longer winters mean rabbits and mice use more energy staying warm and will have fewer, smaller litters later. In lower elevations, long winters also mean more days without worrying about slithery visitors.

February is a good month for gardeners because many garden centers, especially national home-improvement stores, start their spring special offers and sales on all manner of gardening items. There can be some real deals. Containers and potting soil at a good price are always welcome. In all zones, plump, firm bulbs make a nice addition to your garden. You can also stock up on items with a long shelf life, such as fertilizer. But just because you buy it, doesn't mean it's time to apply it!

No matter where you live in the Southwest, from below sea level to high in the mountains, we still experience many more days of blue skies and sunshine than back East. In the warmer areas of our region, this causes long-forgotten friends and distant relatives from colder regions to come for a visit. Put them to work in the garden with you; they may appreciate it. Or, just sit in the sunshine and enjoy our winter weather. Even without company around, take some time to stroll and savor our Southwest sunshine.

PLAN

While winter is still upon us, it's a good time to check your garden for any barren-looking areas. Consider what to add for winter interest next year. In lower elevations, this means winter-blooming shrubs, such as chuparosa (*Justicia californica*), and groundcovers, such as the native verbenas. In upper elevations, consider adding evergreen shrubs and, depending on your snow levels, evergreen groundcovers.

Garden clubs may seem quaint and old-fashioned in the Internet era, but members and presenters have a wealth of information about local growing conditions. And, members will freely share plants tolerant of local conditions when they thin beds.

ANNUALS & BULBS

In lower elevations, it's time to think of where you will plant warm-season annuals. If you plant from seed, you will need bare earth, which may mean digging out something else. Many winter annuals, such as pansy, snapdragon, and Johnny-jump-ups, tolerate transplanting into containers to extend your enjoyment of them while you get the warm-season annuals into the ground.

In upper elevations, you can shop for annual seeds. Cool-season annuals, such as calendula, pansy, and viola, can be started indoors six weeks before last frost date for your area.

EDIBLES

Plan your deciduous fruit trees now for planting in the coming months. Visit your local nursery to order them, or see Resources. In all elevations except zone 10, there are many European fruits that do well in our Southwest soils and aridity. When selecting pome and stone fruit varieties of apple, apricot, mountain ash, peach, plum, and quince, take into account the number of chill hours required by various varieties, and make sure your area provides the amount of chilling needed. Fig, jujube, persimmon, and pomegranate are all good low-care options. Don't forget nut trees such as almond, pecan, and walnut.

In all elevations, if you have not yet planned your spring vegetable garden, it's not too late to do so. Purchase seed now to get growing as soon as conditions are ideal.

LAWNS

If you don't service your own lawn mower, February is a nice, quiet time to take it in to be serviced, with no long waits. Then it will be ready when the lawn is.

PERENNIALS

Perennials are pleasing in the landscape because they persist year after year, with little care required. If you have to spend a great deal of time with frost protection in winter or sun protection in summer, now is a good time to select plants better adapted to your area. Most local nurseries routinely stock perennial plants best suited to local climate, soil, and weather extremes.

ROSES

Instead of a bouquet of roses for Valentine's Day, why not a give a rose bush? Perhaps your sweetheart can give you a coupon good for one rose bush and one dug hole. Shop rose catalogs for the rose of your dreams and order this month for later delivery of bare-root roses—now through April, depending on your zone.

SHRUBS

Shrubs are versatile landscape elements. They offer privacy from neighbors, provide a backdrop for lower-growing perennials, block unsightly views, impede unwanted foot traffic, enclose a deck or patio, and can serve as a windbreak. When planning for shrubs in your landscape, note their mature size. Tiny plants in one-gallon pots may reach 8 feet high and 8 feet around. Planted close to the sidewalk, these young plants mature into hulking nuisances rather than charming additions.

TREES

Why should trees be merely ornamental? Have you ever eaten a persimmon? They're a delicious fall fruit, and the trees are very useful in the landscape. They provide dense shade in summer yet drop their leaves in winter, letting the sun help warm your home/yard, and pests of persimmons are virtually unknown here. In upper elevations, now is a good time to order bare-root persimmon trees for planting in March. Gardeners below 6,000 feet

Ornamental grasses come in a variety of textures and colors, including naturally brown.

can opt for the black or Texas persimmon (*Diospyros texana*). It can be shrubby, but with careful pruning it will turn into a nice patio tree around 20 feet tall. Upper elevations should plant in March, but lower elevations can plant persimmons from container plants now.

VINES, GROUNDCOVERS & ORNAMENTAL GRASSES

Even in the sunny Southwest, gardens are charming in winter. To add interest next year, consider ornamental grasses. Covered in snow, they make beautiful arching mounds. Birds will visit your yard to forage them for seed, and later for nesting material. Depending on the species, you can use the dried seedheads yourself in arrangements. Ornamental grasses also add the element of movement to a landscape, swaying in the breeze. They use less water than similarly sized shrubs, and they are one of the lowest-care plants available.

PLANT

ANNUALS & BULBS

Lower-elevation gardeners can sow seed of warm-season annuals, such as coreopsis, cosmos, gaillardia, gomphrena (globe amaranth), Mexican sunflower (*Tithonia*), sunflower (*Helianthus*), and zinnia.

In upper elevations, it's too cold for outdoor planting, but you can plant bulbs in containers. No space? Tuck a bulb or two in with other plants. Miniature roses and rosemary will kindly share their pots with one or two bulbs for years.

EDIBLES

Lower elevations can start seeds of warm-season spring garden vegetables indoors now. This is roughly ten weeks prior to the time when nighttime temperatures will not drop below 50°F. Tomatoes, peppers, cucumber, melons, okra, and basil are some crops to start now. Start slips of sweet potatoes (see December, Here's How to Grow Sweet Potato Slips).

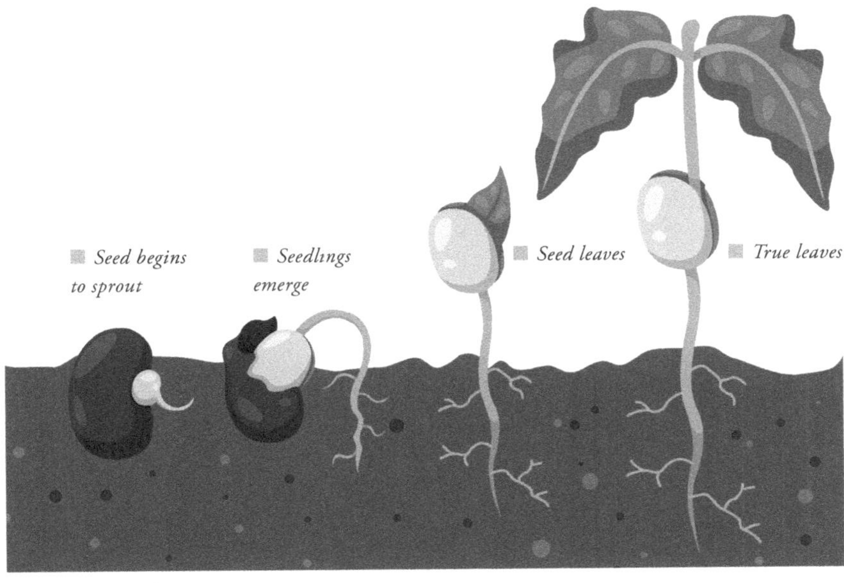

The four stages of growth of a seedling are illustrated here. Note that seed leaves and true leaves serve different purposes and will look different. When a plant has 8 to 12 leaves, it is ready for transplanting.

HERE'S HOW

TO SELECT A GREAT GARDEN CENTER

Whether you have lived in Arizona, Nevada, or New Mexico all your life or are new to this area, there's always something to learn about growing in our unique region. A nursery or garden center staffed with competent employees can help you in your quest for gardening success. Things to consider:

- **Professional affiliations.** Garden centers and nurseries that belong to professional trade associations are committed to maintaining a knowledgeable staff. Ask if they have certified or licensed professionals on staff. Look for this information in advertisements, or in the store itself.
- **Willingness to educate.** Garden centers that want their customers to succeed demonstrate a desire to educate. They hold seminars and demonstrations throughout the year and often have informational handouts in the store, or possibly a monthly newsletter.

- **Commitment to community.** Look for a place where gardening is the focus, not building materials or housewares. A demonstration garden is one indication, as it allows you to see plants *in situ*. These nurseries often host seasonal festivals and holiday events.
- **Help them help you.** If you have a major landscape project in mind, be ready with measurements and photos of the site. Do some prior research to identify plants you like. Know if you want a formal or informal design. Some plants lend themselves to certain design styles.

- **Shop smart.** Saturdays are notoriously busy. If you require a great deal of help, phone ahead and ask when an off-peak time might be. Courtesy pays.
- **Shop local.** Online and national chains can save you money, but part of a great garden center is the relationship you forge with the people who work there. Your shopping is more than a paycheck to them—it is their livelihood. If you want helpful gardeners available for years to come, it may cost some extra money, but the benefits are incalculable.

Upper elevations can start seeds of cool-season vegetables indoors six to eight weeks prior to your last frost day. This includes the cole crops: cabbage, broccoli, kohlrabi, kale, and many Asian vegetables, such as Chinese cabbage and bok choy. Carrot family members with taproots (carrots, parsnips) dislike transplanting. Carrot members you can transplant are herbs, including dill, cilantro, and cumin. Fennel, either bulbing or leaf, is good to start now.

Zones 7 and 6 gardeners should start seed of cool-season herbs indoors this month, including the carrot family members plus French sorrel, salad burnet, and winter savory. Zones 5 and 4 gardeners will start these in March.

For all elevations, the keys to starting seed indoors are light, water, and sterility. Sterile seed-starting soil is a must, since starting life indoors in an artificial environment is stressful to most garden vegetables. Water enough to start the seeds, but resist overwatering, which can easily drown tiny seedlings. (See January, Here's How to Start Seed Indoors.)

LAWNS

Lawns from seed or sod can be planted this month, once daytime temperatures are consistently above 55 to 60°F in your area.

PERENNIALS

In lower elevations, aloes, bulbines, and iceplants—native to Southern Africa—bloom now, which means that you suddenly notice them and want some. Although they come from deserts, their native deserts are not as bright and scorching as ours, so plant them where they get afternoon shade in midsummer. Aloe and bulbine are long-lasting cut flowers.

ROSES

In lower elevations, if temperatures remain below 75°F, you can plant bare-root roses; otherwise, plant roses from containers.

In upper elevations, it's too early to plant roses outdoors. If you're growing miniature roses indoors, now, before spring bloom begins, re-pot them if they need it. Check the root system by

Many species of iceplant do well throughout the Southwest. There are even species for areas that freeze.

carefully slipping the plant out of its pot. If a dense mat of roots greets you, or if roots are escaping through drainage holes, it's time to move them to a larger pot. Use high-quality potting soil that provides ample drainage, since roses do not tolerate waterlogged soils.

SHRUBS

In upper elevations, bare-root shrubs may be arriving now. If the ground is still frozen, keep the roots moist but not soaking. Wrap roots in burlap or an old towel and place the plant upright in just enough water to keep the covering moist. Place in a cool site, such as an unheated garage or basement.

Lower-elevation gardeners can plant container shrubs now. Be prepared to protect them in case of frost.

TREES

In zone 10, you can plant container trees now. In zones 9 and 8, it's better to plant after the last frost date in your area. Don't plant trees in the upper elevations.

VINES, GROUNDCOVERS & ORNAMENTAL GRASSES

Annual vines such as morning glory and hyacinth bean can be planted now in the lower elevations and ordered from seed catalogs in the upper elevations.

Lawmakers in Arizona made it illegal to plant morning glory without listing any scientific name in the law. Morning glory vine is commonly *Ipomea*

There are advantages and disadvantages to each type of nursery stock: bare root, balled and burlapped, or container grown. Select the best for your area and time of year, as recommended in these pages.

tricolor or *I. purpurea*. While you can't buy seeds of these morning glories in Arizona, there are a number of charming relatives to plant instead. Throughout our region consider moon vine (*I. alba*) with white blooms and heavenly nighttime fragrance. Firecracker vine (*I. lobata*) with orange-red blooms is a charmer. Cypress vine or cardinal creeper (*I. quamoclit*) has tiny leaves that help it survive better in xeriscapes. Cypress vine self-sows reliably, making it one of those good "perennial" annuals.

In zone 10, you can plant groundcovers and ornamental grasses. All other zones should wait until two weeks before last frost for both seed- and container-grown plants.

CARE

Dormant season pruning is done now for zones 8 to 6. Don't prune anything with leaves on it unless you live in zone 10. Especially resist the urge to prune frost-damaged plants. The earliest you should prune off any frost damage is mid-March in zone 9.

In lower elevations, frost happens. I let hard freezes kill what they will. What is left is what I grow. But if you don't mind fussing over plants, continue to cover tender plants to trap warmth around them. You can use blankets, sheets, or paper products such as bags, newspapers, and corrugated cartons. Frost blankets of spun fiber are also useful for frost-tender plants.

ANNUALS & PERENNIALS

Spring wildflowers may start to bloom now in sunnier locations in the lower elevations, and depending on your elevation, early spring bulbs might be emerging. While they need no specific care now, make sure to enjoy them.

If you have summer-flowering bulbs (or tubers or corms) that you're overwintering indoors, such as dahlias, cannas, or gladiolus, keep them cool so they don't sprout. Gladiolus corms need to be kept dry, say in a mesh bag formerly used for onions, and 45 to 50°F is ideal. Inspect them this month. If any have turned mushy, throw them out before any infection spreads. If any have sprouted, pot them up for a head start on spring.

EDIBLES

Berry plants need pruning after mid-month in the upper elevations. Prune currants, blackberries, loganberries, and single-fruiting raspberries by first removing all dead wood. Next, remove any weak, spindly canes. Finally, rejuvenate plants by pruning them back to the ground, leaving only six

Frost damage looks unsightly, but it is best to leave it in place until after the last frost day in your area. This layer of dead foliage helps protect the remaining parts of the plant.

HERE'S HOW

TO PRUNE CITRUS

Citrus has specific pruning requirements and only a one-month time frame in which to do it. Find the official last frost date for your area and trim citrus only until four weeks *after* that date. Pruning later isn't good for tree health.

Trim off any dead or broken branches. Remove any branches crossing back through the center. Remove any branches with an exceedingly narrow crotch angle. Find the graft union and remove any sprouts growing below it.

Resist the urge to prune citrus into "trees." Genetically, citrus are large shrubs, not trees. They require shade on their delicate bark, especially in the Southwest, with our higher concentration of UV rays. Expose citrus trunks and branches to a minimal amount of sunlight, because sunscald and the often-subsequent gummosis are generally deadly results.

Cracking, peeling bark on citrus is a sign of sunscald. Prevent this injury by resisting the urge to overprune.

Gummosis or bubbling of sap out of a trunk has a number of causes. In citrus, it's commonly due to sunscald.

to eight older canes 18 inches high to help feed the vigorous new growth that will appear soon. Some people opt to tie these canes to supports for easier maintenance and harvest. If you grow the ever-bearing raspberry for a late-summer crop, simply cut the entire plant to ground level. Gooseberry and elderberry are in different plant families and should be lightly pruned in fall, after fruit harvest.

Prune grape vines in the lower elevations, but wait until March in upper elevations. Do not prune evergreen fruits, including dates, olive, loquat, or jaboticaba, this month. Citrus has special pruning needs. (See Here's How to Prune Citrus.)

Young deciduous fruit and nut trees can be pruned now. The first three years are when you shape them for future production. If you have never done this and are uncertain how to proceed, look for classes in your area. You may not need to travel; the Information Age has led to some handy online tutorials.

LAWNS

Continue mowing overseeded lawns between 2 to 3 inches high. No care is needed for winter-dormant lawns. In upper elevations, if your soil is still frozen, or if it's wet, avoid walking on your lawn. It compacts the soil and leads to a host of problems.

PERENNIALS

If you have a well-lit indoor area (or growing bench), now's a good time to take cuttings. Frost-tender perennials that overwinter indoors, such as geranium, begonia, and coleus, can be rooted now as daylight hours lengthen.

In the upper elevations, when weather permits, walk around your yard to check on perennials. Protective mulch may have blown off, or frost heaves can expose the crowns and roots of plants to drying winds. Recover, replant, or reset as needed. If the ground is still frozen, pile mulch up around frost-heaved plants as temporary protection.

Lower-elevation perennials need little care this month. Zones 10 and 9 can divide summer and fall blooming perennials, such as yarrow, Mexican bush sage (*Salvia leucantha*), and mistflower (*Conoclinium dissectum*, also sold as *Eupatorium greggii*) now or next month. Zone 8 gardeners should wait until next month.

ROSES

In zones 8 and 7b, prune roses now. In zones 7a, 6, and upper elevations, check the mulch around the base of roses to be sure there's still a good layer of insulation from temperature fluctuations. They need a 2- to 3-inch layer covering the graft union. Hybrid teas are typically grafted, and thus more susceptible to winter injury.

SHRUBS

Avoid pruning evergreen shrubs in all elevations. This includes both traditional evergreens such as juniper or cedar, and leafy evergreens such as pyracantha, nandina, or Indian hawthorn.

Deciduous shrubs can be pruned now, but if you live in an area with deer or elk, be sure to discard any pruned branches in the trash. Otherwise, you're inviting these destructive mammals to visit your garden.

TREES

In the lower elevations, avoid pruning any evergreens, including eucalyptus, bottlebrush, silk floss, or mastic trees. Do not prune semideciduous trees, such as mesquite, kidneywood, Mexican ebony, or Indian rosewood, when nights are below 55°F.

In all elevations, deciduous trees such as ash, sycamore, poplar, and mountain ash can be pruned now. Avoid pruning oaks and little-leaf elm this month, unless there's storm damage to remove.

VINES, GROUNDCOVERS & ORNAMENTAL GRASSES

Perennial vines can be cleaned of any dead wood. This opens space for more light and encourages flowers.

Winter-flowering groundcovers could be pruned in zones 10 and 9 if they are done blooming. For all other species and all other zones, do not prune groundcovers this month.

Winter is a good time to observe the structure of deciduous trees and see if there are any branches with poor crotch angles or crossing back through the tree. If so, prune them out.

HERE'S HOW

TO PRUNE ROSES

Pruning roses is a matter of getting the right time, right amount, and right place on the plant.

- **Right time.** Prune eight weeks before last frost in your area.
- **Right amount.** Your bush is going to be reduced to three to ten main branches (canes). Start by removing any dead canes, as well as small twiggy growth. Remove any canes that are crossing through the middle of the bush or rubbing against other canes.

Cut just above the bud, at a diagonal angle, to help shed water.

Now look at your bush and pick out the best canes that remain. Measure with your eye from two different directions before you cut.

The main canes are going to be short—around 1 foot tall. Exact height depends on type of rose bush. You'll leave enough so the plant has enough energy to grow lots of sweet flowers to enjoy later.

Final height and number of canes depends on rose type:

TYPE	HEIGHT AFTER PRUNING	NUMBER OF CANES
Hybrid Tea	8 to 12 inches	3 or 4
Grandiflora	up to 18 inches	up to 6
Floribunda	6 to 12 inches	up to 10
Miniature	reduce by two-thirds	4 to 6

- **Right place.** Look for the eye of a new bud near the base of the canes you have selected to remain. The bud is usually pinkish. Select one around a foot above the ground and on the outside of the cane. Because this bud will grow into a whole new cane, you want the right one—one that will grow outward, opening the shape of the rose bush and letting light into the central portion of the plant. Cut ¼ inch *above* this bud. Cut at a slight diagonal to help shed rainwater once it's healed.

Ornamental grasses may begin to sprout after mid-month in the lower elevations, especially zones 10 and 9. In these zones, trim off last year's growth. (See Here's How to Prune Ornamental Grasses.) In all other zones, prune after the official last frost in your area.

WATER

Plants don't need much water in winter, but they do need some. The cool season means that most plants slow down, but they haven't stopped.

Avoid using a sprinkler to apply water in the Southwest. Due to our low humidity, you lose as much as 50 percent of water to evaporation before it hits the ground. That's not only costly, but it wastes an increasingly scarce natural resource. If you don't install a drip irrigation system, soaker hoses are a better option than sprinklers.

If you live in an area where freezing may still occur, simply lay a hose on the ground near where you wish to water. Allow it to trickle and soak into the soil. Soaker hoses work well, especially the type

HERE'S HOW

TO PRUNE ORNAMENTAL GRASSES

Ornamental grasses need a crew cut once a year. Right after last frost day in your area is the ideal time. Sooner, and they may be frost-damaged; later, and you may kill new growth. Give them a real Marine haircut!

If the species reaches less than 1 foot high, cut the entire plant down to 4 inches. One- to two-foot grass species should be chopped down to 6 to 8 inches. Grasses over 2 feet should be cut to 8 to 12 inches high. This may seem extreme, but the goal is to remove all older brown growth and open the central crown to sunlight. Use the trimmed tops for mulch or add to the compost.

Just after last frost in your area is the time to remove unsightly older growth on ornamental grasses.

Cut ornamental grasses short enough to expose the central crown to sunlight.

One month later, you don't notice where this grass has been trimmed. It shows only lush new growth.

made from fabric, which resists sun rot better than plastic compounds and is easier to roll up and store.

Lower-elevation irrigation system maintenance this month is to move emitters out to the dripline of all trees and shrubs as they grow.

ANNUALS & BULBS

February is when lower elevations may experience temperatures in the 80s during the day, and cool-season annuals need extra water to survive. Don't neglect any wildflower seed you scattered. A watering wand will help apply a gentle, rain-like shower. In-ground annuals need water every three to seven days.

Add a layer of gravel to the plant saucer and fill it with water so the water covers the gravel. This creates a microclimate of extra humidity around indoor plants, helpful during furnace season. Don't let the pot sit in water.

In all elevations, monitor the soil moisture of bulb beds. In a dry winter, and in drier or windier areas, you'll need to water, applying it early in the day when soil is not frozen.

EDIBLES

Cool-season vegetable crops and annual herbs will be stressed as temperatures rise. Make sure their soil remains evenly moist, or leafy greens may become bitter tasting.

In all elevations, fruiting trees and shrubs need water this month since they are gearing up for flowering; monitor their soil moisture to ensure a good crop. Lower elevations may need water every 14 to 21 days. Upper elevations should water at least once this month. Water early on a day when the ground is unfrozen. Even drought-adapted fruits such as wolfberry, sand cherry, and jujube will need water this month.

Herbs should be watered according to their growth form (perennial, shrub, or groundcover).

LAWNS

Both overseeded lawns and dormant warm-season lawns need water this month. Yes, even a straw-colored Bermudagrass lawn needs water in winter. Avoid overwatering if winter rains fall, but do water if the lawn soil is drying out.

In the upper elevations, if there's no snow and no precipitation in the past four weeks, be sure to water your lawn if the soil isn't frozen.

PERENNIALS

If you live in the Mojave or Sonoran Desert regions and no rain falls this month, do water your succulents, including hesperaloe, yucca, and ocotillo. In other areas succulents do not need water in this cool month.

ROSES

In lower elevations, monitor your newly planted roses and any that have already leafed out. Water when their soil is dry below 1 inch. Established roses will need less water, but you need to pamper the youngsters to help them become established. Besides, drought now means fewer blooms later.

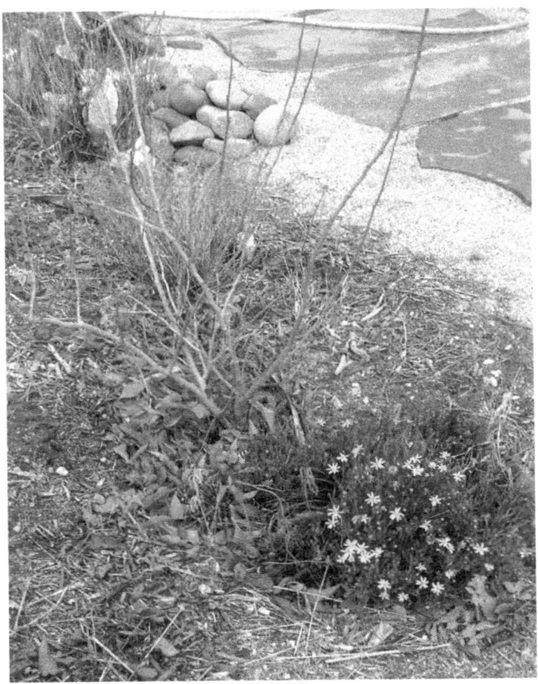

Winter-blooming plants such as damianita need extra water for more prolific bloom.

In all elevations, watch the weather and your roses. Water roses if there is a stretch of clear, dry weather—a three-week stretch in the lower elevations, a five-week stretch in the upper elevations.

SHRUBS

Common names can be confusing. True myrtle (*Myrtus communis*) is native to the Mediterranean and actively grows in the winter. It should bloom soon, so monitor moisture for best bloom and berry production (the birds love these bitter fruits). A different myrtle, the crape myrtle (*Lagerstromia*), is a semideciduous, semitropical from India and needs little water in winter. There are a number of other nonnative tropicals that are winter dormant, including mimosa and red bird of paradise (*Caesalpinia pulcherrima*).

In the upper elevations, keep your eye on the weather and your plants. Water shrubs if there is a five-week stretch of clear weather—sooner if it has been windy. Be sure to water on a nonfreezing day and only if the ground is not frozen.

Taller succulents don't require water in winter—except for Mojave desert plants, such as the Joshua tree (*Yucca brevifolia*), which actively grow in winter. If it does not rain, give them water once this month to a depth of 2 feet.

TREES

In lower elevations, drought-tolerant trees in full leaf need water at least once every 30 to 60 days. Water should penetrate the soil 3 feet deep. If the rains provide this, you're off the hook. Otherwise, get out the hose (or turn on the irrigation). Non-drought-tolerant trees with leaves need water every 14 to 30 days.

In the upper elevations, check both deciduous and evergreen trees. Even dormant evergreen trees need winter watering. Plan on watering at least once every four to five weeks if there is no precipitation. Pick a day when the ground is unfrozen and water early in the day.

VINES, GROUNDCOVERS & ORNAMENTAL GRASSES

In the upper elevations, water plants in this category once this month if warm, windy, dry weather occurs.

In the lower elevations, vines and groundcovers may start to bloom and ornamental grasses may begin to sprout. Water any actively growing plants to 2 feet deep whenever the soil is dry below 3 inches. Same watering advice for the still dormant plants, but it will take them longer to dry out and need water.

FERTILIZE

Little fertilizer is needed this month in lower elevations. In zones 7 and cooler, now is not the time to fertilize outdoor plants.

ANNUALS & BULBS

In zone 10, winter annuals are ending their season and don't require fertilizer. In zones 9 and 8, you could fertilize winter annuals if you wish. In all zones where bulbs are just showing, do not fertilize yet.

EDIBLES

In all zones where gardeners are starting seed, indoors or out, you can apply half-strength fertilizer once seedlings have 8 to 12 true leaves.

In zones 10 and 9, the winter vegetable garden is winding down, and there's no need to fertilize.

After mid-month, in zones 10 and 9, apply fertilizer to evergreen edible trees and shrubs, such as pineapple guava, Natal plum, loquat, and citrus. Use a fruiting fertilizer that's high in phosphorus (the middle number). If you prefer, add a layer of well-composted steer manure around all edible landscape plants, and water it into the soil. In all other zones, edible trees and shrubs do not require fertilizer this month.

LAWNS

Fertilize your lawn if it's a frost-free month in your zone. A balanced lawn fertilizer that contains

■ *Select a lawn fertilizer with more than just nitrogen in it. If you prefer them, OMRI certified organic fertilizers for lawns do exist.*

nitrogen, phosphorus, and potassium (N-P-K) in a ratio of 3-1-2 is best (the package may read 21-7-14 but the ratio remains the same). Many lawn fertilizers contain only nitrogen and are not optimal for healthy lawns in the Southwest. Consider using some of the newer products that include sulfur, a soil penetrant, and microorganisms, which help foster a healthy, biologically active soil. These can be applied quarterly.

PERENNIALS

In zones 10 and 9, fertilize perennials breaking dormancy. Spring-flowering plants, such as salvias and evening primroses (*Oenothera*), should get a bloom fertilizer. Summer- and fall-bloomers, such as ruellia and aloysia, will only need a general-purpose fertilizer. In zones 8 to 4, it's too early to fertilize.

ROSES

Every rosarian has their own formula for getting the best blooms for the annual rose show. If you simply want nice flowers, use a bloom fertilizer for the first two months after roses break dormancy and a general-purpose fertilizer the rest of the time. For optimal rose health, apply fertilizer every two to four weeks. Always follow directions and water fertilizer in after application. Too much fertilizer can kill, so when in doubt, err on the side of caution.

In the lower elevations, shower established roses with love (in the form of fertilizer) on Valentine's Day. Newly planted roses should not be fertilized until they show new growth. In the upper elevations, fertilize roses after the official last frost day.

SHRUBS & TREES

In zones 10 and 9, fertilize plants breaking dormancy. In zones 8 to 4, it is too early to fertilize.

VINES, GROUNDCOVERS & ORNAMENTAL GRASSES

In zones 10 and 9, fertilize vines and groundcovers blooming now, such as verbena and germander, with a bloom fertilizer. Vines and groundcovers actively growing but not blooming can be fertilized with a general-purpose fertilizer. Don't fertilize plants in the legume or pea family, such as lilac vine (*Hardenbergia*), wisteria, and dalea. In zones 8 to 4, it is too early to fertilize.

Ornamental grasses that have broken dormancy need a general-purpose fertilizer. They can be side-dressed with a granular fertilizer.

PROBLEM-SOLVE

In the lower elevations weeds can be an issue, especially if there were winter rains. Remove weeds while they are still small, before they get a chance to release their seeds all over the yard.

In all elevations, hungry herbivores enjoy shrubs and trees, perennials, and perhaps even bulbs. Smaller herbivores such as mice and rabbits gnaw

■ *Weedy mustards thrive in cooler weather and can be difficult to remove due to a thick tap root. Ideally, remove them before they get this large, but certainly before they set seed.*

off bark, while larger ones, such as javelina, elk, and deer, eat entire plants. The only defense is a sturdy fence or wall.

ANNUALS & BULBS

Whitefly may appear in zones 10 and 9 on winter annuals. Since these plants are near the end of their life cycle, your best option may be to yank the plants and compost them now, thus avoiding the infestation. Otherwise, your choices are to daily spray the pest off plants with a jet of water, or use a soapy spray. If you choose composting, dunk the plant in a bucket of soapy water first to kill the pests. The soap will not harm the compost heap.

EDIBLES

In zones 10 and 9, cool-season vegetable crops may suffer whitefly infestations. This is a sign that the plants are nearing the end of their life cycle. At this stage they spend energy making seed, not pest-deterring phytochemicals. Rather than fight Mother Nature, go with the flow. Save a few plants for seed and yank the rest to make room for the next season's crops. Don't put materials infested with whitefly into your compost unless you dunk them first in soapy water.

If you are growing vegetable seedlings indoors, watch for signs of *damping off*, a fungal disease that attacks plants at the soil line. At the first sign, get rid of all infested material, because it can rapidly spread—plus, the spores persist for years. Your best defense is *culture*. Avoid overwatering and start with sterile soil media and sterile containers.

Check the stems of fruit trees and shrubs in the rose family now for early signs of a bacterial infection called *fireblight*. The family includes many fruits we hold dear: almond, apple, apricot, blackberry, loquat, mountain ash, peach, pear, plum, quince, and raspberry. Fireblight can kill an entire commercial orchard in a single year.

LAWNS

Few lawn pests are active in cooler months but fungal problems can arise if grass remains overly wet. Avoid this by watering early in the morning, allowing ample daylight hours for lawn to dry.

HERE'S HOW

TO IDENTIFY & TREAT FIREBLIGHT

Fireblight affects all members of the rose family, including ornamentals such as rose bushes and pyracantha. But it is especially heartbreaking in fruit trees. Fireblight is a bacterial infection that causes affected branches and leaves to appear blackened, shrunken, and cracked, as if scorched by fire. The bacteria spreads rapidly, including by wind and pollinating bees, so catch it early. A plant can be saved if the blighted wood is removed before the infection spreads to its roots, but there is no known cure other than amputation.

You will need clippers, a trash bag, and a container of 70 percent isopropyl alcohol. Cut off and discard infected stems. Cut at least 6 inches beneath the apparently infected area. Dip and swirl your clippers in the alcohol after each cut to thoroughly sterilize them. A strong bleach solution can be used instead of alcohol (¼ cup bleach in 2½ cups of water), but if you choose this method I advocate rubber gloves and old clothing. Once you're done, oil your equipment to prevent rust.

Fireblight causes leaves and stems to appear as if scorched by fire.

Begin treating weeds while a lawn is still coming out of dormancy, like this one.

You can never entirely eliminate weeds, because the wind always brings new seed, but you can minimize them locally, if you remove them as soon as they sprout. If you have a dormant lawn, this is especially easy. Watch for carpetweed, chickweed, crabgrass, henbit, and nutsedge. Digging down and getting their roots is your best defense. There are commercial poisons that kill many of these weeds, but use them with extreme caution—used improperly, they can kill other plants or even your lawn. Keep pets and children away from sprayed areas for at least 48 hours.

PERENNIALS

Most pests of perennials in this cooler month have four legs, not six. Deer- or javelina-proof fencing may be required to protect plants from these hungry herbivores.

ROSES

To prevent rose diseases in the coming months, remove any spotted or yellow leaves. Additionally, rake up and discard fallen leaves in the trash. Fireblight can affect roses. (See Here's How to Identify & Treat Fireblight.)

In the lower elevations, if we have a wet spring, powdery mildew may appear on rose leaves, though it is more commonly a late summer problem. (See August, Here's How to Identify & Treat Powdery Mildew.)

SHRUBS

Fireblight affects a number of ornamental shrubs in the Rose family, including pyracantha, flowering quince, and cotoneaster. (See Here's How to Identify & Treat Fireblight for the treatment of this lethal problem.)

TREES

In the lower elevations, evergreens such as cypress and cedar may be browning due to sap-sucking spider mites. Get out the hose—but don't water the tree! Use the hose to spray a vigorous stream of water up into the tree, giving it a good blast all the way around. Repeat every three to four days for three weeks. This washes the mites off, and they can't climb back up. You need to repeat the process, because spider mite eggs keep hatching. Three weeks of treatment knocks the mite population down to levels the tree can tolerate.

VINES, GROUNDCOVERS & ORNAMENTAL GRASSES

This group of plants will be bothered mostly by four-legged pests this month, because food is getting scarce in the wild. Check for areas where critters might have dug under your walls or fences, and repair as needed.

Hungry javelina are strong diggers, creating and then using holes under fencing you would not think is large enough.

March

March is a month to march into chores—or not. The weather is generally so nice it's more fun to relax in the garden than to work in it. There are few gardening chores that absolutely must be taken care of in March, yet more than enough chores that can be done if you simply want an excuse to putter around the garden.

There's nothing wrong with puttering. My favorite kind of day is when I can putter around the garden doing this and that as needed. Perhaps the intention is to fertilize the roses that are tucked in around the landscape, but then you stop to pick up twigs fallen from the trees in the last storm. While you are doing that you notice a crab spider on a rosemary flower, and then you realize the rosemary needs a little trimming and get out the clippers. Doing some of this and some of that. Puttering!

When you have a garden you will always have more tasks than time. There is always something else that needs to be done, another plant that should be potted up, one more perennial to divide, something that needs a little pruning, a little deadheading, a little weeding, et cetera.

Part of enjoying your garden is learning when to say when! Just like washing clothing, gardening chores will never be completely done, or at least not completely done for very long. You'll have to learn to be okay with leaving some things undone. Don't feel guilty. Relax and look at how much you *did* get done.

Spring is a good time to go on a garden tour and get ideas for your own garden. You may discover plants you hadn't thought about growing in your yard. Or you may see the same plants you have, yet combined in different ways. If you live in a small town and there are no garden tours, perhaps you can get some friends together and visit each other's gardens.

No matter how you use your spring days, do take time to smell the flowers. All flowers, not just the roses!

PLAN

Take a stroll around your yard to see how various plants fared over winter, and note this in your journal. If you had a winter vegetable garden, make notes on the performance of your vegetable selections. This will help you select varieties for next year.

Notice how the sun's arc is shifting in the sky. Does this expose shade-loving plants to too much light? Or does it highlight a specific spot in the garden that might be the perfect spot to add some summer plants?

ANNUALS & BULBS

Before you purchase spring annuals, leaf through your garden journal to see which varieties performed best last spring and which didn't do so well. Perhaps it wasn't the species or variety but the *brand* you purchased that was not ideal. Were you honest in your journal notes? Many factors can lead to the failure of a plant to thrive. By being honest in the pages of your journal, you can help yourself become a better gardener.

In all elevations, check on your bulbs. Some spring bulb beds may be blooming sparsely. Did you remember to fertilize last year after they were done blooming, so they stored enough energy for this year's display? This is another item to add to your journal.

EDIBLES

In lower elevations, now is the time to tear out winter vegetables and plant spring crops. Are your seedlings ready? Plan for harvest of winter herbs you grow for seed, such as caraway, cumin, and coriander. Are your drying sacks emptied of the last harvest?

Bulb beds with bald spots may be due to lack of fertilizer last summer.

Upper-elevation gardeners may have trays of seedlings bursting at the seams. It's time to warm your garden soil. Black plastic sheets can help moist soils warm up. Dry soil may warm, but it also rapidly cools. Our ancestors used to add a layer of dark, rich, composted cow manure. Gardeners today may not care for that barnyard fragrance, but for some of us it brings to mind chilly spring mornings working beside Dad, or perhaps Grandma, helping spread manure with our trowels and four-year-old fingers. Precious memories.

Upper elevations can plant bare-root fruit trees this month and, in the coldest zones, next month as well. Never done it before? Bare-root planting helps deciduous trees get established in your yard quickly and easily. Because they are planted before they break dormancy, they experience less transplant shock. Honesty compels me to admit that I killed the first bare-root plants I tried. My advice: Start small! Buy only one or two trees, or maybe a bare-root rose bush. Once you've taught yourself how to do this, then you can order ten trees at once.

LAWNS

Lawns in upper elevations will still be dormant, but it's not too soon to plan any necessary repairs or changes. As your landscape matures, trees grow, shading more of the yard. Since lawn grasses don't grow well in shade, consider a bed of shade-loving, low-water perennials or groundcovers, such as lirope, coral bells (*Heuchera*), or foamflower (*Tiarella*).

PERENNIALS

Depending on where you live, penstemon are starting to bloom. With over 150 species native to the alkaline soils of the Southwest, there is a penstemon for every elevation. In the colder zones, penstemon bloom in June and July, so everyone can have charming, hummingbird-pollinated penstemon in their yard.

In upper elevations, as the snow melts, the wonderful Lenten rose or hellebore (*Helleborus*),

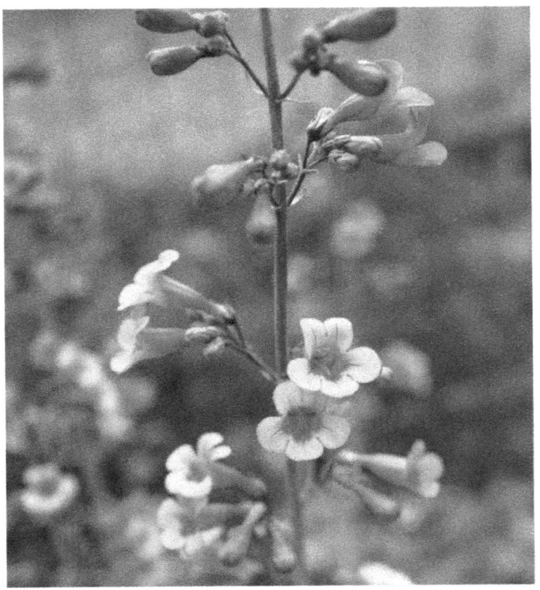

Parry's penstemon grows well in the lower elevations. All penstemons attract hummingbirds to the garden.

begin to bloom. Don't have any? If you are willing to acidify your soil regularly, they're worth considering. They have specific chill hour requirements, so they will not grow in the lower elevations.

In all elevations, perennials require periodic dividing. Plan now where you will place the divisions.

ROSES

In all elevations, consider adding roses. Roses are remarkably tolerant of heat and alkaline soils. (See Here's How to Help Roses Thrive.) In lower elevations, a site with afternoon shade in summer is ideal.

In upper elevations, buds are breaking on roses. Pull the winter mulch back and check the condition of the canes. If they're green and firm, your roses have survived winter. If the bushes have no sign of green, or if the canes have turned brown or black down to the graft union, it's time to order replacement bushes. Or perhaps it's time to fuss over your garden less. Zones 8 to 4 gardeners can replace roses with their edible cousin, aronia berries. (See this month's Shrubs section.)

SHRUBS

Check the mature size of shrubs you are considering for planting. Some get tall and are not appropriate under windows.

Zones 8 to 4 gardeners can consider a shrub that provides edible berries—the aronia (*Aronia*). Its pretty white flowers are followed by tart, black berries and later by attractive red fall foliage. If you don't like the berries, the birds do, and the plants are virtually maintenance-free in Southwest gardens. Three-, six-, and nine-foot-tall varieties are currently available. Which reminds me . . . currants (*Ribes*) are another option! They're lovely shrubs with fragrant flowers and delicious berries.

HERE'S HOW

TO HELP ROSES THRIVE

In all zones, roses do best if the following requirements are met:

- They receive at least six hours of light per day all year, especially in the shorter days of spring and autumn. If possible, light should be morning light. In the lower elevations, some afternoon shade in summer helps roses thrive. Reflected light, like near a pool, is often deadly for roses.
- Well-drained soil is a must. If you have heavy clay soil, this may mean growing roses in containers.
- Space roses at least 1 foot away from walls and fences. Good air circulation helps roses fight off disease and insect pests.
- Plant as early in the year as you possibly can. Roses can survive our summers, but they need a head start.
- Place an organic mulch under your roses in summer to help keep the soil cool and retain moisture.
- Remove fallen rose leaves regularly to prevent providing food and shelter for rose pests and diseases.

Aronia comes in a number of cultivars and makes a durable landscape shrub in zones 8 to 4.

TREES

Nevada and New Mexico celebrate Arbor Day this month (second Friday of the month). Celebrate by planting a tree—if not in your yard, then perhaps in a community space.

VINES, GROUNDCOVERS & ORNAMENTAL GRASSES

Low-growing perennial groundcovers are an indispensable part of any well-designed garden, providing colorful flowers and attractive foliage. They're great for filling spaces between flagstones or pavers, using as a low-maintenance lawn replacement (especially in shaded areas), or for creating a living mulch that cools the ground and suppresses weed growth.

There are numerous groundcover species to choose from, many with charming and long-lasting bloom. But as you contemplate groundcover choices, consider more than simply how they will look. Do you have pets? Lantana can be fatal to dogs. Can snakes get in your yard? If yes, select a ground-hugging species such as myoporum or snow-in-summer that snakes can't hide under. Severe bee allergy? Select a butterfly-pollinated species such as verbena. Use herbs in cooking? Many herbs are groundcovers, including thyme, oregano, and marjoram.

PLANT

Before you start planting, file a sharp edge onto your shovels and spades. It will help slice through soil, roots, and sod with ease. A flat file, also called a mill bastard file, is good for this task. A bench grinder does the work quicker, if you have one. You aren't trying for knife-edge keenness, just a less than blunt edge. Once you have sharpened your spade, oil the blade to protect it from rust. If it has a wooden handle, oil that as well.

ANNUALS & BULBS

The next crop of annuals can be sown this month. In lower elevations, these are the late spring-flowering annuals such as sunflower, zinnia, and moss rose (*Portulaca*). In upper elevations, it's time for cool-loving annuals, such as snapdragon, sweet pea, pansy, and viola. You can sow outdoors once the last-frost day is past for your area; otherwise, sow seed indoors for later transplant. In the upper elevations, if you've been overwintering summer bulbs indoors, it's time to pot them up. Use a soil mix that drains well, and place pots in a cool but not freezing area. Once sprouts appear, move to a brightly lit area.

EDIBLES

In the lower elevations, start seeds of basil and tomato family members indoors or in a sheltered area if you haven't already. You want tomatoes, peppers, eggplant and tomatillos to flower as early as possible, because their pollen dies once air temperatures enter the low 90s. Planting sooner is better if you want ample fruit before temperatures climb—just be ready to protect tender young plants from temperatures below 45°F. Select varieties that produce smaller fruits and are thus less susceptible to blossom end rot, seen as tan or black lesions on the blossom end.

Select smaller varieties of tomato-family vegetables. Larger varieties of tomatoes and peppers may develop blossom end rot.

In the upper elevations, check soil moisture before you plant. Take a handful of soil and squeeze it; if water drips out or it turns into a sodden ball, it's too wet. Wait a week and try again. If it breaks apart or crumbles, it's gardening time!

Upper-elevation gardeners can plant bare-root horseradish and onion family sets (onion, scallion, leek) two weeks before the last frost day. If your soil is amended enough to be acidic, you can plant bare-root asparagus and rhubarb.

Cool-season vegetables can be planted in workable ground, generally after St. Patrick's Day in zone 7; after April Fool's Day in zone 6; Tax Day, April 15, in zone 5; and May Day in zone 4. Better yet, just get a soil thermometer. Plant once the soil is above 45°F.

An often-overlooked edible is Jerusalem artichoke (*Helianthus tuberosus*), also called sunchoke. It does not easily tolerate summers in zones 10 and 9, but the other elevations can plant this delightful edible rhizome now. If your soils are still frozen, plant in containers. You may wish to keep it in containers—if you water often and have rich soils, it can be invasive.

Speaking of edibles with "tuberous" in the name, garlic chives (*Allium tuberosum*) make a great addition to the garden. Originally from the Mongolian steppes, these plants tolerate our alkaline soils and thrive in zones 10 to 4. Despite the species name of *tuberosum*, it's the leaves that are eaten. Harvest anytime and add raw or cooked to any dish where you desire a mild garlic flavor. The plants grow readily from seed and can spread through the garden, appearing in watered areas.

Plant deciduous fruiting trees and shrubs now. In zones 10 and 9, plant container-grown plants; zones 8, 7, and 6 can plant bare-root plants. Zones 5 and 4 should wait until next month.

LAWNS

In the lower elevations, warm-season Bermudagrass or St. Augustine lawns can be planted from sod or seed.

Upper elevations should generally wait until April to plant lawns, but you can prepare the area while you wait. Zone 7b gardeners can sod or seed now if nights have been consistently above 55°F.

There are no entirely deer-resistant plants, but deer rarely bother strongly flavored plants such as garlic chives.

PERENNIALS

Once nights are consistently above freezing, you can divide and transplant summer- and fall-blooming perennials. This may reduce bloom the first year, but plants will recover, and over time they'll bloom better and be less susceptible to disease if they're not crowded.

Upper-elevation gardeners should confirm that the soil isn't too wet before starting. You can divide asters, coneflowers, chrysanthemum, daylily, phlox, and sedum. At lower elevations, you can divide any summer- and fall-bloomers you did not divide last month, plus winter-blooming perennials that are done blooming, such as sweet marigold (*Tagetes lucida*).

ROSES

Plant bare-root roses one month before last frost. If it's too late in your area, plant container roses.

SHRUBS & TREES

In the lower elevations, plant deciduous species of container-grown shrubs and trees now. But wait until April to plant palms, citrus, and other tropicals.

In the upper elevations, plant bare-root shrubs and trees one month before last frost. If it's too late in your zone, plant container-grown shrubs and trees.

HERE'S HOW

TO HARDEN OFF PLANTS

Any plants that have been growing inside your home (or inside a greenhouse) need to be hardened off before they're planted outside. Hardening off refers to acclimating plants to changes in temperature and light. The process is the same for vegetable seedlings, shrubs, and living Christmas trees. Even if you buy plants that were outside at a garden center, it's a good idea to harden them off before planting. (They may have been grown in a greenhouse and delivered to the garden center the same day you bought them.)

1. Place plants in a sheltered location such as a porch or patio during the day, and bring them in at night. Do this for three or four days.
2. Next, leave them outside all day and night in this sheltered location. Do this for about a week. Don't forget to water!
3. Finally, move the plants from the sheltered location to a more exposed location (next to the garden). Leave them there for three or four days.
4. Plant early in the day, so plants have some time before nightfall to recover from the stress of planting. If you have a cloudy day for planting, even better.

Harden off plants gradually before planting them in the garden.

VINES, GROUNDCOVERS & ORNAMENTAL GRASSES

Add the element of movement to your garden with ornamental grasses that sway in the breeze. They can be planted now in lower elevations, and as early as two weeks before last frost in upper elevations. This includes dividing clumps of ornamental grasses.

Vines and groundcovers can be planted after last frost in all elevations.

CARE

Do not prune spring-flowering plants—you'll cut off the buds they will flower from! Wait until they are done blooming (generally June).

In zone 8, don't prune off any frost damage, even now. In zone 9, the earliest you should prune is mid-March, but better yet, wait until April. Always wait at least until last frost is past, because once plants resprout you can better see what did survive. If this messiness truly bothers you, remove the frost-damaged plants and replace them with more frost-tolerant species.

ANNUALS & BULBS

In upper elevations, you may still be taking care of annuals indoors. Simulate breezes to strengthen their stems by gently brushing your hand across them. Indoors or out, leggy growth can be pinched back, helping plants develop evenly.

Forced bulbs are often used to celebrate spring holidays. Keep them indoors in their pot as long as they are flowering. If nights are above 45°F in your area, you can move them outdoors and even plant them into the garden. Leave the green leaves intact.

In all elevations, divide bulbs after they are done flowering. If you don't divide them, they can become overly crowded and some will die. Rather than let that happen, find other parts of the yard where spring color will delight you. Divide irises with bulbs, such as Spanish iris and Juno iris, now (irises with rhizomes will be divided in fall). Resist the urge to trim the fallen-over green leaves of bulbs, divided or not. Bulbs need the sugars leaves are making for luscious bloom next year.

In the Southwest, dig a wide hole for plants, three times as wide as the pot they come from.

EDIBLES

In the lower elevations, adding a mulch layer around winter vegetables helps keep the soil cool and prolongs their growing season. You may be able to keep chard and kale going into May with a thick layer of straw mulch.

Upper-elevation gardeners should avoid mulching tender vegetable seedlings; instead, allow the sun to warm the soil. A thin top-dressing of dark soil can help these youngsters get ahead. Mulch after the soil temperature is above 65°F.

In the upper elevations, if you've overwintered root crops such as carrots and parsnips in the ground, dig them out before they start to grow. You should harvest those tasty roots before they spend their stored sugars making new leaves and seeds.

Potatoes need soil hilled or piled up around the stems, leaving a little of the leafy top sticking out. Because the tasty tubers form on offshoots from the main stem, these soil mounds give them a place to develop. The ancestors to the Incas developed this method over 4,000 years ago, and the varieties we grow all perform best with this care.

There are two reasons to prune fruiting trees and shrubs. One is to help them develop good branching form, and another is to reduce branches that may break under fruit load. Depending on what you're growing, it may be time to prune deciduous fruits. The calendar is only a guide—look at your plants and see what state they are in. In all elevations, fruits with chilling requirements over 200 hours must have pruning completed prior to spring blooms and the emergence of new growth.

For fruits with chilling requirements less than 200 hours (zones 10, 9, and some areas in 8), if plants were hit by hard frost, you need to wait to prune until after fruit set. Guava, pineapple guava, and Natal plum are evergreen tropical species; prune them when you do citrus, in the four weeks after last frost day in your area.

In upper elevations, prune grape vines now.

Clean up herb beds. Vigorously prune any rosemary or lavender plants that are getting leggy, once they are done blooming. Take cuttings of any herbs—many root readily in spring. You can also layer many herbs. (See June, Here's How to Start New Plants by Layering.) Lower-elevation gardeners should harvest and enjoy cool-season herbs such as cilantro, dill, and parsley. The heat that kills them is coming in April or May.

LAWNS

Annual rye overseeded on lawns starts to die as it heats up in the lower elevations. Perennial rye should carry through until the Bermudagrass begins to break dormancy, generally by May.

Close mowing is important in this transitional month. First, weeds should be kept short and kept from seeding (ideally, dig them out). Second, overseeded lawns need sunlight to reach the grasses beneath so they can start to grow.

Do not mow if the soil is wet or waterlogged; you'll do more harm than good. Do not mow newly planted lawn until it has grown to the recommended height.

PERENNIALS

Some popular perennials are considered weakly woody. Plants such as autumn sage (*Salvia greggii*),

Lawn clippings are fine for the compost bin as long as the clippings don't include seeds of weeds or Bermudagrass.

damianita (*Chrysactinia mexicana*), and blue euphorbia (*Euphorbia rigida*) are examples. Due to their woody genes, they require periodic rejuvenation pruning, just like a shrub. If the center is a large bald patch and flowering is sparse, severe rejuvenation time is here. (See Here's How to Rejuvenation Prune Woody Plants.)

In lower elevations, prune winter-flowering perennials that are done blooming. In the upper elevations, little care is required this month.

ROSES

For gardening in zones 6 and cooler, this is the month to prune roses. In zones 10 to 7, if you didn't prune roses earlier you can still do it now, but do not delay. Avoid pruning roses once it's consistently above 85°F.

SHRUBS

In all elevations, rejuvenation pruning can help shrubs that have become leggy or have dead patches. After last frost and up to daytime highs in the 80s is the time to perform this work. (See Here's How to Rejuvenation Prune Woody Plants.) *Do not* rejuvenation prune every year!

In lower elevations, you can prune winter-flowering shrubs that are done blooming, such as sennas, emu bushes, and Mount Lemmon marigolds. These species require gradual rejuvenation pruning every three to five years.

After mid-month you can prune oleanders. If they're getting too large and are not green at the bottom anymore, consider extreme rejuvenation pruning—they will regrow with a more robustly bushy form. You could eliminate the poisonous oleander altogether and plant low-water native (and butterfly pollinated) Arizona rosewood (*Vaquelinia californica*). In zones 10 and 9, loquat (*Eriobotrya japonica*) and pineapple guava (*Acca sellowiana*) are fruit-bearing alternatives to oleander.

After last frost, all elevations should tidy up under shrubs, removing fallen leaves you left as winter mulch. As they decay, they use nutrients. Replace the leaves with inert cedar bark mulch. You can compost the leaves.

TREES

Complete any pruning of deciduous trees with temperate genes, such as apples and ash, before they break dormancy.

The pruned tops from ornamental grasses can be reused as mulch in the garden or added to the compost bin.

HERE'S HOW

TO REJUVENATION PRUNE WOODY PLANTS

Rejuvenation pruning can help shrubs that have become leggy and full of dead patches. Different species need it on different timetables. Some species respond better to gradual rejuvenation, whereas others do best with the extreme form.

Renew a long established shrub by cutting some stems to ground level.

Gradual rejuvenation. A number of shrubs become overgrown with tangled growth and flower less and less as time goes by. These can be renewed through a gradual rejuvenation process in which one-third of growth is removed each year over three consecutive years.

Extreme rejuvenation. Many desert plants, as well as species native to areas of periodic fire, respond better to extreme rather than gradual rejuvenation. Chop the entire plant back at once, generally to 6 to 12 inches high. This results in new growth that is full and even throughout the entire plant. Weakly woody plants such as autumn sage can be pruned annually, but larger shrubs such as squawbush or Texas ranger require such drastic measures only every three to five years. Ornamental grasses get an extreme rejuvenation pruning every spring. (See February, Here's How to Prune Ornamental Grass.)

Over time, the lower branches of many shrubs become shaded by their own top growth and lose their leaves. Rejuvenation pruning is required.

One year after the entire shrub was cut to 6 inches tall, this plant is bushy and full.

Within six months of extreme rejuvenation pruning, the plants were covered in blooms and were visited by pollinators.

Recent research shows that desert trees with tropical genes, such as mesquite (*Prosopis*) and ironwood (*Olneya tesota*), should not be pruned when dormant. This is especially true if the trees are only semi-deciduous, like many mesquites. Not sure about your tree's genes? Find where they are native. Africa and South America are clear indicators of tropical genes. Prune these trees once they are actively growing and can heal wounds, generally in May.

In zone 10, you should be done pruning deciduous trees.

In zones 9 and 8, prune only deciduous trees with temperate ancestors now.

In zones 7b to 4, you have few tropical species and can complete pruning tasks before trees break dormancy without concern.

VINES, GROUNDCOVERS & ORNAMENTAL GRASSES

Upper elevations can wait until next month to prune all plants in this category.

Lower-elevation gardeners have little pruning yet. Ornamental grasses need a crew cut once a year, right after last frost day in your area. (See February, Here's How to Prune Ornamental Grasses.)

WATER

In lower elevations, the irrigation system maintenance this month is to adjust your controller to the spring schedule.

In the upper elevations, continue to monitor indoor plants—especially any seedlings—and allow soil to dry out slightly between waterings.

ANNUALS & BULBS

In all elevations, indoors or out, young annual seedlings need water every one to three days, depending on your soil. Allow them to dry slightly between watering. Water mature annuals every three to seven days.

If you have a bed of wildflowers, a periodic rain shower from your garden hose will extend blooming for months rather than weeks, if the weather remains cool enough.

In all elevations, bulbs need moisture to maintain strong growth—even after flowering. Watering also helps cool the soil, which helps prolong bloom in lower elevations. In the upper elevations, cooling the soil helps prevent premature emergence of late-spring bulbs.

EDIBLES

Because of our dry climate, irrigation is essential. Too little water stresses plants, reducing quality and yield. Overwatering can cause root rot or may cause plants to remain vegetative rather than produce fruit. A careful balance of providing the optimal irrigation to plants as they grow prevents stress and contributes to healthy, high-yielding crops.

After planting a vegetable garden, irrigate lightly every day, until seeds germinate and plants are established. After plant establishment, water less frequently but more deeply, to at least 12 inches deep. Allow the top 1 inch of surface soil to dry out between irrigations, which will promote deeper

HERE'S HOW

TO GAUGE HOW DEEP IRRIGATION GOES

A direction to irrigate "until water reaches 3 feet deep" may sound impossible at first—but you can quickly learn what this means in your yard.

Find something long and narrow to probe the soil with. I use a foot-long knitting needle, but a long, narrow screwdriver will work. You can buy a soil probe, but unless you test soil for a living, save your money.

Water for 20 minutes. Now check how deep into the soil your probe will easily slip. If it's 4 inches, you can calculate that it will take 3 × 20 minutes (60 minutes) for the water to go three times as deep (4 inches × 3 times = 12 inches, or one foot). If it penetrates one foot in one hour, trees will need 3 hours of irrigation for water to reach 3 feet deep.

Apply water to young plants with a hose nozzle that mimics a gentle rain shower. You may need to stand there for some time while the water soaks in.

root growth, helping even vegetable plants become more drought tolerant.

Watering frequency for the vegetable garden depends on soil. If it's sandy, it may be necessary to water every two to five days. Loamy soils generally require water every four to seven days. Heavier (clay) soils may need water every 8 to 12 days. The watering frequency also depends on weather—more often during hot or windy weather and less when it's cool.

Water for fruiting plants that bloom in spring is especially important. Wine growers in France and California know how critical spring rains are for good grape production. If you have fruit-producing vines, shrubs, and trees, monitor soil moisture carefully, especially if we have a windy month. Use a trowel to dig a hole near the drip line, or use a probe. If soil is dry below 3 inches, water.

LAWNS

In the lower elevations, monitor soil moisture. As heat increases, you'll need to water overseeded lawns more often, every five to seven days.

Newly planted sod lawns need daily watering for two weeks to keep the soil moist. Taper to every other day for two weeks. After a month, water less often depending on conditions. In all cases, water should penetrate to 6 inches deep. Six inches is less than the depth of your prepared lawn soil, but it's greater than the roots found on your sod, thus encouraging the roots to seek deeper soils. Use a probe to monitor soil moisture in newly planted lawns.

Don't let fruit or nut trees and shrubs dry out as they break dormancy and bloom.

In upper elevations, water as the lawn breaks dormancy. This may be every 7 to 10 days, depending on wind and other conditions. Water deeply and infrequently to encourage deep rooting for the summer ahead.

PERENNIALS

In all elevations, perennials need moisture to maintain strong growth, even after flowering. Watering helps cool the soil, which helps prolong bloom in lower elevations and prevents premature blooming in the upper elevations. If you lack an irrigation system (or it's still turned off because of chance of freeze) a soaker hose will help you water the soil and not the crowns of plants. Check perennials weekly and water as needed once soil is dry lower than 2 inches.

In lower elevations, many succulents (agave, prickly pear) are breaking dormancy now. Water once this month after the last frost.

ROSES

In lower elevations, roses may be blooming. Monitor soil moisture and water when soil is dry lower than 3 inches deep, to a depth of 2 feet. Check roses once a week.

In the upper elevations, if clear, dry conditions persist and soil is dry below 3 inches, water roses on a warm, sunny day when temperatures are above freezing. As temperatures warm, this may be as often as once a week. Water to a depth of 2 feet.

SHRUBS

In the lower elevations, spring-flowering shrubs such as senna, bottlebrush, and little leaf cordia perform better with water. Monitor soil moisture on all shrubs and water when it is dry below 3 inches. Water to a depth of 2 feet. For drought-tolerant species, this means every 14 to 30 days. Non-drought-tolerant species need water every 10 to 14 days.

In the upper elevations, if clear, dry conditions persist, water established non-drought-tolerant shrubs every three to five weeks on a warm, sunny day when temperatures are above freezing. Water fall-planted shrubs more often. Newly planted bare-root shrubs need water as soon as the soil begins to dry below 2 inches deep. Established drought-tolerant shrubs should not need water this month.

TREES

Established trees have anchor roots near the trunk and water-absorbing roots at the edges of the canopy or foliage line, called the *drip line*. The drip line is the area where a light rain would drip off the leaves to water the plant; this is the area where the water-absorbing roots are genetically programmed to grow. This is where you need to water and fertilize trees. By watering deeply and less frequently, these water-absorbing roots can be trained to grow deeply in search of moisture, avoiding surface evaporation and requiring you to water less often.

If there has been little winter precipitation, water trees at the drip line to a depth of 3 feet. This is notably important if March comes in like a lion. Wind can quickly desiccate any plant. Especially monitor any newly planted trees.

Non-drought-tolerant trees that are leafed out need water every 21 to 30 days. Drought-tolerant trees need water every 30 to 60 days.

VINES, GROUNDCOVERS & ORNAMENTAL GRASSES

In all elevations, monitor moisture under all plants in this category, especially any newly planted ones. Wind can easily desiccate all plants, even low-growing ones.

In lower elevations, drought-tolerant vines and groundcovers need water every 21 to 30 days; non-drought-tolerant plants, every 10 to 14 days.

Water ornamental grasses after their annual severe rejuvenation pruning. If they have broken dormancy, water every 14 to 21 days.

In zones 7 and 6, overwintering plants need water at least once this month to help them break dormancy. If they're mulched for winter, leave the mulch in place until after the last frost, but check beneath. If the soil is dry lower than 3 inches, water.

In zones 5 and 4, you should not need to water established plants in this category. Fall-planted plants should be checked if the soil is not frozen. If the soil is dry lower than 3 inches, water.

FERTILIZE

Fertilizer will help plants, but the wrong amount or the wrong kind can harm or even kill them. While many fertilizers call themselves "plant food," this is inaccurate. Plants *make* their own food, via photosynthesis. Fertilizer for plants is like vitamins for humans. These elements are needed so vital biological processes, such as making new cells, can happen.

ANNUALS & BULBS

Annuals perform better with fertilizer, but avoid fertilizing newly planted seedlings. Two weeks after planting, lightly fertilize by applying fertilizer at half-strength. Alternatively, use a slow-release fertilizer when you plant, and reapply as stated on the package. Since annuals are grown for their bloom, use a bloom fertilizer high in phosphorus, such as an 8-12-6 compound.

Bulbs perform better the next year if you fertilize them after they flower, while they still have green leaves. Use a general-purpose fertilizer high in nitrogen.

EDIBLES

Citrus and other spring-flowering evergreen fruits need help to set ample fruit. Fertilize citrus now if you didn't in February, before the end of the month. Use a citrus or fruiting fertilizer in the amount indicated. If you miss this deadline or if they have started to flower, wait until Memorial Day. Too much fertilizer, or fertilizer at the wrong time, can lead to poor fruit set, fruit drop, or poor quality fruit.

Fertilize deciduous fruit and nut trees and shrubs as they break dormancy, using a bloom fertilizer. Grapes and deciduous berries (brambleberries, currants, aronia) bear better with a fruiting fertilizer applied within two weeks of breaking dormancy.

Vegetable gardens probably don't need fertilizer, depending on what stage they are in. Newly planted seeds and seedlings do not need fertilizer for at least two weeks. In the lower elevations, the winter garden is ending and doesn't need fertilizer.

Fertilize perennial herbs if the days are consistently above 55°F. If you planted herbs to encourage pollinators, then fertilize the spring-blooming species with a bloom fertilizer.

LAWNS

It's tempting to purchase weed-and-feed fertilizer, but use these with care. If you have trees, shrubs, or perennials anywhere near your lawn, you may kill them.

For the lower elevations, fertilize lawns overseeded with perennial rye. Do not fertilize plain Bermudagrass lawns or those overseeded with annual rye. Upper-elevation gardeners don't need to fertilize lawns this month.

PERENNIALS

In all elevations, you can start to fertilize once perennials start to emerge. Use a slow-release formula or apply a general-purpose fertilizer at half strength every two weeks.

In lower elevations, flowering succulent perennials, such as bulbine, aloe, and haworthia, will bloom better next year with a general-purpose fertilizer, used at half strength and applied every two to four weeks from now until Memorial Day.

ROSES

In the lower elevations, fertilize with a bloom fertilizer at recommended strength while roses are blooming. In upper elevations, fertilize only after your roses have leafed out. Use a slow-release formula or apply a general-purpose fertilizer at half strength every two weeks.

SHRUBS

At lower elevations, fertilize spring-blooming shrubs with a bloom fertilizer. Exceptions are senna, cassia, and others in the legume or pea family, which don't require fertilizer.

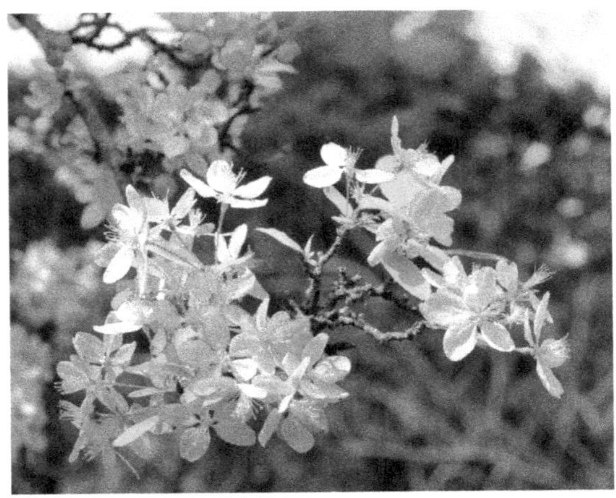

Spring-blooming deciduous trees and shrubs, including edibles, should be fertilized as they break dormancy in spring.

In upper elevations, you don't need to be in a rush to fertilize your shrubs. Instead, wait until April.

TREES

In all elevations, the best time to fertilize deciduous trees is at budbreak. Use a balanced fertilizer, such as 10-10-10. Apply fertilizer around the drip line of the tree where the feeder roots live. Follow label directions and water fertilizer into the soil.

Fertilize spring-blooming trees with a bloom fertilizer. Exceptions are the many desert trees, including mesquite and palo verde, which are in the legume or pea family; they don't require fertilizer.

VINES, GROUNDCOVERS & ORNAMENTAL GRASSES

Spring-flowering vines benefit from flowering formulation within two weeks of breaking dormancy. In lower elevations, this is generally now. One more reason to get rid of a grass lawn is that groundcovers need less fertilizer than turf grasses. Instead of fertilizer, you could sprinkle compost over groundcovers—this will supply necessary minerals for the plants, supply microorganisms to help nourish the soil, and supply organic matter to improve the water-holding capacity of the soil. If you have a blooming groundcover, add a bloom formulation of fertilizer.

Don't fertilize groundcovers in the legume or pea family, such as acacia or dalea.

Ornamental grasses need a general-purpose or lawn-type fertilizer in spring, especially after their annual rejuvenation pruning. Wait until nights are above 45°F to fertilize.

PROBLEM-SOLVE

The main March pest is weeds. Just when you think you got them all, they're back! Grandpa taught me, "One year's seeding is seven years weeding."

Lower-elevation gardens may be visited now by leafcutter bees, a solitary bee. The mother bee will cut small circular holes out of leaves. She uses this leaf circle to make a case she packs with one egg and a nectar and pollen blend. These cases are tucked in rock or wood cavities and earn these important pollinators the name of mason or carpenter bee. While the circular holes in leaves are unsightly, plants do recover. I have never had a plant killed by these bees, although one rose bush looked quite bedraggled for a while. Some gardeners apply soapy spray onto their plants to deter bee visits. It is mildly effective.

ANNUALS & BULBS

Monitor for aphid and whitefly, both a common problem as the days warm. Both can be hosed off with a stream of water or sprayed with insecticidal soap.

In the upper elevations, frost heaving can be an issue for shallow-rooted annuals and bulbs in this month of shifting weather. Check and gently rebury as necessary.

Leafcutter bees are active in spring and use the leaf circles to build nests for their young.

Floating row covers can help protect vegetables from frost.

EDIBLES

In all elevations, late frosts can harm new transplants and tender sprouts. If a hard frost is predicted, you can cover them with frost cloth, specifically designed for this task. Also called floating row covers, these can be left in place for several days. If you don't have frost cloth, then cardboard boxes, buckets, burlap, or even shade cloth can be used. Remove any opaque coverings each day so plants can get the light and air movement they need for healthy growth.

In the lower elevations, if you started your spring garden outdoors, be especially alert for night temperatures below 40°F, and protect tender seedlings and transplants.

Flea beetles appear as temperatures reach 50°F. Variously colored black to tan, solid, or spotted, they hop like fleas when approached. Look for holes in leaves, especially on young seedlings, where damage is most rapid and will cause the most harm.

Early in spring, flea beetles emerge from leaf debris and wait to feast on your garden. If they were a problem last year, cut off their food supply by delaying planting for two to three weeks. Homemade sprays can work to control flea beetles but those with alcohol can burn plants.

Citrus thrips appear in March and cause scarring on the fruit rind in a circle around the stem. They don't harm fruit production or flavor, but they are of concern in commercial orchards because consumers don't buy scarred fruit. A number of natural enemies attack citrus thrips, including a predatory mite (*Euseius tularensis*), hunting spiders, lacewings, dustywings, and minute pirate bugs.

LAWNS

Watch for spring weeds and eliminate them before they bloom and go to seed. The sooner you do this, the smaller the weeds and the quicker the lawn grasses will grow and cover any bare patches.

PERENNIALS

Flea beetles may bother some perennials. Generally, well-established plants recover, but if you also have a vegetable garden, you should control this pest.

In upper elevations, shallow-rooted perennials, especially small ones such as hellebores and dianthus, could suffer frost heaving. Check them periodically and gently rebury as necessary. Add a layer of mulch to help prevent recurrence.

ROSES

Continue to monitor for aphids and powdery mildew, both a common problem as the days warm. Treat aphids with insecticidal soap.

Powdery mildew spores are easily spread by the splashing from overhead watering, especially if you let fallen rose leaves remain under your shrubs. Keep the area under roses free of fallen rose leaves, and mulch with cedar bark or similar inert mulch to help prevent splashing.

SHRUBS

In the lower elevations, agaves, especially larger species, may suffer from agave snout nose weevils (*Scyphophorus acupunctatus*). They prefer large plants on the verge of flowering. Female weevils puncture a plant to lay their eggs, and they carry bacteria in their saliva that rots the plant, making it easier for the larvae to feed. This is one case where toxic compounds are required just as soon as you notice any wilting or collapsing of agave leaves. Read and follow directions! To prevent their spread, you need to get the weevils when they're grubs. Treat with a granular grub killer applied to a large area of soil around the agaves. It's best applied in March and again in June, when the beetles are most active. Infected agaves are doomed, but you can prevent the spread of this pest.

Desert broom is a useful shrub, but can become weedy in the landscape as seedlings pop up everywhere. Learn to recognize them and pull them when they are small, before their extensive taproot is fully developed.

In upper elevations, check bare stems of deciduous shrubs for overwintering scale and aphid pests. Treat with a dormant oil spray before bud break. Such sprays kill all insects, even beneficial species, so unless you had a severe infestation last year, you may opt not to spray. Do not spray succulents or evergreen species with needles; the oil removes their protective coating.

TREES

There are few tree pests to watch for in nonfruit trees this month.

VINES, GROUNDCOVERS & ORNAMENTAL GRASSES

Just the weeds! Especially eliminate weeds in groundcovers before they take over.

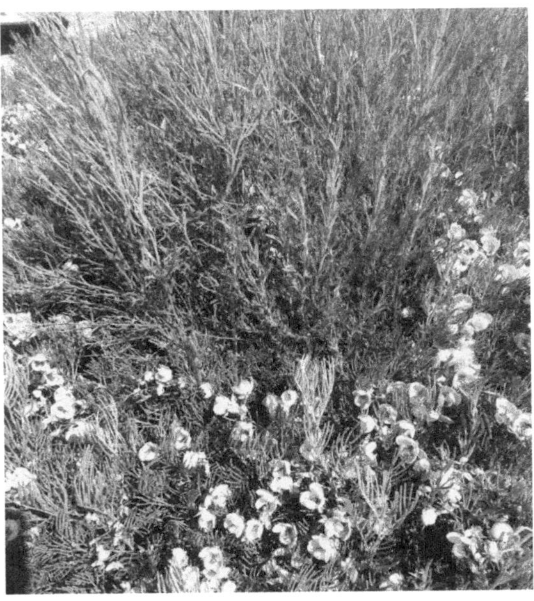

The green splotch in center of this flowering cassia is a weedy desert broom. It sprouted in the shade of the cassia and was not removed by the landscaping crew.

April

April is awesome. *The days are sunny and warm while the nights are crisp and cool. That's great for us humans, and great for plants as well.*

While it was okay to play hooky in March and ignore some garden chores, the summer heat ahead makes it important to buckle down and complete certain chores in April. The first two weekends of the month are ideal for a good spring cleaning. Then there is planting to complete, and spring pruning, and fertilizing—but once all that is done, it will be time to relax and enjoy your garden all summer long.

Now is a good time to plan and prepare the garden for summer enjoyment. Summer is the time of year that many of us use our yards more in the evenings than during the daylight hours. Creating a garden to enjoy at night will take some effort now, but is highly worth it.

As the sun sinks slowly in the west, most plants shut down for the night. Lucky for us in this region, there are a number of local plants that do not; instead, they drench the night air with alluring fragrance, trying to attract some of the nighttime animals to come and pollinate them. It makes sense. Without hot sunshine to wilt flowers or dry up nectar, flowers last longer. The drawback is that there are relatively few pollinators active at night. Plants share pollinators by timing when they bloom over the course of the summer. This creates a win-win situation for Southwest gardeners. By planting a variety of plants, you can have a delightful palette of ever-changing fragrances in your evening garden all summer long.

Night bloomers abound—annuals, perennials, groundcovers, shrubs, succulents, and even some herbs. But they need not bloom at night; some plants have leaves whose fragrance can waft across the garden at night. A number of native plants have foliage that gleams silvery in the light of the moon. Some people cultivate Moon Gardens specifically to be viewed after sundown.

PLAN

As you formulate your checklist of April chores, look for places you can add night-blooming and fragrant plants. There are many choices, including some with pink, lavender, and yellow blooms.

ANNUALS & BULBS

Spring-clean your pots and containers. Potting mix degrades with use, and you should replace at least half with fresh media each year. You can use the old potting soil as the brown component in your compost.

Take a few moments to record in your garden journal which bulb is blooming when, and which annuals do well. If you maintain an electronic journal, you can easily add photos.

If you'd like to add fragrance to the garden this summer, plan on adding some lemon lily (*Lilium parryi*), a native of the Southwest mountains. Lemon lily is very easy to grow—it just needs water and cool winter temperatures. With part shade in summer, it can survive in zones 9 to 6. The shady north side of a home is ideal in the lower elevations.

EDIBLES

Lower elevation gardeners rip out the last of the cool season garden and install spring and summer vegetables this month. Plan this carefully and resist the temptation to stuff in one extra plant. Vegetable plants produce better if they're not overly crowded.

Fragrant and delicate, this Southwest-native lemon lily is a charmer for your summer garden.

Those in the upper elevations still have time to start warm-season seedlings if your planning reveals you'll have a slot for them.

Annual herbs that thrive in the warmth ahead include basil, epazote, perilla (shiso), and stevia. They can be planted in beds, pots, or in the landscape. Order seed now if you haven't yet.

LAWNS

Xeriscape principles state that an appropriate-sized lawn in the oasis zone is just fine. If your eye craves grassy green, you should plant what makes you happy. But to follow the ideals of xeriscape, you should choose the type of grass best adapted to your area and prepare the lawn site well.

For lower elevations, hybrid Bermudagrass is ideal. It can take triple-digit heat and survive on relatively little water compared to other grasses. The hybrids don't flower and won't torture allergy sufferers with pollen. In upper elevations, xeriscape lawn choices include buffalograss, blue grama, and turf-type tall fescue. For higher altitudes or colder sites, fine fescue works well.

Sprinklers are not ideal for watering in the Southwest. Up to 50 percent of water is lost to evaporation before it even hits the lawn. If you're installing or redoing a lawn, look into some of the newer technologies, including drip mats and drip tubes that are installed under the soil. These drip products have been honed to virtually trouble-free products for homeowners.

PERENNIALS

Plant sales at area botanical gardens generally offer plants that do best in your area. Purchase only what you can plant within a decent time frame; there will be more next year.

Gardeners at lower elevations: look for some of the smaller clumping succulent perennials, such as aloe, hesperaloe, bulbine, and manfreda (also called tuberose). These are attractive, low-care additions to the garden.

Zones 9 to 4 can consider the night-blooming daylily (*Hemerocallis lilioasphodelus*), also confusingly called lemon lily, although it is not

HERE'S HOW

TO PREPARE TO INSTALL A LAWN

The secret to having a healthy lawn is planting it well below the level of your patio and other areas of the yard. The top of the mown grass should be 2 to 3 inches below grade. This allows you to water your lawn, and for the water to soak down into the lawn, not run over your patio.

The area must be well prepared by removing all rocks, debris, old turf, and weeds. Water the entire area to a depth of 12 to 14 inches and leave it overnight. This makes the soil easier to dig and blend in the following key ingredients to help your lawn thrive: compost, soil sulfur (to help alleviate caliche), and optionally a high-nitrogen fertilizer. You need to dig these components in a full 12 or more inches deep to create a good home for lawn grasses. Lay down and dig in 4 to 6 inches of compost, soil sulfur at 5 pounds per 1,000 square feet, and fertilizer as specified on the container. As you work, remove any rocks larger than a quarter.

Installation of the irrigation system happens after the soil is prepared. Once all this is done, use a lawn roller to even out the soil, so there are no trip hazards and so the lawn can be evenly mowed. Now you are ready to plant.

Growing lawn from sod looks easy, but there are a number of critical steps to be taken ahead of time to ensure success.

a true lily (*Lilium*). This charming daylily has fragrant blooms that open at dusk.

ROSES

While lower-elevation gardeners collect rose petals for cooking and crafts, upper elevations could still be visited by snow. But upper-elevation gardeners can *plan* to replace underperforming roses. Gardeners in lower elevations now have to wait for fall to plant roses, because summer is too close. (See March, Here's How to Help Roses Thrive.)

SHRUBS

Spring-flowering shrubs delight the eye. Record bloom times in your journal, or note a lovely shrub seen elsewhere that you'd like for your garden. As tempting as it is to have one of every beautiful plant, it can turn your yard into a tangled, chaotic mess. Plan your garden design to avoid this.

TREES

Arizona celebrates Arbor Day the last Friday of April. Sad to say, many trees do not tolerate planting this close to summer. To celebrate in lower elevations consider planting trees with tropical genes, such as palms.

Container-grown trees can be planted in upper elevations. Plan their placement based on the mature size of the tree and avoid planting too close to structures.

VINES, GROUNDCOVERS & ORNAMENTAL GRASSES

Arbors, ramadas, or pergolas can add an enticing destination area in your garden, especially when covered with flowering and fruit-producing vines, such as the native passionflower. Such a structure replaces a tree in landscape design, providing a shady seating area in much less time than it takes a tree to grow. Alternatively, you can place an arbor under a mature tree and add shade-loving vines. Those in zones 10 and 9 may consider snapdragon vine (*Maurandya antirrhiniflora*), yuca (*Merremia aurea*), and lilac vine (*Hardenbergia violacea*). Those in zones 9 to 4 have a number of varieties of fragrant, evening-blooming honeysuckle (*Lonicera*) to select from, as well trumpet vine (*Campsis radicans*).

Mature size matters. Trees and large cacti are hard to move once established in the landscape, so plan your planting.

Ornamental grasses have a place in any garden—perhaps not as a centerpiece, but tucked in here and there or scattered in blank areas. Planted with spring bulbs at their base, they provide year-round interest as well as food and shelter for birds and some species of butterfly. There are so many grass species to choose from! See the Resources at the end of this book for some nurseries that offer a wide selection of plants that will thrive here.

PLANT

This book is a guide, but you still need to pay attention to what the weather is doing any particular year. El Niño and La Niña patterns aside, other shifts and droughts do occur. A garden journal will help you garden better in future years if you record weather conditions and overall trends.

ANNUALS & BULBS

Throughout the Southwest there are a number of species of datura, a night-blooming wildflower. Also called jimsonweed, or locoweed, datura fills the night with a musky fragrance that attracts the large hummingbird moths to pollinate them. The plants survive on rainfall alone and can be planted from seed once soils are above 45°F. Datura plants are poisonous, but that can be a plus, because their presence helps prevent hungry herbivores from examining your yard too closely and finding the more tasty plants.

Lower elevation gardeners can plant summer annuals, including zinnia, periwinkle, and moss rose. Add night-scented stock (*Matthiola longipetala*) to this list. You may have to order seed and grow it yourself, in which case you start it at the same time you start mustard greens for the garden (they're in the same family).

In the upper elevations, you may be just now taking annuals out of their protective cold frame and planting them into the ground. You can plant now, but zones 6 and 5 gardeners should keep frost protection handy. Zone 4 gardeners should wait until next month to set annuals into the soil.

All elevations can thin and transplant bulbs that are done blooming. In upper elevations, this includes snowdrops, glory-of-the-snow, and Siberian squill. Gently lift the clumps out of the soil, separate the bulbs, and plant them to the same depth elsewhere in the landscape, being careful to keep the leaves intact. This is also a good time to plant out any forced bulbs you had growing indoors.

EDIBLES

As lower-elevation gardeners set out vegetable seedlings, be sure to space them as recommended on the seed packet or label. Once soils are above 50°F, plant sweet potato slips. Now is the time to sow seed of hot-season greens such as amaranth, New Zealand spinach, purslane, and Malabar spinach (a perennial vine).

For zones 7 and 6 gardeners, this is the time to plant cool-season vegetables, such as radish, arugula, and European spinach, from seed. Plant slow-growing members of the carrot family, including parsnip, carrot, fennel, parsley, and dill. (In zones 5 and 4, you will plant these next month.)

Plant fruiting shrubs and trees from containers now in all zones except 5 and 4. These uppermost elevations can still plant bare-root or balled-and-burlaped plants.

Lower-elevation gardeners can start summer herbs from seed or seedlings if you haven't yet. Basil, epazote, and perilla are commonly used as herbs. Also consider planting perennial herbs, such as rosemary, bay, and aloysia (also called oreganillo) from containers now. Lemongrass is a lovely addition to the zone 10 garden, but it will need frost protection in zone 9.

Summer herbs for the upper elevations include members of the carrot family, such as anise, caraway, cumin, and dill. Sow seed in zones 7 and 6; in zones 5 and 4 wait until next month. Anise hyssop is a variety of hyssop in the mint family and can be planted from containers now, along with other perennial herbs, such as beebalm, horehound, and valerian.

Aloysias are fragrant, night-blooming, shrubby herbs with a number of species native to the Southwest. Easy to find in the nursery trade are oreganillo (*Aloysia wrightii*), also called Mexican oregano and used in the kitchen, vanilla scented white bush (*A. gratissima*, also sold as *A. lycioides*), and almond verbena (*A. virgata*). Most are hardy to zone 7b.

Zones 10 and 9 can plant the tall and stately Peruvian apple cactus (*Cereus hildmannianus*, also sold as *C. peruvianus*), with massive (and massively fragrant) nighttime flowers. Fruits are large and delightfully edible, but don't bite into them like an apple; instead, slice them open and scoop out the watermelon-sweet flesh with a spoon.

LAWNS

In all zones except 5 and 4, you can establish a lawn this month, but first prepare the area. (See Here's How to Prepare to Install a Lawn.)

Lawns may be planted from sod, plugs, or seed. Both sod and plugs are growing grass with roots and soil. Sod is sold as squares or rectangles, which are laid down like carpet, the sections not overlapping. Sod forms an instant lawn. Plugs are square or round and are spaced 8 to 10 inches apart. A full season is generally needed for a lawn to fill out. Thrifty gardeners buy rolls of sod and cut their own plugs. Even thriftier gardeners plant seed, but this requires vigilance and effort to keep the seed-eating birds away, and the area can't be used until the young grass plants are well established.

PERENNIALS

Gardeners in lower elevations can plant summer- and fall-blooming perennials now. Consider hummingbird trumpet (*Epilobium canum*, formerly *Zauschneria californica*), Mexican bush sage (*Salvia leucantha*), and the colorful hesperaloes (*Hesperaloe parviflora*) or their night-blooming cousin *H. nocturna*.

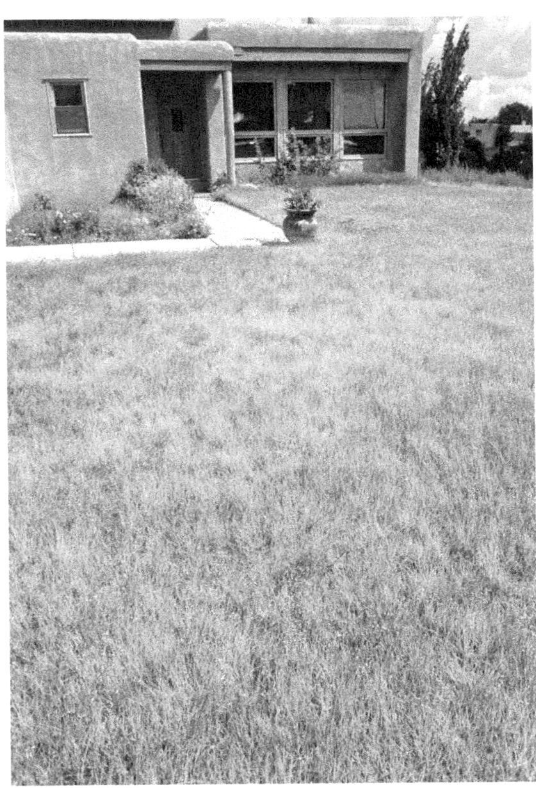

Buffalograss is a tufting ornamental grass commonly used as a groundcover alternative in the upper elevations. April is a good time to plant.

For all but zone 4, two Southwest natives related to bougainvillea are worth mention. Night-blooming angel's trumpet (*Acleisanthes longiflora*) is a New Mexico native sub-shrub; it's hard to find but worth it. It's ideal for the cactus garden or somewhere well away from lawn, because overwatering kills it. Nevada's native wildflower, desert moonflower (*A. nevadensis*) is a fragrant night-bloomer to add to low-water areas. Both can be planted this month from seed or containers.

Upper elevations need to plant any bare-root perennials as soon as they arrive. Ideally, such plants should be in the ground before they break dormancy. You have more leeway with container plants, since there is soil around their roots, but the sooner planted, the better, because summer is coming. Meanwhile, protect plants still in their containers from freezing with blankets around the pots when frost is predicted.

ROSES

All elevations can plant container-grown roses this month. Roses are easy to transplant—just be careful to keep the rootball intact.

SHRUBS

In lower elevations, now that it has warmed up, tropical evergreens such as hopbush (*Dodonaea viscosa*) and true myrtle (*Myrtus communis*) can be planted. Planting sooner is better than later, so plants can grow ample roots prior to summer heat stress. Be careful about overwatering transplants to avoid killing them with kindness.

Roses, especially grafted varieties, should not be planted any deeper than they were in their original container. In winter, you protect this delicate tissue with mulch, but burying the graft union in soil at planting generally leads to failure.

Those in upper elevations can still plant bare-root shrubs if they just now arrive. If you are making your purchase now, a better choice is balled-and-burlapped or container-grown shrubs.

TREES

Those in lower elevations can plant trees this month, but it's not ideal for many species. Palms have tropical genes and should be planted this month, now that it has warmed up.

In upper elevations, it is a good time to plant balled-and-burlapped or container-grown trees.

VINES, GROUNDCOVERS & ORNAMENTAL GRASSES

When planting ornamental grasses and groundcovers, space them according to their mature size.

Gardeners at lower elevations can plant heat-loving and summer-blooming groundcovers such as lantana, black dalea (*Dalea pulchella*), and yellowdot (*Sphagneticola trilobata*). Night-blooming groundcovers feature a number of evening primroses, including tufted evening primrose (*Oenothera caespitosa*), Arizona evening primrose (*O. hookerii*), desert evening primrose (*O. primiveris*), and Mexican primrose (*O. berlandieri*).

Gardeners in upper elevations can plant the tried and true cold hardy snow-in-summer (*Cerastium tomentosum*), bearberry (*Arctostaphylos*), and hardy iceplant (*Delosperma*). This allows them sufficient time to establish prior to the heat of summer. Now is also a good time to plant vines such as Virginia creeper and honeysuckle. Don't forget ornamental grasses, including ribbon grass (*Phalaris arundinacea*) and maiden grass (*Miscanthus sinensis*).

CARE

April is seed-collecting month in lower elevations. Time to collect and save seed of spring wildflowers as well as cool-season vegetables.

HERE'S HOW

TO SAVE SEED

It is easy to save seeds of annuals, wildflower, vegetables, and herbs. The key is to collect the seed just as it matures and before it starts to drop. You especially want to catch any pods that burst open to scatter seed.

Stalks of pods: Snip off the stalks and invert them into large paper bags. Fold the bags shut. Now, when seedpods shatter, the seeds are trapped in the bag for next year's sowing.

Seedheads: Often these seedheads simply break off in your hand. Hold a container below them as you break them off.

For future sowing, you don't need to clean the seed, although some purists like to. For use as an herb (such as coriander or dill seed), clean the seed. Kitchen colanders and sieves are useful for this.

Store saved seed indoors in jars or paper bags. Just don't forget to accurately and entirely label them, including the date.

Epazote, sorrel, and garlic chives all grow well from seed. Each plant will yield far more seed than you can use the following year.

With some plants, you can shake stalks of seedpods over a bed sheet then pour the collected seed into a container for storage.

ANNUALS & BULBS

Native wildflowers will self-sow, returning year after year. Problem is, our urban areas have more quail and other seed-eating birds than are found in the wilderness. These winged wonders may devour all your wildflower seed over the summer. The solution: save seed as seedheads form, and sow it in autumn when it's time for the plants to grow.

Deadhead spent blooms from iris and larger bulbs, such as tulips and daffodils. This prevents the plant from setting seed and can encourage additional bloom if the bulb has sufficient energy.

EDIBLES

Lower-elevation gardeners should save seed of cool-season vegetables and herbs because the best thing to grow in your yard is what worked for you last year. (See Here's How to Save Seed.)

In all elevations, keep an eye on vegetables sprouting, and thin the plants to the spacing

Pinching encourages more branching and a more compact growth form.

recommended on the seed packet once they are 3 inches tall. Plants need elbow room to perform their best. Use scissors to cut excess seedlings at soil level. This is less disruptive to the soil and roots of the remaining plants than pulling out unwanted plants. Once plants are 4 to 6 inches tall and soil is above 50°F, mulch with an organic material to discourage weeds and help retain soil moisture.

Most herbs benefit from pinching, a type of pruning that removes just the growing tips of a plant, ½ to 2 inches from each tip. Pinching encourages branching and helps plants maintain a more compact form. Pinch spring-blooming herbs such as feverfew and chamomile so they produce more of the blooms used as the herb. Basil should be pinched at the first sign of flower production (nip 'em in the bud!). This ensures that the herb produces more leaves and doesn't spend energy on flowering.

Pinch some of your berries too. Pinching the tips of raspberries and blackberries early in the season promotes branching and thus more fruit. Prune shrubbier berries, such as elderberry and gooseberry, like you would spring-flowering shrubs.

LAWNS

April is a transitional month for lawns in our region, with little specific care. You could aerate a cool-season lawn now, in early spring, or wait until fall.

PERENNIALS

Some semiwoody perennials, such as Palmer's marigold (*Tagetes palmeri*) or Russian sage (*Perovskia atriplicifolia*), require gradual rejuvenation pruning every two to three years. Perform rejuvenation pruning after bloom is past, or two months before it begins. (See March, Here's How to Rejuvenation Prune Woody Plants.)

Some perennials benefit from pinching rather than wholesale pruning. Most members of the sunflower family can be pinched back, including blanketflower (*Gaillardia*), Joe-Pye weed, asters, chrysanthemums, coreopsis, Shasta daisy, and desert zinnia (*Zinnia acerosa*) and prairie zinnia (*Z. grandiflora*). Also pinch 'Autumn Joy' sedum, ruellia, and globe mallow (*Sphaeralcea*).

Lower-elevation gardeners, have you mulched yet this spring? If not, apply a 2- to 3-inch layer of cedar bark or similar mulch of organic material to help the soil retain moisture during summer heat. Select tan or lighter-colored mulch to help reflect summer sun away from soil.

In the upper elevations, if you mounded mulch to protect the crowns of tender perennials, uncover them on last frost day in your area, and certainly by the end of the month. Leave a 2- to 3-inch layer over the roots to help reduce summer evaporation. Excess mulch can go into the compost.

ROSES

Deadhead spent blooms to prolong flowering. Do not drop the spent petals around the plants, no matter how poetic it looks—you'll only have to

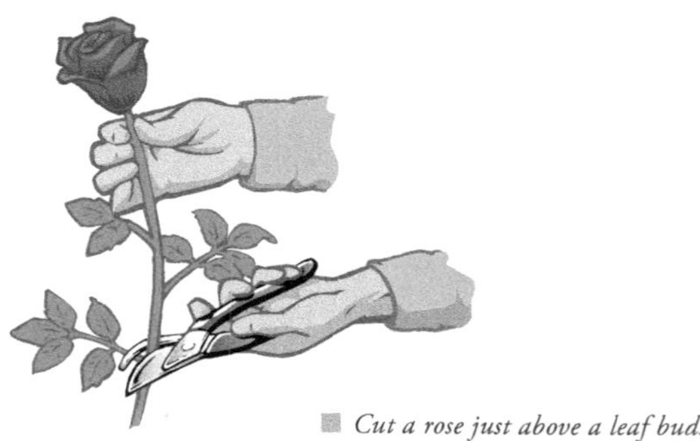

Cut a rose just above a leaf bud.

remove the petals later to protect your roses from disease. Compost bins are kept by gardens for a reason; you can compost rose petals, but avoid composting rose leaves.

Gardeners in upper elevations should remove the protective winter mulch from around the bushes, but leave a 2- to 3-inch layer over the roots. Since the mulch is no longer protecting the crown, keep some garden blankets handy in case of late freeze.

SHRUBS

Gardeners in all elevations can prune spring-flowering shrubs once they complete their bloom. The first step to any pruning job is to remove dead wood and damaged stems or branches. Once that's done, you can treat the plant as needed, perhaps a mild pruning of a few out-of-scale branches or a gradual rejuvenation pruning of a shrub losing its vigor. Avoid topiary pruning (shearing a plant into a specific shape). Plants require a great deal of water and fertilizer to recover from such treatment.

Mulch out to the drip line of shrubs. A 2- to 3-inch layer over the roots helps reduce summer evaporation.

TREES

Did you remove the puny nursery stake when you planted your tree? Most tree species need sturdy tree staking once planted so they will be able to sway in the wind and learn how to stand up on their own. (See October, Here's How to Stake a Tree.)

Avoid excessive pruning that exposes any smooth bark of trees to sunlight. Plants can get sunburned. Called *sunscald*, it can occur on any tree, but especially those with smooth bark, such as most young trees (apple, peach, jujube), many tropicals (citrus, olive), and other species as well (mulberry, aspen). Hot summer sun can heat the water inside the bark so greatly that tissues rupture. Such burn damage leads to cracks in the bark, opening the door to pests and disease. Retain branches on the lower part of the trunk of immature trees to shade the southwest side. You can remove these temporary branches in future years, when higher branches extend far enough to shade the trunk.

VINES, GROUNDCOVERS & ORNAMENTAL GRASSES

Treat groundcovers with bald patches now. For small patches, add compost to improve the soil and encourage the surrounding groundcover to root into the area. For larger patches, install replacement plants as needed.

Remove any dead or damaged stems from established vines once they have leafed out.

Severe rejuvenation pruning of ornamental grasses should be done every year in early spring, just as the plants break dormancy. (See February, Here's How to Prune Ornamental Grass.) Note that just because it has "grass" in its name does not mean it is a grass. Beargrass (*Nolina*) is related to asparagus and will only recover from rejuvenation pruning very slowly. Mexican grass tree (*Dasylirion longissimum*) will be outright killed.

WATER

An irrigation system can save money and time compared to hand watering. It does not need to be elaborate. A garden hose can feed one irrigation line at a time and be moved to other lines as needed. Quick connectors help the process.

Any irrigation system in the Southwest should include three things. First, a filter (left) that can be cleaned out on a regular basis; second, a pressure regulator (center) to keep water pressure at a level that won't blow off emitters. Third is a back-flow preventer (not shown). This basic system is simply attached to a garden hose (right).

In lower elevations, the irrigation system maintenance this month is the big one before summer comes. Thoroughly check the entire system. Make sure all emitters are working. Replace the backup battery in the controller (timer) before summer power bumps cause the controller to forget its programming.

ANNUALS & BULBS

If you have sown seed for seasonal annuals, lightly moisten the soil daily to a depth of 1 inch or so to help germination and give tiny plants a head start.

Monitor moisture levels for bulb beds. Summer bulbs that have been planted need moisture to grow as soils warm. Bulbs that still have green leaves need water to make ample sugars for next year's bloom.

EDIBLES

As you get ready to place transplants into the garden, water them the day before. This ensures they'll be moist but not waterlogged when it comes time to plant, reducing the chance of their tiny rootballs breaking. Moist soil also helps reduce transplant shock. Water again after they're in the ground, so the two soils merge and any large air pockets are driven out. Use a nozzle that will apply water like a gentle rainfall.

Most herbs require well-drained soil and can be killed if overwatered. Rosemary, thyme, and lavender, including desert lavender (*Hyptis emoryi*), are some of the herbs that like to dry well between watering. Check the soil with a probe or dig down 2 inches to see if they have used the water you last applied.

Don't skimp on water for plants that are flowering and setting fruit or nuts. If drought stress occurs at this point, you may lose an entire year's crop.

LAWNS

The secret to maintaining a xeriscape lawn is to water deeply and not too often. Once established, a deep-rooted lawn needs a good soak every week or two in summer. In the wild, grass roots grow downwards 6 to 12 *feet* in search of water. By soaking your lawn deeply, you encourage your cultivated lawn to follow its genetic programming and grow nice, deep roots. Deep watering also takes longer to evaporate, saving you money.

Short, frequent waterings lead to shallow roots, while deeper waterings, less frequently applied, encourage deep roots.

In the lower elevations, overseeded lawns need water as they transition to the warm-season grass. In the upper elevations, be sure to water as lawns break dormancy. Last frost day is only a guideline—if spring arrives early, you will need to nurture the emerging lawn.

Maintain good moisture levels for any newly seeded or sodded lawn. Frequent light waterings of newly seeded lawns help grass germinate. Sodded lawns need daily soaking at first. Even if you have an irrigation system, check the edges of any new lawn. Edges next to hardscapes can dry out more quickly than the center of the lawn and may require additional watering with a hose.

PERENNIALS

In all elevations, monitor perennials blooming now. Anything in bloom will need water more often than discussed in Here's How Often to Water Your Landscape.

Many native succulents begin flowering now and will bloom better if watered. If you grow prickly pear, barrel cactus, or banana yucca for their edible fruit, help them by watering every two weeks. Water all small succulents at least once this month, more often if they're in containers.

ROSES

Roses are fairly drought tolerant; unless they are in bloom or it gets windy, every 7 to 14 days is often enough to water established roses. Roses you planted this spring require daily water at first, tapering to twice a week, and gradually less until established.

Try to water in the morning, when plants need it. Books may advise you to avoid water on top of rose leaves, but that is only an issue in humid areas. You don't hold an umbrella over your roses when it rains.

SHRUBS

Newly planted shrubs can be killed by kindness! If the soil remains waterlogged, it will kill them as quickly as drought will. Check the soil with a probe or dig down 3 inches to see if they've used the water you last applied.

TREES

April showers may arrive, but in our region they rarely bring enough moisture for trees. Use a trowel to dig a test hole out at the edge of the canopy (the drip line), and check moisture levels at 4 inches' depth. If the soil is dry, apply water to a depth of 3 feet. For most gardeners, this will be every three weeks to help trees get ready for summer. Even drought-tolerant natives such as oaks, palms, and mesquite need water when they're growing in urban yards, generally every 14 to 30 days in spring. High-water-use trees such as ash or sycamore need water every 7 to 12 days. They're native to riparian areas of the Southwest, so while they're "native," they're not drought-adapted natives.

VINES, GROUNDCOVERS & ORNAMENTAL GRASSES

Depending on the size of the vine, the species, and its exposure, you may need to water once a month to once a week. Although they may be as tall as a tree, vine roots are more like that of a shrub, thus watering to 2 feet deep is sufficient. Plan on 7- to 12-day intervals for high-water users, such as wisteria or potato vine (*Solanum jasminoides*). Drought-tolerant vines, such as Baja passionflower

Most drought-tolerant groundcover, such as this Mexican evening primrose, will bloom for many extra weeks, if given a little extra water while it's in bloom.

(*Passiflora foetida*) or creeping fig (*Ficus pumila*), need watering every 14 to 30 days.

Groundcovers shade their own roots and need less water than similarly sized lawn areas. Shorter species have shallower roots. My rule of thumb is water to a depth twice as deep as the groundcover's height: thus a 6-inch-high thyme plant gets watered to 12 inches deep.

Ornamental grasses easily grow roots twice as deep as plants are tall, and since they're mostly native to grasslands where rainfall is around 20 inches per year, they need less water than other perennials. That said, summer is coming—be sure you water them this month.

FERTILIZE

In the Southwest, we have a plant nutrient issue different from most of the country—alkaline-induced iron chlorosis. Plant leaves yellow while the veins remain green, and the diagnosis is lack of iron *in the plant.* Southwest soils almost universally have more than enough iron, but plants can't absorb the iron out of alkaline soils. (See June, Here's How to Recognize & Treat Chlorosis.)

ANNUALS & BULBS

If you have annual beds, help plants by helping the soil with soil-enhancing organic matter, such

HERE'S HOW

OFTEN TO WATER YOUR LANDSCAPE

The guidelines in this chart are to help you plan how often to go out and water or have your irrigation timer turn on. Exact timing depends on your soil texture (sand, loam, clay), soil status (unfrozen), and local weather conditions (windy, record highs), as well as plant condition (flowering, dormant). This guide is for established plants (1 year for shrubs, 3 years for trees). Newly planted plants and those in containers will need additional water.

Water to the depth indicated and out at the canopy drip line of the plants, not at the trunk.

PLANT TYPE		SPRING	SUMMER	FALL	WINTER	DEPTH
	Zones 10, 9, 8	Mar.-May	May-Oct.	Oct.-Dec.	Dec.-Mar.	
	Zones 7, 6	Apr.-May	June-Sep.	Sep.-Oct.	Dec.-Apr.	
	Zones 5, 4	Apr.-May	June-Aug.	Sep.	Dec.-Apr.	
ANNUALS		3-7 days	2-5 days	3-7 days	5-10 days	1 foot
LAWNS	warm-season turfgrass	7-10 days	3-7 days	7-10 days	20-30 days	2 feet
	cool-season turfgrass	3-5 days	none	3-5 days	5-10 days	2 feet
ORNAMENTAL GRASSES		10-21 days	7-18 days	14-30 days	21-45 days	2 feet
PERENNIALS	drought-adapted	7-10 days	5-7 days	7-10 days	10-14 days	2 feet
	non-drought-adapted	5-8 days	3-5 days	5-8 days	8-14 days	2 feet
PERENNIAL SUCCULENTS		14-30 days	7-21 days	14-30 days	21-45 days	6-10 inches
ROSES		7-10 days	5-7 days	7-10 days	10-14 days	2 feet
SHRUBS	drought-adapted	14-30 days	7-21 days	14-30 days	30-45 days	2 feet
	non-drought-adapted	7-10 days	5-7 days	7-10 days	10-14 days	2 feet
TREES	drought-adapted	14-30 days	7-21 days	14-30 days	30-60 days	3 feet
	non-drought-adapted	7-12 days	5-10 days	7-12 days	14-30 days	3 feet
VINES & GROUNDCOVERS	drought-adapted	14-30 days	7-21 days	14-30 days	21-45 days	1-2 feet
	non-drought-adapted	7-10 days	5-7 days	7-10 days	10-14 days	1-2 feet

Alkaline-induced iron chlorosis shows up as yellowing leaves with green around the veins. It's easily treated by acidifying the soil around the affected plant.

as compost, aged steer manure, or peat moss. As well as releasing essential minerals into the soil, these amendments improve soil's moisture-holding capacity. If you wish, add a slow-release granular fertilizer and mix it in well as you prepare the soil. Although it releases slowly, you can still add too much, so follow the label directions.

If your spring-flowering bulbs are done blooming but still have green leaves, help them produce better blooms next year with a general-purpose or high-nitrogen fertilizer now. Be sure to water it into the soil.

EDIBLES

Lower-elevation gardeners with warm-season vegetables should fertilize with a general-purpose fertilizer in the early stages of growth. You can switch to a bloom fertilizer once plants near their flowering state, generally indicated by the production of side branches. Exceptions abound—beans and other legume family members need no fertilizer. Corn needs a great deal of nitrogen fertilizer right up to harvest. Many melons simply have one long vine; you can switch to a fruiting fertilizer once they start to bloom.

Gardeners at upper elevations with cool-season gardens should help the soil as described for annuals. Once the garden is planted, apply a slow-release granular fertilizer according to label directions. If you don't use a slow-release fertilizer, apply a general-purpose fertilizer at half strength every other week.

Fruit and nut shrubs and trees in bloom or starting to set fruit need fertilizer. A general-purpose fertilizer, such as a 12-12-12, is the best option. Less is better than too much. I pre-mix half the recommended fertilizer with water in a bucket and tip it into the plant basin. This way I am sure it is entirely dissolved and delivered where needed.

Many herbs are most flavorful and fragrant just as they get ready to bloom. A bloom fertilizer now is good for spring- and summer-flowering herbs.

LAWNS

The more you fertilize, the more you'll need to mow. However, some fertilizer is needed to help keep a lawn healthy and better able to withstand stress.

In lower elevations, it's not necessary to fertilize a non-overseeded Bermudagrass lawn in April.

HERE'S HOW

TO FERTILIZE THE FORGETFUL GARDENER'S WAY

Whether forgetful or just really busy, some of us neglect fertilizing. But providing fertilizer every so often will help plants thrive, provide flowers and fruits, and survive the slings and arrows of fortune. Just think, "Happy holiday to my garden!" and celebrate by fertilizing on these noteworthy days.

Zones 10 and 9: Fertilize on St. Patrick's Day, Memorial Day, and Labor Day (skip Fourth of July; it's too hot).

Zones 8 and 7: Fertilize on Tax Day (April 15), Memorial Day, Fourth of July, and Labor Day.

Zones 6 and 5: Fertilize on May Day (May 1), Memorial Day, Fourth of July, and National Sneak Some Zucchini onto Your Neighbor's Porch Day (August 8).

Zone 4: Fertilize on Memorial Day, Fourth of July, and National Sneak Some Zucchini onto Your Neighbor's Porch Day (August 8).

Lawns overseeded with perennial grass should be fertilized with a product high in both nitrogen and potassium to help the grass plants prepare for summer dormancy.

In upper elevations, it's not necessary to fertilize until a lawn is breaking dormancy and the grass is starting to grow, which may be the case now in some zones. Then, use a fertilizer that includes nitrogen and potassium.

Alkaline-induced iron chlorosis is difficult to treat in a lawn. It may be necessary to apply a lawn fertilizer containing iron or apply a chelated iron supplement.

PERENNIALS

In all elevations, wait until perennials break dormancy to fertilize. Even native perennials do better with some fertilizer. A bloom fertilizer is good for spring- and summer-flowering perennials. A general-purpose fertilizer is an option, and better now for fall-blooming species.

Because our soils lack organic matter, you can avoid fertilizer if you sprinkle compost around the plants and gently rake it into the soil around the roots. Cover with a plant-based mulch when you're done. This will act both as a soil builder and slow-release fertilizer.

ROSES

Bloom fertilizer or general-purpose? It depends on what state your roses are in: flowering or done for now. You can't go wrong with a general-purpose fertilizer applied at half the recommended strength, or a granular slow-release fertilizer.

SHRUBS

Avoid fertilizing newly planted shrubs for their first month in the landscape. Compost is not the same as chemical fertilizer; applied to the well around their base, it will slowly release the nutrients plants need.

Established, non-legume shrubs can be fertilized with a general-purpose fertilizer after the last frost day in your area this month.

Fragrant acacias are in the legume family and do not need fertilizer.

TREES

Gardeners in the lower elevations can fertilize this month, or wait until Memorial Day. (See Here's How to Fertilize the Forgetful Gardener's Way.)

In the upper elevations, established trees are breaking dormancy. Apply a general-purpose or slow-release granular fertilizer at half strength, and water in well. Do not fertilize newly planted trees or members of the legume family.

VINES, GROUNDCOVERS & ORNAMENTAL GRASSES

Established, non-legume vines and groundcovers can be fertilized with a general-purpose fertilizer after last frost in your area.

Fertilize ornamental grasses with a lawn fertilizer if you have some available; otherwise, use a general-purpose fertilizer at half the recommended dose.

PROBLEM-SOLVE

Weeds will be weeds. They will be growing alongside desired plants no matter what you do. Some are edible, such as lamb's quarter, a close relative of spinach. Look for a class or information on edible weeds. It somehow makes weeding less tedious if you get to eat the little rascals.

Speaking of rascals, little varmints are out in force in April. Lower-elevation critters, including rabbits, ground squirrels, pack rats, birds, and javelina, all have hungry babies in tow by now. In the upper elevations, you can add deer, elk, mice, and chipmunks to the list. Protect any newly planted plants, as they're the tastiest. As plants get older, many start to produce anti-herbivore compounds.

ANNUALS & BULBS

Bird netting or even chicken wire placed over newly planted annuals can prevent herbivore attacks. Remove it after the plants get taller (and to make it easier to weed).

Bulbs are gourmet morsels for many animals, and they *will* dig them up and devour them. A layer of chicken wire placed under the soil when you first plant can help discourage herbivores, but once bulb foliage is up, repellent sprays or a stout fence may be your only option.

EDIBLES

A number of Southwest birds adore seedlings. Avoid attracting quail and other herbivorous birds while your vegetable garden has small tender plants in it. Bird netting over your garden may be required until vegetables are larger.

Common now are cutworms and armyworms. These moth caterpillars especially attack young vegetable plants. Crawling along the soil, they eat the first part of the plant they encounter—the stem—and thus cut it down; hence the name. Collars of plastic or paper cups with the bottoms cut off can be gently placed around the stems of seedlings to discourage these pests.

Southwestern native insect eaters, such as this gentle and non-toxic minature red-spotted toad (Anaxyrus punctatus), *may make your garden home, even in highly urban areas.*

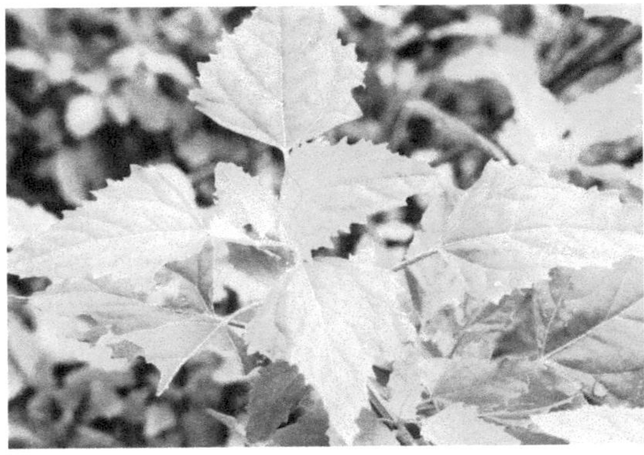

Lamb's quarter is now considered a weed, but it was originally brought here by the pioneers for food. It can be eaten in salads or cooked like spinach.

Gardeners growing melons, cucumbers, or any member of the squash family should watch for squash vine-borer caterpillars. The mother moth looks more like a fat black and red wasp, but don't be fooled. Mama moth lays her eggs on squash vines near the base and her babies bore inside the central stem, carefully not killing the plant until their last feeding frenzy before they form a chrysalis. Discourage egg laying by wrapping squash family stems with aluminum foil before they are the thickness of a pencil. Smearing them with petroleum jelly also works.

Deciduous fruit trees, especially those related to apples (including peach and almond) can suffer the depredations of the codling moth (apple worm) or tent caterpillars. Avoid using a toxic spray, as it also kills the pollinators as well as the beneficials that help control these pests. There are a number of IPM (Integrated Pest Management) products available, as well as traps that lure and kill the adults before they lay eggs. These insect traps work well if placed according to directions, plus they reduce the populations for several years.

An easy and chemical-free way to protect plants against cutworm damage is to place cardboard collars around small seedlings.

To treat tent caterpillars, simply wrap the tent in plastic and cut the tent out of the tree when they are all in it—in early morning or after dark. Dispose of it in the trash.

LAWNS

Few lawn pests are troublesome this month. If you find insects or their larvae in your lawn, identify them before you panic. Most insects are either neutral or beneficial for growing plants; a rare few are the "one-percenters" that cause major harm. Collect a sample or two of the insect in question, preserve them in rubbing alcohol if you wish, and take it to the local extension service or a reputable local nursery for identification before spending time and money on treatment.

As warm-season lawns break dormancy, you may discover patches of the lawn that fail to green. Two common causes are pet waste (generally urine) and, in the upper elevations, damage from deicing salts. Rinse the affected area well and dig out the dead patches. If the patch is large you may have to replant, but generally lawn grasses can fill in a small patch on their own.

PERENNIALS

In all elevations, leafminers may attack a number of perennials. These miners are tiny insect larvae that live and feed inside leaves, digging translucent tunnels through the flesh of the leaf and leaving their frass (droppings) behind as black spots. Leafminers may be moths, sawflies (a type of wasp), true flies, or beetle grubs. Their tunnels and frass patterns can help determine what insect they are and what control is needed. If their attack is limited to a few leaves, you can remove and discard the leaves in the trash. If the attack is widespread, there are highly effective IPM products. Foliar sprays such as insecticidal soap are ineffective, since the pests are inside the leaves.

ROSES

Aphids and thrips leave the lower elevations as temperatures rise. This also means that spider mites start to appear. They can be washed off with a jet of water or with insecticidal soap.

Aphids and thrips start to be a problem in the upper elevations. Remove them by hand, spray with a jet from the hose, or squirt soapy water from a spray bottle. You need to repeat every other day for at least three weeks.

Bare spots in the lawn often indicate chemical burning caused by pet urine.

Leaf miners live inside their tunnels and are thus hard to treat.

SHRUBS

Newly planted shrubs and those just starting to bloom are moving ample sugars in their sap and are doubly enticing to aphids. One indication of aphids is ant activity around the base of a shrub. Some species of ants "farm" aphids, collecting the "honeydew" aphids release. These farm ants protect their herd of aphids by fighting off aphid predators. If your shrubs are not suffering unduly, let nature take its course. Despite the ants, predators often prevail. One surprising predator is the hummingbird. The extra protein they get eating these insects helps them raise healthy babies.

TREES

Trees may get aphids, and a strong stream of water can knock their flightless young to the ground. Repeat every other day for three weeks.

VINES, GROUNDCOVERS & ORNAMENTAL GRASSES

The main problem this month in this category is weeds. It is especially hard to spot weedy grasses mixed in your ornamental grasses. Buffelgrass is a particularly nasty invasive. It is handy to have images of your planted species stored in your garden journal for reference.

Bald patches in groundcovers (not just lawns) could be due to pet waste (dog and cats) or salt damage. Rinse the affected area well and clip out the dead patches. If the patch is large, you may have to replant, but generally a groundcover can fill in a small patch on its own. For the future, your own dog can be trained to use one section of the yard, and be careful with deicing salts next year.

Are stray animals a problem? They can be deterred with liberal sprinkling of dried chili peppers. If you have an old chili ristra, break it up over the target area. Many Southwest supermarkets sell dried chili by the pound, also a good option. There are a number of deterrent sprays you can purchase, but wear latex gloves when you apply them. Their scent can linger on your skin for days.

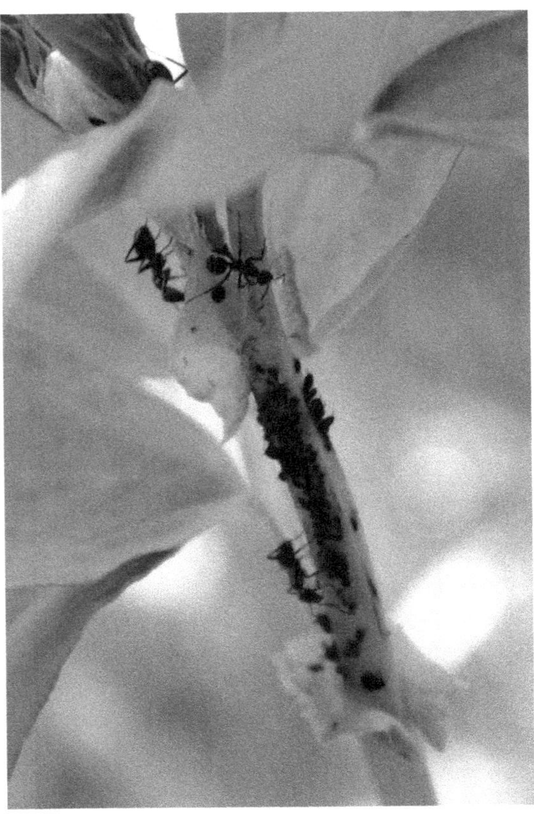

Ants farming aphids help the gardener because the "farmers" like to keep their herd in one field, and thus the aphids don't spread through the garden quite so much.

May

May is a month where temperatures may be in the triple digits by mid-day in the lowest elevations while the uppermost elevations are just starting to plant their cool-season vegetable gardens. It does make it hard to let you know which garden tasks you should tackle!

One gardener explained that summer in Yuma is her equivalent of a back-East winter. She stays indoors, gets inside tasks done, putters with houseplants, and dreams of the garden she will plant next season.

As summer approaches many municipalities in our region become more concerned over water use and ask consumers to plant native plants. In most elevations, you should plan now for fall planting of natives. The problem is that being a "native" plant does not necessarily mean it's a drought-tolerant or low-water-use plant. Trees such as sycamore, ash, and cottonwood are native throughout the Southwest along streams and rivers. They grow with their feet in the water! And thus being native becomes a slippery term.

Consider a native plant as one that is not simply from your state or even your bioregion (such as the Mojave Desert). Look for plants that are native to the growing region *and* conditions found around your home. I don't mean just the plants that grow in your area—that might leave you with too few choices for charming garden plants. Instead, consider the elevation, natural precipitation, weather patterns, and overall heat load a plant may face. Then look for Southwest natives from the surrounding 500 miles to best fit your yard.

You don't need a degree in botany or horticulture to discover these plants; all you need to do is visit your local arboretum, botanical garden, or a reputable garden nursery. In the age of the Internet, you don't even need to leave the comfort of your own home to do this. Visit these places online!

PLAN

Plan for the heat ahead. Water demands of all plants growing closely together in your landscape will need to be dealt with. Plan to install a drip system if you don't have one. Drip systems make watering in hard-to-reach corners of a yard easier; plus a system can slowly apply the deeply penetrating water that plants need to thrive in the Southwest. Even in the highest elevations, aboveground irrigation drip lines can be laid out for summer use and simply drained, coiled up, and stored for winter.

ANNUALS & BULBS

For annual plantings, now is the time for the heat-lovers. Heat-lovers in the upper elevations include snapdragon, pot marigold (*Calendula*), marigold (*Tagetes*), cosmos, and sunflower. Heat-lovers in the lower elevations include zinnia, celosia, castor bean, and portulaca.

Summer-flowering bulbs are such a charming addition. Gladiolus, calla lilies, crocosmia, and Sonoran spider lilies (*Hymenocallis*) add grace and beauty with their foliage as well as their bloom. Depending on your elevation, there may be many others to choose from (or not); the lower elevations are left out of many of these choices because it is too blasted hot. Before ordering any bulb, be sure it is rated for your zone.

Consider adding a fire pit area for evening entertaining. It can mean less lawn to care for.

It is not too early to purchase and plant fall-blooming bulbs, such as squill, ornamental allium, and starflower (*Ipheon*).

EDIBLES

Plan on purchasing mulch for edibles this month. All edibles will require mulching this month: vegetable gardens, deciduous fruit trees, evergreen fruiting shrubs, and groundcovering herbs. All these edibles will do well from having a 2- to 3-inch layer of moisture-preserving organic mulch over the soil as summer arrives.

LAWNS

May is a good month to downsize your lawn. The active growth phase of most lawn grasses will help eliminate all the sprouts that will reoccur as you try to kill the lawn. Bermudagrass is especially persistent, and it may take several tries to get rid of it all. Solarization of the soil helps kill Bermudagrass, weeds, and soil-dwelling plant pests. (See Here's How to Solarize Soil.)

There are five great reasons to reduce lawn size:

1. Save time and money on mowing, fertilizer, chemicals, water, and irrigation repair.
2. Conserve water because many shrubs and perennials use less water than lawns.
3. Attract and provide for butterflies and hummingbirds.
4. Get rid of all the lawn-care clutter in your garage or shed.
5. Reduce pollution and live more lightly upon the earth.

PERENNIALS

Lower-elevation gardeners should not plan on planting perennials this month. Upper-elevation gardeners can still plant perennials from containers or divisions through May.

ROSES

Those in the lower elevations should not plan on planting roses this month, but those in the upper

An arbor planted with deciduous vines provides much-needed summer shade, yet serves as a sunny nook in winter.

elevations can still plant roses from containers through May.

SHRUBS & TREES

Lower-elevation gardeners should have plants in the ground already. The exceptions are palms and succulents, which need to wait for warmer soils. Plan on helping them become established with a covering of shade cloth.

Gardeners in the upper elevations can still plant trees and shrubs, but consider covering them with some shade cloth to help them become established. If yours is a windy site, a side wall of shade cloth will help reduce wind stress.

VINES, GROUNDCOVERS & ORNAMENTAL GRASSES

As it heats up, the need for shade becomes more evident. An arbor planted with a deciduous vine is one quick solution for needed shade.

Those in the lower elevations might enjoy pink- or white-flowering queen's wreath (*Antigonon leptopus*). This vine easily grows 40 feet over a summer and dies to the ground when temperatures dip into the 20s. Upper-elevation gardeners can plant hops (*Humulus lupulus*). If you order hops now, you can get them in the ground in time for some shade this summer. (A note about hops: catalogs may list male and female plants with

HERE'S HOW

TO SOLARIZE SOIL

Soil solarization uses the sun's rays instead of chemicals to kill unwanted plants and control soil-borne pests. In our region, this works well to kill unwanted lawns, because we have ample sunshine. The soil must be covered with a clear (see-through) plastic tarp for four to eight weeks during the hottest period of the year, and during the time when the soil receives the most direct sunlight. The top 6 inches of the soil can heat up to as high as 140°F. There are four steps to solarization:

1. Dig to remove as much lawn or plant material as you can. Expose as much bare soil as possible.
2. Level and smooth the soil so the plastic cover will lie flat.
3. Irrigate to encourage plants to resprout, and thus scorch. Moist soil also transfers heat better.
4. Lay the clear plastic tarp as flat as possible on the soil's surface for four to eight weeks. Weight the edges of the tarp down against wind. Every two weeks, lift the tarp, water the soil, and lay the tarp down again.

If you start this in mid-May, your old lawn should be killed by mid-July, and you can plant your new yard in fall.

Clear plastic for solarization needs to be as flat on the soil as possible. Here, drip lines were left in place to water the soil and increase heat transfer.

differing prices; you can plant either males or females for shade but if you want hops for beer making, you need to order female plants, which have the flower structures, called seed cones or strobiles, that are used in making beer. You won't need male plants in your garden to get these flowers.)

See the Plant, Lawns section to read about a number of groundcovers that can be used instead of lawns. Some you can walk on! Since groundcovers have roots less deep than trees, there are a number of shade-lovers suitable for under trees where lawns will not readily grow. (See Here's How to Plant a Groundcover Bed.)

Ornamental grasses can make good foundation plantings near the walls of your home, because they use little water. Avoid planting high-water-use plants too close to the walls of your home. Moist soils will attract house-eating termites. Low-water ornamental grasses offer an aesthetically pleasing solution for foundation planting.

A shrub that needs acid soil, such as this camellia, must remain in acidic potting soil in our region, but it can be underplanted with annuals for summer color.

PLANT

Most landscape plants have a difficult time developing a healthy root system during the heat of summer. In all but the uppermost zones, mid-May is the latest you should be plant. All gardeners tend to push the boundaries, but it is hard on the plants.

ANNUALS & BULBS

Annuals generally require a lot of water, but don't feel guilty about planting them. According to the rules of xeriscaping, such high-water-use plants belong in the oasis zone, closest to the home where you can easily enjoy them. Consider container gardens for your porch.

No matter which annuals are available to you, you can create lovely container combination plantings if you remember to add three elements: *thriller*, *filler*, and *spiller*. The thriller is the central focal point, and can even be a plant that might later be planted in the yard, such as a yucca or an aloe. The filler is a plant that fills in around the edges of the thriller. A spiller spills over the edges of the container, helping the whole ensemble appear lush and full. Follow a less-is-more approach. The filler should be two or maybe three different species, and not wildly different color; the same is true for the spiller. This gives the combo an enchanting look, not a chaotic one.

EDIBLES

Lower-elevation gardeners can plant a second sowing of the warm-season vegetables now, including corn and greens. Melons have a long growing season and need to be in the ground before mid-month. Sow more annual heat-loving herb seed such as basil if you wish.

Upper-elevation gardeners can plant peas if they haven't yet. Set out young tomato family seedlings (eggplant, pepper) three weeks after final frost in your area, along with seedlings of other warm-season edibles. If the soils are warm enough, you could plant seed of the three sisters (corn, beans, and squash). Sow seed of warm-season annual herbs, such as basil, epazote, and perilla.

Annual herbs don't have to grow in rows in the vegetable garden. If you have any trees or shrubs for which you'll be monitoring the water, plant herb seedlings around them and mulch everything. The herbs, together with the mulch, will shade the roots of the growing tree, reducing evaporation loss. Since they're annuals, they will be composted long before they're shaded out. Gardeners in the lower elevations should avoid planting non-drought-tolerant fruit trees and shrubs this month. Those in upper elevations can still plant container-grown plants.

LAWNS

Lawns can be planted this month, and better now than in June. Grass lawns are traditionally Bermudagrass or St. Augustine in the lower elevations, perennial rye and zoysiagrass in the upper elevations. Many New Mexico residents in upper elevations report success with buffalograss lawns.

There are low-water plants to use as lawn alternatives, and many can still be planted as transplants now (or better yet, in fall). If you want to walk on a nongrass lawn, that's still an option if you select the right species. In the lower elevations, creeping herbs such as thyme, oregano, and germander stay around 2 to 3 inches high. The native phyla, also called frogfruit, is becoming increasingly popular. For shady situations, dichondra can be planted either from seed or plugs. In the upper elevations, clover, dwarf buffalograss, creeping potentilla, moneywort, sedges, and cold-tolerant creeping herbs are all popular lawn alternatives.

PERENNIALS

Gardeners in the lower elevations can plant perennials from containers or divisions before mid-month. If you purchased plants last month, get them in the ground as early in the month as you can, because the coming summer can be brutal on plants left in black plastic nursery containers. Upper-elevation gardeners can plant perennials from containers or divisions through May.

ROSES

Roses kept in containers can be repotted in all elevations this month. Select a container that's generously proportioned for the plant. Roses do best when they aren't pot-bound. Another reason for generously sized pots is that extra potting soil will help protect the roots from excessive heat now and winter cold later.

SHRUBS & TREES

What to plant? Consider a plant's life history. Many tropical and semitropical tree and shrub species naturally grow from seed dispersed in late summer, thus it can be better to plant them at the end of summer rather than during the hottest time of the year.

Lower-elevation gardeners should plant tropical plants, including succulents and palms, this month. Most semitropicals, such as mesquite, do better planted during the monsoon season (if you have one) or early in the autumn.

Upper-elevation gardeners can plant trees and shrubs from containers all through May. Just be careful to avoid overwatering and thus drowning these new plantings.

VINES, GROUNDCOVERS & ORNAMENTAL GRASSES

Most evergreen vines and groundcovers will have a hard time developing healthy root systems during the heat of summer. Lower-elevation gardeners should plant them as early in the month as possible. Upper-elevation gardeners should get landscape plants into the ground by mid-May.

I keep touting the durability of ornamental grasses, and many of them will survive transplanting this month, especially in upper elevations.

HERE'S HOW

TO PLANT A GROUNDCOVER BED

1

2

3

4

1 *Prepare the soil by digging with a spade to a depth of 8 to 12 inches. Break up large clods with a hoe or cultivator. Dig in and incorporate up to 50 percent organic matter, such as compost or peat moss. Add sand if you have clay soils. Smooth the planting area with a rake until level.*

2 *Lay out plants in a staggered grid pattern, not in straight rows. Refer to the informational stake from the nursery for guidance on how close together plants should be placed. While the area might look sparse at first, groundcover plants will rapidly fill it in.*

3 *Using a hand trowel, dig a hole for each plant in your prepared bed. Remove the plant from the pot and set it in the hole, gently pressing down roots so they make contact with soil. Repeat this process for each plant. Backfill over the top of the plant hole as necessary.*

4 *Water in the plants to drive out any air pockets. Water the plants deeply and ensure that the soil is constantly moist for at least the first two weeks after planting. Do not overwater—don't allow standing pools of water to remain at the bases of plants. Spread a 1- to 2-inch layer of mulch around young plants to prevent soil from losing moisture and to protect against erosion.*

CARE

There is little extreme pruning to be done this month in most elevations. A gentle pruning that is always a good idea is deadheading—the act of removing dead flowers to encourage further blooms and prevent the plant from going to seed. Pinch or cut back to the first set of leaves beneath the bloom rather than leaving an unsightly dead stalk.

ANNUALS & BULBS

Some annuals deadhead themselves and some need human intervention. Cosmos, marigold, calendula, geranium, and zinnia all need deadheading. Snapdragon will continue to bloom if you carefully cut off any developing seedpods. Many deadheaded flower petals dry well and can be used for potpourri.

Protect tall annuals (such as hollyhock and sunflower) from getting knocked over by wind. Tomato cages or bamboo stakes work well. As the plants grow, their foliage hides this protection.

Depending on your zone, either late spring or early summer bulbs may be emerging. If you live in a windy area, gently insert a stake or bulb cage around them to prevent bloom stalks from breaking. If your bulbs are done blooming and the leaves have all turned brown, clean up this debris.

EDIBLES

Thin cool-season vegetables that come up densely, such as carrots, beets, and lettuce. Ideally, use garden scissors for this task rather than tugging them out of the soil and disturbing their neighbors. Water when you're done to settle any soil disturbance that may have occurred.

In the coolest zones, you may still get frost, so keep frost protection handy.

In the lower elevations, the edible onion family bulbs (onion, garlic, shallots) are maturing. Let the leaves turn brown prior to harvest.

In all elevations, train vining plants to climb the trellises, poles, or fencing you've provided. Even watermelons and pumpkins can be trained to grow on a fence as long as you provide support to prevent their heavy developing fruit from breaking the nurturing vines. Tie their vines to the fence with string; or slip a sheer knee-high stocking over young fruit before it gets large, and tie that to the fence. The nylon will expand while supporting the fruit as it gains girth.

Instead of tying, melon family members such as gourds or luffa could be grown under trees that don't have a dense canopy layer. The vines will climb the trees. Pollinators will easily find the flowers, but nibbling creatures won't get at the developing fruits. Since these crops aren't food, a rake or long pole will work well for harvest.

Gardeners in all elevations can reduce excessive June drop (of fruit) if you thin the fruit on trees that bear large fruit, such as apples or grapefruit. (See Here's How to Reduce June Drop.) Prune grape clusters when the grapes are the size of a match head. Leave roughly twenty clusters per plant.

Pinch annual herbs to encourage the plants to maintain a compact form. Pinching also delays flowering so plants will last longer.

LAWNS

Lawns in our climate require aeration every one to three years, depending on your soil type and lawn traffic. The best time for aeration is at the start of the growing season, when the grass can heal and

Brussels sprouts growing in dry grass mulch.

Squash trained on fence.

Gourds grown in trees.

Thin grape clusters when grapes are the size of a match head. You will get fewer fruits, but they will be sweeter—and you'll reduce the chance of disease.

fill in any open areas after soil plugs are removed. Lower-elevation gardeners should aerate in April or before mid-May; those in zones 8 and 7, the sooner the better. In zones 6 and above, complete this task by the end of this month.

PERENNIALS

In the lower elevations, mildly woody perennials, such as whirling butterflies (*Guara*), globe mallow, and autumn sage, are winding down from spring bloom. Late in the month, give them a rejuvenation prune. This will encourage them to take a rest from blooming for a while and focus on growing. They'll regrow in a more compact form, and generally rebloom in autumn.

Keep an eye on perennials that may need support from wind. Delphinium, foxglove, and even daylily and iris all do well with a tomato cage set in place when you first notice the developing flower stalk.

HERE'S HOW

TO REDUCE JUNE DROP

Plants normally shed some of their young fruit after pollination. Termed "June drop," this is normal, healthy, and nothing to panic about. Plants produce fruit so they can spread their seed. Because a too-large crop would strain a tree's resources, it protects itself by self-thinning its fruits. Fruits that contain the fewest seeds are the first to be shed. How does a tree count seeds? It doesn't count, but instead senses the lower draw of nutrients when a fruit has fewer seeds.

As you thin fruit, bear in mind mature size and leave 4 to 6 inches between what will be ripe fruits.

Three actions on your part will help reduce June drop:

Prune. Fruit should be evenly spaced along the branches and around the tree. In general, thin so fruit will be 4 to 6 inches apart when ripe. Space between fruit permits better air circulation around fruit, reducing chances of fungal diseases. The farther apart the fruit is, the less tempting it is to insect pests. And although you may get fewer fruits, what you do get is larger and sweeter.

Fertilize. Do follow label directions. Excessive fertilizer in the soil will cause *all* fruits on the tree to pull nutrients in the race to be the biggest. The tree may simply shed most of them because it doesn't need them all.

Care. Create plant wells (basins) out to the drip line. Fill the wells with compost for a slow and steady release of nutrients. Monitor water and prevent excessive soil drying.

Prune fall-blooming perennials now. Chrysanthemums, along with New England asters, phlox, heliopsis, and sneezeweed (*Helenium*), should be cut back by one-third to promote bushier growth and more flowers.

Mulch perennials now if you haven't yet.

ROSES

If your roses are just starting to bloom or are still blooming, deadhead to encourage better bloom production. Avoid any other rose pruning.

Use well-sharpened clippers to make deadheading easier on the thornier varieties of roses.

In the lower elevations, consider moving container-grown roses to a site where they'll get afternoon shade in summer. This will help them survive the heat ahead.

In all elevations, rake up and discard any leaves fallen off rose bushes. For mulch, use leaves of plants not in the rose family. Pine needles work well if you have them.

SHRUBS

Lightly prune shrubs to remove errant growth, maintaining an even form without unduly stressing plants. Avoid topiary pruning, because shrubs that are topiary-pruned need more water to survive and heal their wounds. Such pruning also removes the chance of sumptuous blooms. If you wish to add a rectilinear form or round ball for your yard, garden art and colorful pottery abound. Such garden art provides the desired shapes without torturing yourself with one more chore and without torturing plants that are only trying to do what their genes demand of them.

TREES

In the wild, many of our native trees look more like giant shrubs, with branches drooping to the ground. Their genes are ordering them to shade their trunks from the intense rays of the sun here in the Southwest. When we bring such species into our urban yards, we need to understand that they should not look like a lollipop. Before you hack a tree into an unnatural shape, consider the reason for the cut you are about to make. If it is damaging property (rubbing on a roof) or a safety

All plants have a natural shape and height to which they will grow. Select a tree form that appeals to you.

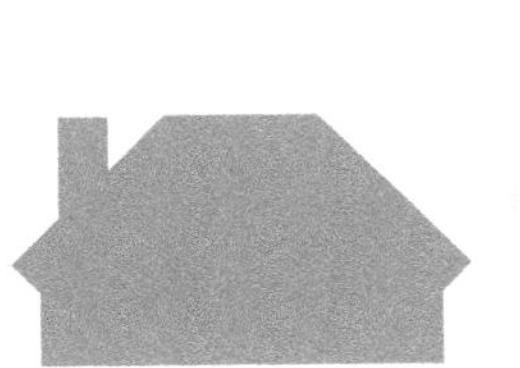

issue (blocking a path), then you certainly need to prune. But if you just want to cut it to meet your mental image of what a tree should look like, then prune it off at ground level and start over with a tree species that has the mature shape you desire.

VINES, GROUNDCOVERS & ORNAMENTAL GRASSES

Some vines, such as grape and wisteria, climb on their own, either twining or using tendrils. Keep an eye on these and gently guide their growth where you wish it to go by tucking in stray tendrils.

Some vine species, such as bougainvillea and Cape honeysuckle (*Tecoma capensis*), are considered shrubby and need to be tied to or woven through their supports. Keep an eye on such vines while they are actively growing in spring, and tie those that need help. You can use twist ties, garden twine, or specially made vine ties.

WATER

May is often a rainless month in most of our region. Thus, you'll need to keep a careful eye on your entire landscape. Some towns celebrate "ice break" on local rivers this month on the first day it hits 100°F. Your plants will need water to help them celebrate.

Lower-elevation gardeners' irrigation system maintenance this month is to set your controller for its summer schedule. If you haven't yet, change the backup battery before the power bumps of summer storms erase all your programming. When upper-elevation gardeners power up your irrigation systems for the year, the first thing to do is to take off the end cap and flush the system. Check and clean the filter. Move drip emitters to the drip lines of trees and shrubs.

ANNUALS & BULBS

Monitor annuals. Those in pots and even those in the ground may need daily watering as temperatures rise, especially if there's a drying wind. Avoid overwatering however, as you can kill with kindness. (See Here's How to Recognize Plant Water Stress.)

HERE'S HOW

TO RECOGNIZE PLANT WATER STRESS

Ironically, some signs of overwatering appear the same as signs of underwatering. We all learn as we go, and gardeners do kill plants. The goal is to learn from our mistakes and not repeat them.

SIGNS OF UNDERWATERING:

- Soil is dry and hard to dig.
- Older leaves turn yellow or brown and drop off.
- Leaves are wilted or drooping and do not recover after sundown.
- Leaves curl around the mid-vein; especially seen in grasses.
- Stems or branches die back.

SIGNS OF OVERWATERING:

- Soil is constantly damp.
- Leaves turn yellow or lighter green throughout.
- Leaves remain green yet are brittle and may crumble.
- Algae or mushrooms appear around plants.

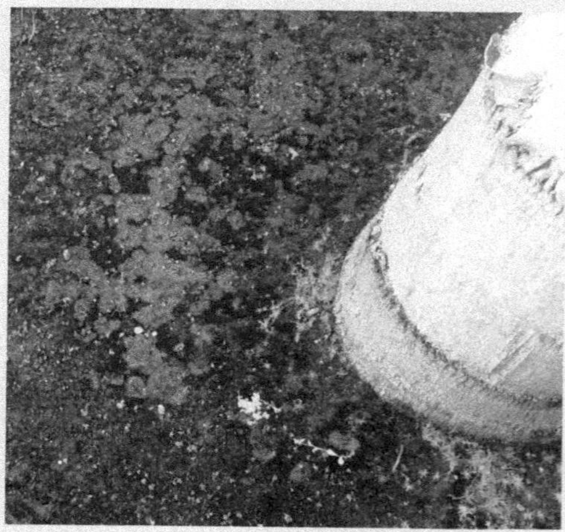

Algae growing in the soil around this palm tree is a clear indicator of overwatering.

Cover soaker hoses with mulch to improve overall landscape appearance as well as to reduce evaporation. Just remember where they are before you dig.

In all elevations, monitor moisture levels for bulb beds. Summer bulbs that have been planted will need moisture to grow as soils warm. Bulbs that still have green leaves need water in order to make ample sugars for bloom next year.

EDIBLES

Water vegetable gardens regularly to help transplants grow and seeds germinate. Transplants need extra water as they spread their roots into their new home. Water established vegetables once soils dry to a depth greater than 1 inch. This may be every three to seven days, depending on conditions.

Don't skimp on water for fruit and nut plants that may still be flowering or are setting or ripening fruit. If drought stress occurs at this point you may lose an entire crop. Monitor water at least weekly, and water as needed. To minimize June drop, make sure trees get ample water but are not waterlogged.

Herbs with large leaves, such as hyssop, lemon balm, beebalm, and mint need extra water as weather warms, perhaps even daily if container grown.

LAWNS

Warmer temperatures mean warm-season lawn grasses are breaking dormancy. If there's no rain, water deeply to a depth of 2 feet once every seven to ten days during May. Deep watering encourages your lawn to grow deeper roots that are better able to withstand drought. If you are unsure how long this takes, see March, Here's How to Gauge How Deep Irrigation Goes.

If you have an overseeded lawn, there is a battle going on between the warm- and cold-season turfgrasses trying to occupy the same space. Overseeded lawns will need irrigation more often than those not overseeded.

PERRENIALS

In lower elevations, the non-drought-tolerant perennials, such as daylily, lily-of-the-Nile, and bleeding hearts, are blooming and will be sucking moisture as temperatures climb. Monitor their water carefully. Water succulents twice this month, especially any cacti in flower.

ROSES

Roses you planted this year need to be monitored for water needs. Be careful not to overwater them, though. Allow the soil to dry out slightly between waterings.

SHRUBS

Some evergreen shrubs commonly planted in our region may not be as drought-adapted as you think. Abelia, photinia, and even Texas rangers are native to areas that get 30 to 50 inches of rainfall per year, and such plants are not truly drought-adapted, although they are commonly sold as such. Regionally native shrubs, such as mountain mahogany, wormwood, saltbush, and juniper, can survive on rainfall alone in the wild, but in an urban yard they will need some supplemental water, because landscape plantings are closer together than in nature.

Native succulents start to flower this month. If you water them at least once at the start of May, you'll help promote blooming. Where is the drip line on a succulent? It's at a distance roughly equal to their height. A 10-foot-high saguaro, yucca, or ocotillo should be watered in a circle 10 feet away from the base. Water only needs to go down 6 to 10 inches for these highly efficient and generally shallow-rooted plants.

A 3-inch layer of organic mulch around the base of trees and shrubs will reduce irrigation requirements. To prevent disease issues, don't mound mulch against the trunks.

TREES

Newly planted trees, no matter the species, need water more often to become established. During establishment, trees need water regularly applied at the drip line, which is an ever-increasing distance from the trunk. Once trees are established, they will need less water overall. The exception is for established but still juvenile trees; just like teenagers, they are growing rapidly and need ample water and nutrients. They will need extra water until they are mature.

VINES, GROUNDCOVERS & ORNAMENTAL GRASSES

Vines need water at their drip line, just like any other plant. But where is their drip line? Like any other leafy plant, the drip line is at the edges of the area covered by the leaf canopy. But what if they are trained vertically up a trellis? In this case, water 2 to 4 feet out from the base of the vine, not right at the trunk. For groundcovers, it is best to soak the entire area they cover, much like you would water an entire lawn. The good news is that groundcovers shade their soil and need water less often than the same area of lawn.

Ornamental grasses are originally from grasslands, which get an average of 20 inches of rain per year. Watch for signs of stress, but watering once every two weeks is often sufficient for species in all but the hottest zones.

FERTILIZE

If you have read the months before this one, you may have notice that I advocate applying *half* the recommend dose. This is because Southwest growing conditions are very different than back East. Low humidity, soil alkalinity, low levels of organic matter in the soil, and myriad other factors combine to make many standard gardening

HERE'S HOW

TO KNOW IF A PLANT IS ESTABLISHED

A plant is considered established when it reaches the point where it can survive without further careful attention on the part of the gardener. It is very hard to know exactly when that is, though generally it means three years for trees and one year for other woody plants (shrubs, groundcovers).

After planting, most plants simply sit in the ground for a while before growing. (Bare-root plants may put out some new growth right away; this is because they were ready to break dormancy.) What you need to look for is *robust* new growth, where a tree may put on several feet in a single year. Continue to water them through this robust growth stage. When they slow down again they can be considered established.

recommendations invalid for our area. After numerous fertilizer mishaps, I now use the half-strength option. Slow-release granular fertilizers are one way around this. However, if you're trying to garden organically, they are currently not an option.

If you haven't fertilized yet this year, May is the month to do it. If you're following Here's How to Fertilize the Forgetful Gardener's Way (see April), then Memorial Day is the holiday to fertilize everything.

ANNUALS & BULBS

Since you plant annuals for their flowers, a half-strength bloom fertilizer every two weeks will help the display. Avoid high-nitrogen fertilizers; they encourage leaves rather than flowers.

If your bulbs have no blooms but green leaves, a general-purpose fertilizer applied this month will help. This includes spring- and summer-blooming bulbs such as rain lilies (*Zephyranthes*).

EDIBLES

Which fertilizer you put on your vegetables this month depends on what you're growing. Warm-season gardens are mostly crops that produce fruits (tomato, corn, melons—if it has seeds, it's a fruit). These plants need a bloom fertilizer with a high middle number, such as 6-12-8. If you still have cool-season leafy crops (lettuce, arugula, kale), then apply a general-purpose fertilizer.

Most fruiting trees and shrubs need a bloom fertilizer this month. The exceptions are those that are done fruiting, such as loquat and some jujube. Half-strength fertilizer is especially important on fruits in order to reduce June drop. Consider organic fertilizers such as bat guano (8-3-1) rather than manufactured fertilizers.

All herbs do well with a general-purpose fertilizer this month. Don't forget herbs that have bulbs, such as garlic chives, society garlic, and I'itoi onions—they, too, can use a general-purpose fertilizer this month.

LAWNS

In all elevations, if you aerated and applied compost topdressing either this month or last month, there's no need to fertilize your lawn now. If you did not treat your lawn recently, fertilize this month with well-composted steer manure, which will fertilize, amend the soil, and help reduce soil alkalinity. Apply the manure in a ½- to 1-inch-thick layer all over the lawn, then rake it down among the grass blades with a leaf rake. If you do not wish to use steer manure, compost will also work, though not as well.

In all elevations, if you recently planted trees, shrubs, or other plants near your lawn, *do not* use a weed-and-feed fertilizer; it will retard the growth of the plants you just labored over and may kill them.

In the upper elevations, you have probably not fertilized lawn since September. If you're not going to aerate or apply a layer of steer manure or compost, select a fertilizer that has both fast-acting

You can side-dress vegetables by spreading slow-release fertilizer around the plants.

HERE'S HOW

TO IDENTIFY & TREAT JUNE BEETLES

May beetle, June bug, June beetle—there are a number of very different species given similar names. They're in the scarab beetle family, related to the East Coast pest, the Japanese beetle. Their larvae (grubs) feed on roots of any number of plants, weakening and even killing them, while adults feed on foliage. Most destructive in our area is the ten-lined June beetle (*Polyphylla decemlineata*), also known as the watermelon beetle. Adults can make a hissing sound when touched or otherwise disturbed. This can be startling when you live in rattlesnake territory! (They make the sound by pushing their wings down, forcing air out between wings and back.)

Large, green figeater beetles look like Japanese beetles but only feed upon already-injured fruits, and their larvae don't damage gardens and lawns as severely as other species of scarab. These are the grubs most commonly encountered in compost piles because, even as larvae, they are better at eating rotting things than they are at consuming living material.

If you have large (2-inch-long) grubs with solid, dark-brown heads, take a sample of the pest (in a jar of alcohol if you wish) to the cooperative extension service for identification and treatment recommendations. One grub is not cause for alarm. Four grubs per square foot of soil is considered an infestation.

An often-recommended treatment is milky spore bacteria. This bacteria (*Paenibacillus popilliae*, formerly *Bacillus popillae*) is lethal to the grubs of Japanese beetle and other scarab species but is technically not listed for a treatment of the ten-lined June beetle. There are also a number of species of beneficial nematodes that infect and kill beetle grubs. If you prefer, there is a toxic soil drench that kills all life in the soil, including earthworms. Keep pets out of the area for 72 hours after using.

The best treatment is prevention. June bug mothers prefer to lay their eggs in sandy soil. If you have sandy soils, add compost to help change the soil's texture. Moms also prefer to lay eggs in moist soils—one reason I encourage you to allow the top inch or more of soil to dry between watering.

Adult ten-lined June beetle

Larvae

Milky spore IPM treatment

(water-soluble) and slow-acting nitrogen. These help the lawn green quickly and maintain health.

PERENNIALS

Bloom fertilizer is good for the spring- and summer-flowering perennials now. General-purpose fertilizer is also an option, and better for the fall-blooming species. Alternatively, use a slow-release fertilizer, which is good for about twelve weeks. If you applied some last month, check the package to see when reapplication is needed.

ROSES

In all elevations, roses need fertilizer this month. Roses, especially the heirlooms, bloom better with a slow, steady release of nutrients. This is one reason many rose growers like slow-release fertilizers, while others prefer to regularly add compost. Your yard; your choice.

SHRUBS

May is an ideal time to fertilize shrubs with a general-purpose fertilizer, unless you just planted them. Always wait two to four weeks after planting to fertilize. This gives plant roots a chance to heal from the breaks and scarring that occur no matter how gentle you are.

TREES

How old are your trees? Mature trees that are well established in the landscape don't need fertilizer. Young trees, generally less than seven years old, can be helped by a general-purpose fertilizer watered into the soil at their drip line. A tree basin or well full of compost is a slow-release option. Legume trees such as locust or redbud don't need a nitrogen fertilizer but will be helped by the trace minerals in compost.

VINES, GROUNDCOVERS & ORNAMENTAL GRASSES

Most drought-adapted vines and groundcovers do not need a great deal of fertilizer, nor do most ornamental grasses—just one more reason to feature these tough plants. A once-per-year fertilization with a general-purpose fertilizer will work for most ornamental grass species.

PROBLEM-SOLVE

ANNUALS & BULBS

Annuals get more water than many other plants in the landscape (except for maybe vegetables), making their tender, juicy plant parts enticing to aphids, flea beetles, leaf-hoppers, and thrips. Soapy sprays and blasts from the hose will help knock these pests off. Record the infestations in your garden journal, and consider planting different species of annuals next year—or opt for more perennials. Most bulbs are not bothered by these pests.

EDIBLES

Grape leaf skeletonizers often appear this month. Small, black-, yellow-, and blue-striped caterpillars feed side-by-side in groups, devouring grape leaves rapidly, leaving only the tough veins. Soon, only the skeleton of the leaf remains. The caterpillars mature into blue-black moths that resemble wasps. Adults and larvae are active at dusk and dawn and can destroy your grape vines in very few days. If you catch them early, hand pick and destroy any adults, larvae, or eggs you see. Wear gloves and a dust mask, because the larvae are covered with stinging hairs that may become airborne. At this time, the approved treatment is to spray the undersurface of your grape leaves with *Bacillus thuringiensis* (Bt).

Bt is a bacteria that will kill *all* members of the butterfly and moth family, so if you are trying to nurture these pollinators, you may want to rethink growing grapes. Bt is rated as an organic pesticide that can be used on fruits, ornamentals, and various other plants. When used as directed, it will not affect birds or beneficial insects such as honeybees and ladybugs.

Stink bugs, also called leaf-footed plant bugs, appear to feed on developing fruits of virtually every species: peaches, pecans, mesquite beans, and even "vegetable" fruits, such as tomatoes, beans, and tender melons. They have several generations a year. Control them with beneficials, such as praying mantis, ladybugs, or green lacewings. While you are waiting for the beneficials to arrive or hatch, you can use Neem oil.

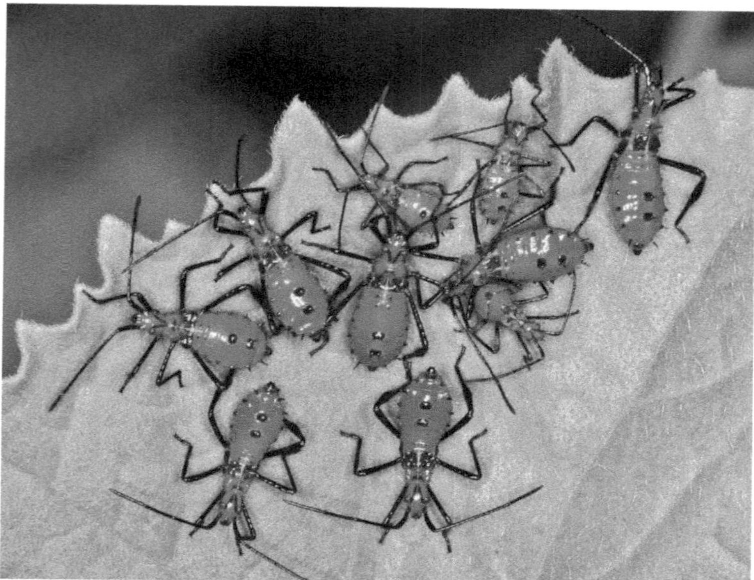

There are many species of stink bugs, and some can ruin fruits. Encourage natural predators in your garden to help keep their populations low.

LAWNS

In the upper elevations, sod webworms may appear. Flocks of birds generally quickly appear to eliminate these pests for you.

Lawn mites occasionally appear now, especially where light reflected off a window dries the lawn quicker than elsewhere in the yard. Aerate these areas and rake in a 1-inch layer of compost to help the soil hold the extra water the lawn needs in such patches.

If your lawn is suffering brown patches and it's not caused by webworms, pet waste, or dry conditions, turn over a shovelful of soil. If you find grubs, see Here's How to Identify & Treat June Beetles.

PERENNIALS

Thrips, leaf hoppers, aphids, and even grasshoppers may arrive to munch on just about any perennial you grow. There are a number of IPM beneficials that feed on these pests. Grasshoppers can be caught in an insect net and squashed, and if you toss the pest corpses into an open area, neighborhood birds will learn that you working in the garden equates to food.

Some rose diseases are best dealt with by shovel pruning—entirely removing the plant from your garden.

ROSES

Be on the lookout for two pernicious rose pests that are best dealt with through shovel pruning—digging up and throwing away infected plants before the infection spreads. These infections are especially insidious, because they can be transmitted to other members of the rose family, such as apple and peach trees. The best defense is prevention. Purchase roses only from well-known, reputable dealers and growers who aggressively manage and eliminate these diseases in their operations.

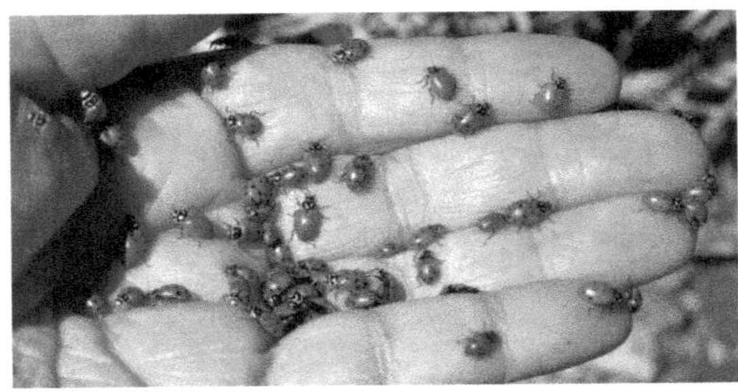

Natural predators of garden pests abound. When possible, avoid toxic sprays that harm them.

Crown gall is a bacterial infection that can spread extremely rapidly and must be eliminated by quickly discarding infected plants. A crusty, black swelling appears at the base of the rose plant where the stem meets the ground. If you are unsure, take a good picture or a well-sealed sample to a nursery or your extension service for verification.

Rose mosaic virus appears as yellow zigzag lines on all or a part of a leaf. A single affected leaf could be due to wind damage, but a number of afflicted leaves are a sure indicator. Infected plants must be destroyed.

SHRUBS

Weeds are annoying if they start growing under shrubs. A nice layer of mulch may not prevent them from sprouting, but it sure makes them easier to pull. Prevent fungal crown rot on mulched shrubs by making sure the mulch is not mounded against the trunks.

Alkaline-induced iron chlorosis often shows now on susceptible shrubs, such as the bottlebrushes (*Callistemon*). Watch for leaves that yellow between the veins and treat by acidifying the soil around the plant with compost or coffee grounds. (See June, Here's How to Treat Chlorosis.)

TREES

If you found grubs in your lawn and your trees are suffering, they may be infested as well. Dig around the roots of wilting trees to search for them; treat grubs before your tree dies. If it has died, solarize your soil to kill the grubs before you replant in that site. (See Here's How to Solarize Your Soil.)

VINES, GROUNDCOVERS & ORNAMENTAL GRASSES

If you found grubs elsewhere in your yard and the groundcovers or vines are having problems, they, too, may be infested. If you didn't find grubs, take a sample of the affected plant to your local extension office with a photo of the overall planting. The age and species of plant, as well as where and when you purchased it, are all helpful data often necessary to accurately diagnose a problem. Proper diagnosis is necessary for proper treatment and future prevention.

One reason to consider ornamental grasses is that so few pests bother them—generally, not even grubs.

June

June is one of my favorite months of the gardening year. It's plenty warm by midday but still cools off at night. Early mornings are cool enough so that it is pleasant to work in the yard. The humidity is still so low that the heat doesn't feel too hot. Best of all, there are few things that must *be done in the garden this month.*

Most schools are on summer break now, but that doesn't mean your kids couldn't spend some time learning. Get them up at their usual school time—but instead of getting them onto a school bus, get them out into the garden. Have them help you water, weed, pick up plant debris, or have a fun "treasure hunt." How many different leaf shapes can they find? How many different kinds of bugs, birds, or lizards? Maybe you can lay back and cloud watch. When is the last time you did that?!

This month brings the summer solstice. I like to celebrate by welcoming the dawn and watching the sunrise, just like all of our ancestors, all around the globe, once did. What's even more fun is to celebrate the solstice the Southwest way. But you need a group of people to join you. Kids too—they will love it!

In centuries past, in areas of the Southwest that got summer rains, solstice was observed with solemn dawn prayers followed by a village-wide water fight. Adults and children alike tossed water on each other. Centuries ago water was a scarce resource, sometimes carried for miles in heavy pottery jars. Now we can turn a faucet handle and have all the water we need. I do appreciate modern technology!

Why not get some friends and family together and celebrate solstice in your garden. You can follow your sunrise watch with a sumptuous breakfast feast, or perhaps have a sunset watch and have a sumptuous dinner feast. Either way, take some time to celebrate the fact that we live in one of the loveliest gardening spots on the globe.

PLAN

After June 21, the days will technically be getting shorter, but they'll be getting hotter, as well. Most yard work this month will be monitoring your garden to head off heat and drought problems before they become major issues.

They say, "It's a dry heat." Ovens are dry too, and Southwest summer is hard on plants in all elevations. Planning garden tasks this month includes helping the plants in your yard do well during June and for the next two sweltering months.

Plants have various ways of dealing with Southwest aridity and heat. All plants have to open their stomates (pores) to take in oxygen, conduct photosynthesis, and form the sugars they need for life. When they open their stomates in our arid climate, the moisture inside them escapes into the air. This process, called *evapotranspiration*, also helps plants cool off. Plants become stressed when the amount of water going out exceeds the amount of water coming in. Many arid-adapted plants solve this problem by conducting all photosynthesis early in the day. They may close their stomates and shut down their sugar factory within an hour or two of sunrise. This is one reason for watering early in the day.

Closing stomates isn't an option for some species, thus they have other strategies. Many heat-tolerant plants have hairs or waxes on them to reduce evaporation. Some plants actively move through the day. Sunflowers track the sun, but did you ever notice how their leaves move too, drooping at noon? This droop helps trap moisture under the leaves. Squash family members are the dukes of droop. At four o'clock in the afternoon, every leaf may look like a furled umbrella. Don't panic and start watering unless they don't unfurl as the sun goes down. Corn leaves curl to trap their moisture, as do lawn and ornamental grasses. Don't panic with them either, unless they don't uncurl after sunset.

Learn to tell the difference between normal heat responses and stress responses in your plants. If you're a visual learner, take photos and tuck them in your garden journal for future reference.

Learn to recognize normal heat responses so you can identify true drought stress.

ANNUALS & BULBS

Summer heat is hard on traditional garden annuals, most of them from cool climates. We think of marigolds (*Tagetes*) as heat-lovers, but although they're native to Mexico, they're from cool, pine-topped Mexican mountains, where they get ample summer rain and cool nights. If your annuals are declining, plan on replacing them with different, more heat-tolerant species such as portulaca or zinnia.

If you want fall-blooming bulbs, plan for and purchase them now for planting as soon as possible. Consider heirloom sternbergia (*Sternbergia lutea*). Also called fall daffodils, sternbergia look more like big, lemon-yellow crocus. They do best in sunny sites that are dryish in summer and not too harsh in winter—in other words, zones 9b to 6a in the Southwest. Two other charming fall bulbs for most of our region are red spider lily (*Lycoris radiata* var. *radiata*) and surprise lily (*Lycoris squamigera*), also called "naked ladies."

EDIBLES

If you decided to skip the hot summer vegetable garden, start planning for the cooler season ahead. You have time, but it's never too soon to start planning. You may need to order seed. In the upper elevations, late summer is the time to plant cool-season crops, such as lettuce and radish. In the lower elevations, plan an August planting of short-season cucumbers and melons, as well as green beans.

If sections of the vegetable garden are empty and fallow, plan on some soil-building work. You'll need to add compost, composted steer manure, or peat moss and *dig it in*. Water the soil to give the myriad microorganisms that live there a chance to blend together the amendment and the soil.

It's not too late to add herbs to your garden or even create an herb bed. Gardeners in the lower elevations can consider what I call the Herculean herbs. Originally from the hot, dry hillsides of the eastern Mediterranean where Hercules once roamed, these herbs do well on our hot, dry hillsides, as well. Rosemary, germander, and even Greek oregano can be added to the landscape in the lower elevations this month. Gardeners in the upper elevations can plant those species in pots to bring inside in winter, plus add sage and thyme to the landscape.

LAWNS

If your lawn isn't working in certain areas, determine why. Heavy shade is a better spot for a seating area or a bed of shade-loving perennials or groundcover.

If you will fallow part or all of your garden for summer, add peat moss compost or other soil amendments now and dig them in.

There are many species and varieties of low-care prickly pear that can be added to the garden.

A heavily trafficked area is the place for a path. Rather than battle a trend of balding lawn, rearrange things so your yard works well for you.

PERENNIALS

Want to add something to the garden, but don't want to add garden chores? How about a prickly pear? You may think of prickly pear cacti as a Southwest plant, but they are native to every state except Hawaii. (Interestingly, rattlesnakes occur in all but Alaska and Hawaii.) This means that even the coolest garden could have a truly plant-it-and-forget-it charmer that produces impressive blooms plus edible fruit. Small species such as the western prickly pear (*Opuntia macrorhiza*) take the place of a low perennial in the landscape, as does Mojave Desert native *O. basilaris*, which does not need the summer rain. Larger species, such as Indian fig (*O. ficus-indica*), are more in the nature of a shrub or maybe even a tree. (Its name refers to the fact that New World natives showed Europeans that the fig-like fruit is highly edible.)

ROSES

Use your garden journal to note how your roses are doing. Take note of the varieties that you appreciate for fragrance, bloom shape, or color. Plan on shovel-pruning the ones that are not working for you. Life is too short!

If your roses are still blooming, cut some and bring them indoors to enjoy. One or one dozen, tall or small, cut flowers inside your home help make the sweat and toil all worthwhile.

SHRUBS

A number of Southwest native shrubs, such as potentilla, snowberry (*Symphoricarpos*), tecoma, and San Marcos hibiscus (*Gossypium harknessii*), begin to bloom now. Take pictures of any that catch your eye around town and consider where you might add some to your yard. Your local garden center should be able to help you with identification.

TREES

Many Southwest native trees bloom now, and they often get blamed for seasonal allergies. But before you chop your trees down, do some research. Bee- and other insect-pollinated plants have large, heavy pollen grains that don't float in the breeze. If bees pollinate your trees, they're not the source of your allergies. The most common wind-pollinated plants found across the Southwest are the various species of ragweed (*Ambrosia*) that are notorious for causing allergic reactions in humans. They may be called bursage or burrobush but they are all in the same genus, and all have highly allergenic pollen.

VINES, GROUNDCOVERS & ORNAMENTAL GRASSES

You could still add an arbor to your yard. If you don't want to plant vines this summer you could cover it with a temporary bamboo shade screen.

It's not too late to add ornamental grasses to landscapes in zones 8 and cooler. Even for smaller plants such as grasses, you have to plan for their mature size.

PLANT

For those in zones 10 to 7—it's time to take a break! There's not much landscape planting to be done during this hot month (but if you absolutely want to, read on for some heat-lovers). Zones 6 to 4 gardeners—go forth and plant.

ANNUALS & BULBS

Lower-elevation gardeners: this is not the month to plant annuals or bulbs. For the upper elevations, replace cool-season annuals that may be flagging. Plant heat-lovers such as zinnia, celosia, and scabiosa, and Southwest sunflowers such as 'Hopi Black Dye' or 'Tarahumara White'.

EDIBLES

In the vegetable garden, plant the heat-lovers. This includes native vegetables such as amaranth, corn, devil's claw, epazote, squash, and tepary beans. Nonnative heat-lovers include black-eyed peas, muskmelon, squash, okra, and watermelon.

Sunflowers are not just for the landscape. Their seeds are edible and rich in vitamins and trace minerals. They're easy to grow here, too, especially varieties that have centuries of cultivation, such as 'Apache Brown Striped' or 'Havasupai'.

In lower elevations, plant date palms now. There are many cultivars available; select depending on how you like your fruit. Just as with figs, some dates are best for drying, others are dandy when eaten fresh. Note that mature date palms can get really large; don't plant them too close to permanent structures.

Heat-loving herbs can be planted, but be ready to pamper them with a shade cloth cover in the lower elevations. Before planting, you may have to add sand to the soil to promote drainage, since most herbs do not like wet soils. Plant the Herculean herbs, including rosemary, germander, thyme, sage, and Greek oregano. There are also tropical perennial herbs, such as turmeric, ginger,

Part of annual flower care is making the seasonal switch. Pull out the cool-season annuals or use pruners to cut them off at the ground to make space for the heat-loving annuals.

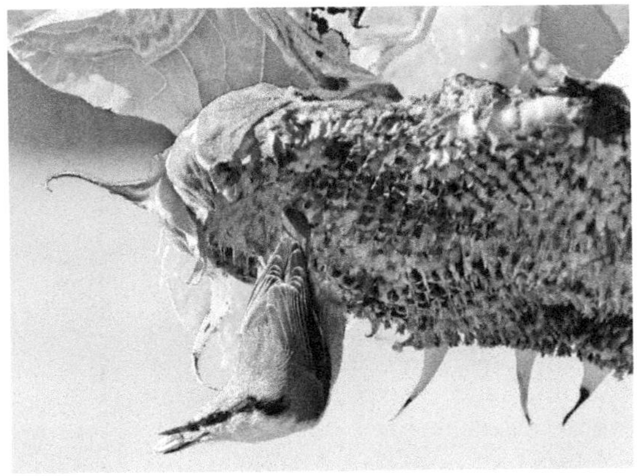

A number of southwestern birds adore sunflower seeds, including nuthatches and Gila woodpeckers.

cat thyme (*Teucrium marum*), and Vietnamese coriander (*Persicaria odorata*, formerly *Polygonum odoratum*). In areas of little frost, gardeners can plant these in the landscape. In other elevations, plant them in containers and bring them indoors in winter.

LAWNS

Repair bare patches in your lawn, as needed. Although not ideal in lower elevations, you can also plant alternatives to lawn grass during this warm month. Be sure you keep any new plantings well watered while they become established.

PERENNIALS

Get the last of any perennials out of their nursery pots and into the ground before mid-month. If you live in the coolest zones, keep planting perennials through summer.

ROSES

Lower-elevation gardeners should be done planting roses before June begins. Upper-elevation gardeners can still plant container-grown roses if you protect them with some shade cloth for their first few weeks.

SHRUBS

All elevations can start some species of shrubs this month through a process called *layering*. Shrubs with flexible stems, such as Texas ranger or honeysuckle, are prime candidates. (See Here's How to Start New Plants by Layering.)

PALMS HAVE PANACHE

Palms come in many sizes and forms and can add a tropical feel to the landscape. Some even offer us dates to eat. Some palms are tall and treelike, while others are short and shrub-like. Some can live their entire lives in containers, and are just fine for the zone 4 gardener. Palms are best planted in June and July.

- Parlor palm (*Chamaedorea elegans*) grows well in containers. It can grace your porch all summer and be moved indoors when temperatures dip towards the mid-40s.
- Mediterranean fan palm (*Chamaerops humilis*) grows to 15 feet high, but spreads to 20 feet wide. The plant clumps and sends out multiple trunks (some gardeners call these "pups"). Avoid planting this species in a tiny space.
- Fan palms such as the California or Mexican palm (*Washingtonia*) have large, fan-shaped leaves and provide a bold, coarse texture in the landscape.
- Feather palms such as the Queen's palm (*Syagrus romanzoffiana*) have a weeping form to their leaves and are considered less coarse.

Many palm species have persistent leaf bases that make a bold statement in the landscape.

HERE'S HOW

TO START NEW PLANTS BY LAYERING

Many species of shrubs, mildly woody perennials (such as autumn sage), herbs, vines, and groundcovers are easily propagated by layering.

- Find a stem on your plant that can be bent to the ground with 6 inches or so to spare. I select branches on the east side of the plant so they will have afternoon shade.
- Wound the branch slightly on the underside where it will touch the ground. Score it with pruners, a knife, or a fingernail.
- Rub rooting hormone into the wound. You can skip this step, but it does aid the process.
- Bend the branch into a little 1-inch-deep hole in the ground and cover with loose soil or potting mix. Be sure the tuft of leaves is not covered.
- Weigh down the buried branch with a rock.

The branch should form roots while still attached to the parent plant. In two to four months (this fall) you can cut the rooted plant off the parent plant and move it to where you want it. It helps if you water the soil under the layering branch on a regular basis.

TREES

All zones can plant seed of trees that are fruiting now, such as oaks, redbuds, and Texas mountain laurel. Collect some seed and plant them where you want them to grow. Keep the seeds watered through the summer and into fall, because some species are slow to emerge.

In lower elevations, now is a good time to plant palms. Be sure to note mature size, because some species get huge. Consider what you are looking for in the landscape, both in color and texture. (See Palms Have Panache.)

In zones 5 and 4, you can plant container-grown trees, but in other zones you should wait until fall.

VINES, GROUNDCOVERS & ORNAMENTAL GRASSES

Bougainvillea is a shrubby vine, or maybe just a shrub. Either way, it can still be planted in-ground in zones 10 and 9, where it will survive the winter. Other zones can grow this charmer in pots on a patio and move it indoors in winter. Dwarf varieties for container growing abound.

Lower-elevation gardeners should avoid adding groundcovers to the landscape this month. Gardeners in the upper elevations can plant groundcovers, but should monitor their water needs.

Ornamental grasses can be planted in upper elevations; sooner is better than later. Avoid planting ornamental grasses in the lower elevations.

CARE

Go easy on plant pruning in this hot month. If at all possible, avoid pruning because it harms tissue, and it's hard for many plants to heal in the heat.

The care that's needed is mulching, especially if you didn't do it already. A nice layer of organic material conserves moisture and helps keep the soil cool. Increase the size of any basins (wells) you have around plants. Basins help hold the mulch in place; they should be the same circumference of the canopy of the plant they are under.

ANNUALS & BULBS

Deadhead flowering annuals to promote new bloom.

You may have bulbs with yellowing leaves. Many bulbs originate from seasonally dry climates and naturally go dormant as temperatures soar. Bulbs store all the energy they can, and their leaves yellow as they transfer precious nutrients down into the bulb. While it's unsightly, resist the urge to trim these yellowing leaves. Let them become entirely brown and dry before you remove spent leaves.

EDIBLES

Mulch vegetables if you haven't yet. This will help keep the soil from getting too hot. In the upper elevations, mulch will increase cool-season vegetables' production. In the lower elevations, mulch is important to reduce evaporation.

If daytime temperatures are over 95°F and corn is producing tassels on top, you'll need to help corn pollination. Shade cloth at least 6 inches above the tops of the plants helps keep crops cooler, holds in some humidity, and increases pollen viability. If it's a windy site, you should add side screening to help keep in the humidity needed to help the pollen adhere to the silks. A light misting of water in early morning can also increase your chances of getting nice full ears of corn. Ideally, you planted Southwest varieties of corn (also called land races); high temperatures are less of an issue with them.

The same high heat and lack of humidity affects tomato fruit set. Shade cloth over plants and a light misting in early morning when pollen is viable will help increase the humidity around the plants. Gently brush the flowers to encourage pollen to release from inside the flowers down onto the stigmas.

Use netting to protect grapes, apricots, and other developing fruits from birds. Harvest early grapes.

The delicious and unique saguaro fruit is ripening. It should be ready to harvest around mid-month. The fruit is full of seeds and sweet pulp and tastes like crunchy watermelon. Scoop the mass of pulp and seed out of the rind and enjoy. The pulp makes a very nice jam, jelly, and wine.

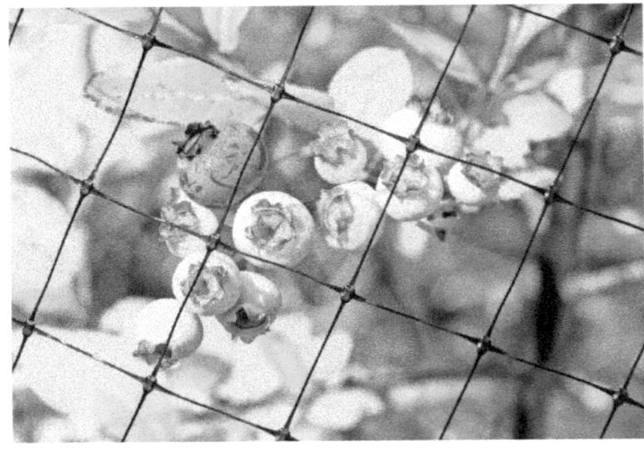

Netting over developing fruits helps protect them from the birds.

Adjust your mower wheels to mow higher as the temperatures rise.

LAWNS

Less mowing is needed as spring growth slows. Speaking of mowing . . . what do you do with your lawn clippings? If you throw them away, you are throwing away valuable (and expensive) lawn nutrients. Consider using a mulching mower, which leaves clippings as a slow-release fertilizer for your lawn. If you don't get a mulching mower, compost any seed-free lawn clippings. Avoid using lawn clippings directly as mulch unless you spread them out in the sun and turn them into hay first.

In most cases, set your mower blade to a height of 2 to 3 inches. This height helps grass better withstand summer heat and drying conditions. Some warm-season grasses can be mowed even higher, including bentgrass, zoysia, and buffalograss. (See Here's How to Select the Mowing Height for Your Lawn.)

PERENNIALS

In all elevations, a layer of mulch will help perennials use less water. Organic mulch, such as cedar bark or pine straw, helps soil remain cooler than rock mulches. If you recently planted perennials, organic mulch over their roots will help them become established.

ROSES

Deadhead spent blooms, but no other pruning is needed. In fact, roses don't respond well to summer pruning in our area. If you want to do something for them, make sure their mulch layer is at least 2 inches deep. Also make sure that mulch isn't mounded up against the stems, creating a shady summer home for bark-munching pests.

HERE'S HOW

TO SELECT THE MOWING HEIGHT FOR YOUR LAWN

Mowing height will shift with the seasons as the needs of your lawn shift. As temperatures rise, so should the mowing height.

Maintaining the lawn at a taller height results in a deeper and more extensive root system for a more drought-resistant lawn. The higher your cut, the less often you will need to mow. The standard rule is to cut off one-third of the turf plant at one time.

Most grasses thrive when cut at 2 to 3 inches in fall and spring. Set your cutting deck higher in summer, so grass can soak in the sun, allowing it to grow and develop.

COOL-SEASON MOWING

Annual rye	1½ to 3 inches
Bluegrass	2 to 3 inches
Perennial rye	2 to 3 inches
St. Augustine	2 to 3 inches
Tall fescue	2½ to 3½ inches

WARM-SEASON MOWING

Bermudagrass	1 to 2½ inches
Bluegrass	2 to 3½ inches
Perennial rye	2 to 3½ inches
St. Augustine	2 to 4 inches

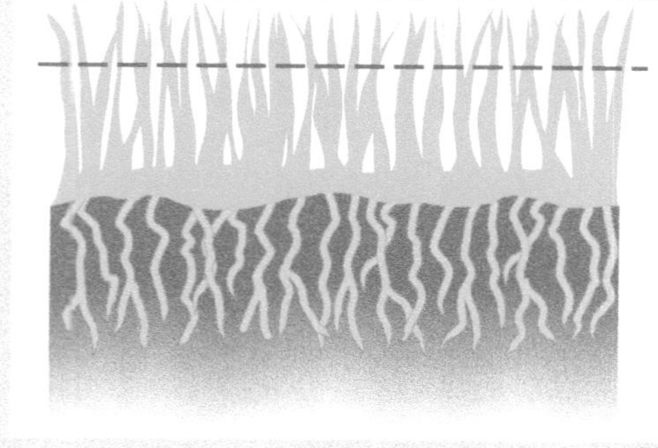

Follow the one-third rule and only cut off one-third of the turfgrass plant at one time.

SHRUBS

There's no major care for shrubs in June. You can always remove dead wood, but ideally you did this earlier in the year.

TREES

Recently, an unnecessary type of care called "thin the crown" gained popularity. The theory is that you need to thin the crown of large trees so they don't blow over in the wind. Rarely, if trees haven't developed anchoring roots, this it might be a good idea; but if you water trees correctly, it is entirely unnecessary. Apply water at the drip line (the edge of the canopy where the feeder roots grow). These feeder roots develop into anchoring roots. If you water at the trunk of a tree, you encourage feeder roots to grow backward toward the trunk where they won't anchor anything. A study of summer urban blow-downs in Tucson showed that lack of good root structure was a contributing factor in over 90 percent of the cases.

Palms are not true trees. Although they are tall and seemingly woody, they're more closely related to grasses, with a structure like a giant straw filled with many smaller straws. The smaller straws are the water-carrying veins running from each individual leaf down into the ground. The wood of the trunk is formed by each individual leaf as it grows. Living bases of leaves intermesh over time to form the giant outer straw for the next generation of leaves.

Because of their structure you should *never* take a green leaf off a palm. A palm needs that green leaf to age in place, sending nutrients to both leaf buds and its future trunk. Allow palm leaves to age and turn brown on the plant so that sturdy trunk tissue is created. Occasional leaf removal will not kill a plant, but repeated removal of green leaves weakens a palm and makes it a target for palm borers. Due to the palm borer life cycle, avoid pruning palms this month.

VINES, GROUNDCOVERS & ORNAMENTAL GRASSES

Train vines as they grow. This is especially important if you have a newly planted twining vine you are training up a trellis. Check on the training often; make it once a week chore all through the

With no anchoring roots, this tree was easily blown down in a summer thunderstorm. Water at the drip line to help trees develop sturdy anchoring roots.

vine's first summer. As they say, "Catch 'em young and bring 'em up right."

Groundcovers cover the ground. That's what they do. This may mean that they creep out of their bed and start to grow where you don't want them. Go ahead and prune them back if they need it. Once again, mature size matters. Remember that they are just fulfilling their genetic destiny; perhaps it would be easier to move surrounding plants rather than to constantly prune your groundcover.

Now is not the time to prune ornamental grasses.

WATER

Weather has always been unpredictable, but it seems more so in recent years. Will we have continued drought or a deluge? Either way, it makes good sense to nurture plants so they are as self-sufficient as possible, with healthy, deep root systems. Don't let plants become "drip-sip" junkies. Water deeply and infrequently, encouraging roots to grow deeply after moisture.

The irrigation system maintenance this month is to check all emitters and sprinklers for proper moisture distribution. Replace any clogged emitters.

ANNUALS & BULBS

Annuals don't have very deep roots. Because they aren't going to be around long, they don't spend much energy making long-lasting root systems. Annuals may need water daily, even the warm-season species.

Spring-flowering bulbs are going summer dormant this month. Taper off their water. Meanwhile, summer-flowering bulbs are emerging and getting ready to flower. For the best display, don't stint their water: irrigate every three to seven days. Make sure any fall-flowering bulbs have their soil moistened every 10 days or so to keep them on schedule to emerge from the soil.

EDIBLES

Tall vegetables can grow deep roots, and you can help. When you water, irrigate enough that the water will sink in to 2 feet for taller plants such as tomato and corn. Water established vegetable gardens once soils are dry deeper than 1 inch. This may be every two to seven days, depending on conditions and how much protective mulch you've laid down.

Water is especially important for fruit and nut crops, such as peaches and pecans. Keep them irrigated to minimize June drop. Some drop is healthy and normal. Depending on the soil, nut trees and tropical evergreen fruits such as citrus and pineapple guava may need water every 7 to 14 days. Plant roots can rot if you water them so often that the soil doesn't dry out between watering.

Watch for winds. Deciduous fruits and especially rose family fruits with large leaves (apple, peach, raspberry) seem to be more sensitive to drying from wind than many other fruits. If wind is predicted, give them some extra water ahead of time. Avoid letting them dry to the point of wilting, because this may make them drop fruit; it also makes them more prone to pests.

Many herbs come to us from the dry, rocky hillsides of the eastern Mediterranean and need little water. They'll need water once every 10 to 21 days depending on the heat load they're experiencing (reflected light is hard on many

The pot of gold at the end of this rainbow is the money out of your pocket. Fifty percent of the water can evaporate before it reaches the ground.

plants). Native herbs, such as Mormon tea (*Ephedra*) or slender poreleaf (*Porophyllum gracile*), could be watered once this month. Or not.

LAWN

In our arid Southwest, overhead sprinkler watering means that you lose up to 50 percent—*half*—of your water to evaporation before it ever hits the ground. You can lose even more than that on a windy day. (See Here's How to Check on Lawn Irrigation to gauge how much water your lawn is actually getting.) A number of homeowners are switching to flood irrigation for their lawns.

No matter what type of irrigation you use, avoid evaporation loss (and disease issues) by applying water early in the morning just before the sun rises, not in the afternoon or evening. Practice good lawn care, including mowing less often. A healthy, unstressed lawn will require less water.

PERENNIALS

Perennials with large leaves dry rapidly in our low humidity, even if it isn't hot. They will need ample water to stay hydrated. Avoid letting them dry out too much; ideally water as often as needed, and *before* it's needed. This may be as often as every two to seven days. Drought-adapted species, such as paperflower (*Psilostrophe cooperi*) or Russian sage, may only need water every 7 to 14 days.

Water succulents every two to three weeks in this dry month. Water more often if the plants are growing in containers.

ROSES

Watch for winds. Although they tolerate low humidity on a calm day, roses are sensitive to drying winds. If your roses are consistently water stressed, plan to move them or plant a windbreak this fall.

HERE'S HOW

TO CHECK ON LAWN IRRIGATION

Sprinkler output can vary depending on the design of the system, water pressure, and age of the pipes. Check it once a year.

- Collect six to eight shallow cans such as tuna or cat food cans. They should all be the same size.
- Spread the cans around your lawn, 3 to 5 feet apart.
- Turn on the irrigation or your sprinkler for 15 minutes.
- Leave the cans in place to measure the depth of water in each can. (Leaving the cans in place lets you note if one area gets significantly more or less water.)
- Record the water depths. Add them up and divide the total by the number of cans to get an average depth. This is the amount that your sprinkler system applies in 15 minutes.
- Now use your soil probe to see how far down into the soil the water has reached. If it's 6 inches, you know that you'll need to run your sprinkler for four times 15 minutes in order for water to penetrate to the recommended 2 feet.

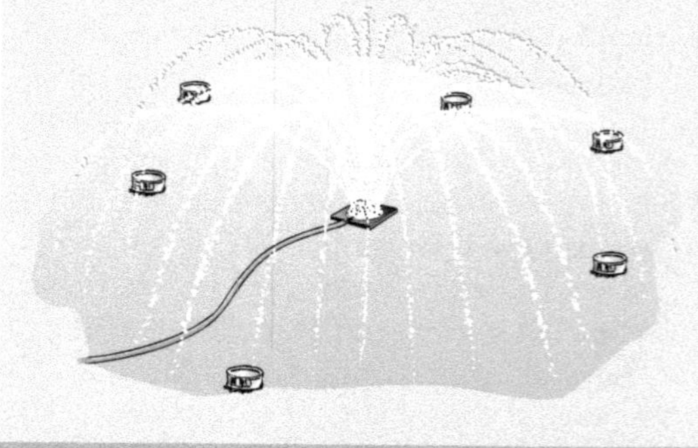

SHRUBS

Shrubs planted in the last twelve months are still in their establishment stage and should be closely monitored for water needs. (See May, Here's How to Know if a Plant is Established.) While they are still becoming established, non-drought-adapted shrubs such as pyracantha or viburnum may need water every three to seven days, while drought-adapted shrubs such as littleleaf cordia or winterfat (*Krascheninnikovia lanata*, formerly *Ceratoides lanata*) every 7 to 14 days.

TREES

The summer heat is here, and trees will perform best if they are not drought stressed. Water slowly, deeply, and at the drip line, where the feeder roots grow. Water long enough so the water penetrates 3 feet deep. If you have sandy soil, gravity more quickly pulls the water below the 3-foot-deep root zone, and you will have to water more often. In clay soil, it takes longer for water to penetrate to 3 feet and saturate the root zone, and it takes longer for it to leave the soil.

VINES, GROUNDCOVERS & ORNAMENTAL GRASSES

Since summer officially arrives this month, you will need to increase water for your vines, groundcovers, and ornamental grasses—but perhaps not if they're shaded by recently leafed-out trees. Check by digging down 3 to 4 inches with a garden trowel. If the soil is dry to the touch, it is time to irrigate. Most of these plants do best with infrequent watering to 2 feet deep, rather than frequent shallow watering.

Ornamental grasses are generally well able to handle drought, if you planted them in the right place. Some, such as bamboo mulhy (*Muhlenbergia dumosa*), do best in part shade, while their cousin pink mulhy (*Muhlenbergia capillaris*) does well in full sun. If your ornamental grass consistently becomes stressed, note this in your garden journal so you can move it to a more favorable location this fall or next spring.

FERTILIZE

If you fertilized on Memorial Day, there's very little to fertilize this month. If you missed this Memorial Day chore, fertilize early in June before temperatures rise. In uppermost elevations, you will fertilize on Flag Day (June 14). In zones 10 and 9, you won't need to fertilize most plants again until Labor Day (there are some exceptions).

ANNUALS & BULBS

In the upper elevations, fertilize annuals mid-month with a half-strength, general-purpose fertilizer. If you want a holiday to do this on, use Flag Day, June 14.

In all elevations, any bulbs still in leaf, as well as summer-blooming bulbs, can be fertilized with half-strength, general-purpose fertilizer this month.

EDIBLES

Fertilize vegetables with a fertilizer appropriate for the crop you're growing. Warm-season crops (the ones that produce fruits, such as tomato, corn, melon) will benefit from a bloom fertilizer. If you still have cool-season leafy crops (lettuce, arugula, kale), then apply a general-purpose fertilizer.

Some fertilizer can be spread by using hose attachments that do the mixing for you. Use these early in the morning and rinse off leaves with plain water afterwards to avoid sunburn from our intense Southwest sun.

Most important is to fertilize citrus before mid-month if you didn't at the end of May. For citrus, use a well-rounded fertilizer high in phosphorus. If you don't fertilize citrus by Flag Day (June 14), skip it until Labor Day. Date palms require a nitrogen-rich fertilizer this month.

Herbs don't require fertilizer this month in lower elevations. Upper-elevation gardeners use a half-strength, general-purpose fertilizer.

LAWNS

You can skip lawn fertilizer, since your spring care should have given your lawn a good start. As temperatures soar, it's healthier for lawns to slow their growth rate.

PERENNIALS

June is a good month to slow the growth on perennials by not fertilizing them. Container-grown succulents are in their warm-weather, active growth phase, so fertilize them once a month through summer. You can purchase specific succulent fertilizers, or use a standard fertilizer at half-strength. Some cacti-philes like to use bat guano dissolved in water, since it's not an overly rich fertilizer. Even then they use it at half-strength to ensure succulents don't grow so quickly that they rupture their skin.

ROSES

Repeat-blooming roses aren't done blooming. Fertilize them mid-month (Flag Day) if you didn't last month, using a bloom fertilizer.

SHRUBS

In all elevations, fertilize summer-flowering shrubs with a bloom fertilizer this month to promote bloom. Nonblooming shrubs could be given a month off from fertilizer.

In the lower elevations, this is a good month to slow the growth on all nonblooming shrubs by not fertilizing them.

TREES

In all elevations, fertilize trees you planted this spring or last fall with a general-purpose fertilizer. This applies to any young tree still in establishment phase of growth. Reminder! Trees in the legume or pea family, such as Mexican ebony and locust, can be stunted by fertilizer.

Palms require a nitrogen-rich fertilizer. They can be fertilized once each month in any month where temperatures stay above 80°F. Skip fertilizer for palms you plan to prune next month.

VINES, GROUNDCOVERS & ORNAMENTAL GRASSES

Plants in this category that were planted last fall or this spring should get a dose of general-purpose fertilizer. As for established plants, this is a good month to slow their growth by not fertilizing.

PROBLEM-SOLVE

Insects of all sorts become active as the weather warms. Watch for tiny young praying mantis emerging now. Don't mistake the tiny baby green walkers for aphids, their prey.

Many Southwest ant species like warm weather and may swarm now to start new colonies. Most species of ants are helpful for the soil, and a number of them are predatory, consuming garden pests. They in turn are eaten by many species of lizard, including the unique Southwest lizard known as the "horny toad" (*Phrynosoma*). Many lizards are eaten in turn by roadrunners, a member of the cuckoo family that is a pure delight to watch, not to mention the state bird of New Mexico. Try to tolerate ants in your yard for all the other native wildlife they will attract.

Leaf-cutter ants are hard to tolerate. Common in New Mexico and Arizona, in areas of summer rain, leaf-cutter ants don't eat the leaves they cut, but instead carry cut leaves back to their nest, where they grow a fungus on the leaves and then eat the fungus. As far as native desert plants are concerned, most of them tolerate this harvesting and grow better for the soil aeration the ants supply. If you have nonnative plants such as jasmine and rose bushes, you are this ant's new

HERE'S HOW

TO RECOGNIZE & TREAT CHLOROSIS

In our region, chlorosis is generally easily treated by acidifying the soil. In a few rare cases, additional treatment may be required.

Some plants may become chlorotic as summer rains or irrigation cycles leach nutrients out of the soil. Chlorosis is indicated by yellowish leaves that remain green around the veins. In our area, the cause is almost always alkaline-induced iron chlorosis. Although there is iron in the soil, plants can't absorb it because the soil is so highly alkaline. The solution is to make soil more acidic. Roses, citrus, and bottlebrush are especially susceptible to alkaline-induced iron chlorosis.

To quickly treat the problem, coffee grounds are handy if you have them. Toss used coffee grounds under plants every day, or save them up and dig them into the soil. For even quicker treatment, acidify soil with white vinegar, but make sure to mix the vinegar in water first! Use 1 cup white vinegar in 4 gallons of water. Pour this around the roots once a week until the leaves improve. Then, do it once a month throughout the warm season.

You can also treat iron chlorosis with powdered sulfur. Sprinkle this product over the root zone and water it in. Wear protective gear when handling sulfur; some people have strong adverse reactions when it gets on their skin. Be very careful not to inhale the powder.

Help prevent chlorosis by adding a 2-inch layer of compost to the plant basin at least twice a year.

Leaf-cutter ants are fungus farmers. They use the leaves they harvest to grow the fungus that is their food.

best friend. Due to the feeding habits of leaf-cutter ants, most common ant poisons don't kill them. Their nests can be 12 feet deep, so boiling water also does not kill them. Diatomaceous earth repeatedly applied around plants you wish to protect throughout the warm season seems to be the only recourse.

Lucky for us, the invasive fire ants (*Solenopsis*) found in the humid areas of Southeast US are not known to occur in the arid Southwest.

If you live in an area that gets summer rains, you may wish to apply preemergent weed control before the rainy season starts. It's one way to keep ahead of weeds, but be very careful using it anywhere near bulbs, vegetable gardens, and wildflower beds. Most types will stop any seed from sprouting, and one study suggests that they negatively affect a number of flowering bulbs.

ANNUALS & BULBS

Warm-weather equals pests, including aphids on annuals. Hose them off or use a soapy spray. Don't use the soapy spray on moss rose (*Portulaca*); it removes the plant's natural protective coating, leading to possible sunscald.

EDIBLES

The vegetable garden may be afflicted by a number of pests when it's so nice and warm out.

Squash vine borers can infest any member of the squash family and will kill the plant. Look for a hole near the base of the vine that has frass around it. You can spot the borers by identifying a darker patch seen through the translucent stem. Pierce them with an ice pick or similar slender sharp object. To prevent re-infestation, coat the stem with petroleum jelly anywhere the diameter of the stem is larger than a pencil. (Some gardeners prefer to wrap aluminum foil around the stems.) If your plants wilt and don't recover after water and after the sun goes down, this is an indicator of squash vine borer. Bt is not the best option against this pest, since they are inside the stem.

Know your neighbors. This pretty pale butterfly is a garden white. Its babies are voracious consumers of all your cabbage-family crops.

Leaf-hoppers are not welcome in the garden, because they hop from plant to plant, sucking sap. While they feed, they can spread curly top virus to cucumber, melon, and tomato plants. Row covers are one way to avoid this problem.

Peaches and grapes are just some of the fruits nearing harvest, and the birds know it. Bird netting over the plants is one way to deter them. If you have a choice on grapes to plant, lighter-colored green table grapes seem to be less bothered by birds, perhaps because they don't turn dark and more noticeable as they ripen.

As irrigation of fruiting trees and shrubs increases, so does the chance of their developing alkaline-induced iron chlorosis. (See Here's How to Identify & Treat Chlorosis.)

Green fig beetles appear throughout much of the Southwest about the time figs ripen. They look like their distant cousin, the Japanese beetle, but larger and with a charming, iridescent green body. Lucky for us, they're nowhere near as destructive as their cousins. The adults only eat fruit that's already damaged.

LAWNS

Lawns may suffer browning patches as the heat increases. This is rarely caused by disease but is generally due to care issues. Common causes of lawn browning are pet waste, excessive fertilizer, mowing too short (scalping), and water issues. Excess water is just as bad as lack of water for lawns.

You may have patches of inordinate drying in one part of your lawn due to soil compaction or reflected light from a pool, fountain, or off windows. If reflected light is the problem, consider replacing the lawn in that area with a bed of plants that tolerate reflected light.

PERENNIALS

If your perennials are summer-flowering and they make lovely buds that fail to open, the problem may not be in your care—most likely you have thrips. Most likely they're the western flower thrip, a tiny, tan insect that hides inside over 500 species of flowers. They use their rasping mouths to damage tender flower petals, which prevents the buds from opening. These thrips are attracted to bright-colored flowers, especially white, blue, and yellow. Flower thrips are also know to rasp on humans wearing bright clothing. Thrips don't feed on blood, and such biting doesn't result in any known disease, but skin irritations do occur. There are a number of IPM products that are effective at controlling thrips. Avoid toxic sprays that could kill their natural predators, such as ladybugs.

Aphids love plants about to bloom. You may spot them on flower stalks of daylilies, hesperaloe, and even the poisonous succulent lady's slipper (*Pedilanthus macrocarpus*). You can brush aphids off plants with your hand (gloved or bare), or blast them off with a stream of water from the hose. Do not use a soapy spray on succulents; the soap removes the plant's natural protective coating, and it may suffer sunscald.

ROSES

Spider mites can be an issue in this warm weather. Treat with blasts of water or insecticidal soap applied every two to three days for a month until they are gone. Culture is important to prevent their recurrence. Rake up any leaves fallen from rose bushes and discard them in the trash.

SHRUBS

Prickly pear cacti may suffer cochineal insects in this hot, dry month. This scale insect produces a white, cottony-looking mass to protect itself as it sucks sap. The insect hidden beneath this distasteful coating is the source of a royal purple clothing dye that was a well-protected trade secret for centuries. It's now being used as a food dye. In your yard, cochineal looks unsightly and can be eliminated by repeatedly hosing off the prickly pear with a strong jet of water. The water will also help the plants recover. Don't use insecticidal soap on prickly pear.

TREES

Evergreens in lower elevations, including cedars, junipers and Italian cypress, are especially susceptible to spider mites as the temperatures climb. Foliage becomes mottled and can start to drop. Eliminate spider mites with blasts of water from the hose. Blasting them three times a week for a month seems to do the trick.

Cochineal insects try to protect themselves from their predators with a waxy white froth.

Palm borer beetles mate and move this month and next. Their young are grubs that can live in a palm for up to nine years before emerging. Infested fronds turn yellow and plants generally die, although healthy, properly pruned palms are known to recover. Borer-weakened palms may topple in wind, or the bored-out tops may snap off. Palms are very heavy and can cause great havoc when they fall. The only sure treatment for palm borers is prevention through proper cultural practices. Leave all green leaves on your palms, removing them only once they turn brown. Make it clear to anyone working on your palms that they're not allowed to use climbing spikes. Prune only in late summer, when adult borers are inactive but plants are still actively growing and can heal the pruning injury.

VINES, GROUNDCOVERS & ORNAMENTAL GRASSES

Aphids and spider mites are two main pests. They even bother tough, prickly plants such as junipers. Blasts of water really do work to knock back their infestations, but you have to be consistent and do it every two to three days, treating undersides of foliage as well. Part of what these blasts of water do is knock the pests off, but they also add extra water and humidity to the area around the affected plants, helping them recover from pest attacks.

July

As temperatures remain nice and hot, few folks want to spend time working up a sweat in the yard. Luckily, there isn't all that much you should be doing in the yard this month—except, perhaps, enjoying the summer with a little brew and barbecue.

In Arizona and New Mexico, July brings rain. These summer rains are what some tribes call "male rains." They arrive with thunderous noise and aggressive deluges. The rain pounds down for minutes, each raindrop landing with arrow-like force; and then, as fast as it started, the storm disappears. These rain cells can be so localized that rain falls in the backyard while the street in front bakes in the sun. Winter rains are called "female rains." They quietly roll in and gently drop their water almost as a mist across vast stretches of land. Sometimes they stay for days to nurture the area.

When our summer male rains arrive, they can wreak havoc in the garden, breaking branches, toppling trees, removing soil from newly installed plants. Often, they are accompanied by hail, which can damage plants, shatter pots, and bring down garden structures. The idea of rain—some free water falling out of the sky—sounds nice, but the aftermath can be a major headache.

Summer rains are capricious—they may not fall at all. This means that a major July task may be irrigating your landscape. On average, 50 percent of household water is used on the landscape, and that number can go up in a hot, dry summer.

The good news is that there are numerous ways to reduce the amount of water you have to buy and apply to your landscape. As you spend time in your garden this month, think about how you might lighten the chore load in the future and have more time to simply enjoy your garden.

PLAN

You can install an active rainwater harvest system that uses barrels or a passive one that uses a series of berms and basins to slow the flow and hold the rainwater in your yard. While some states in the West have laws against interfering with the flow of water across your land, this is not yet the case in our three states. Harvest away!

To plan water harvesting, take out your scale map of your property. It should include home, sidewalks, patios, and any other impervious surfaces (hardscapes), which will shed water onto the landscape. Make copies, and start marking them up. Sketch arrows to indicate water-flow directions across each surface. Mark landscaped areas, types of vegetation, and number of plants. Mark where you can add catchment areas.

Catchment areas catch and hold the water so it can soak down into the soil. In most modern yards, this involves building soil berms or dikes across the water draining from your land. Construct a curving berm, and plant on the upslope side of the berm. Better yet, make a series of berms. Amend the soil for planting and include up to 50 percent added organic matter (compost) to help the rain soak into your soil.

Already have rain gutters? Instead of letting water run down the drain, reroute them to run out onto the landscape and add berms and catchment basins so downspout water flows into a series of planting beds.

Powerful summer rains can sweep in, bringing needed rain but also causing damage in the garden.

ANNUALS & BULBS

Many annuals are not very heat tolerant. Note in your journal which ones perform well in your garden and which underperform. This will help with your purchases next year. If you have a good relationship with your local nursery, share your information with them.

It's not too soon to think about spring-blooming bulbs for next year. Do get on the phone and discuss our Southwest temperatures as you place your order. For our region, they shouldn't ship bulbs until after Labor Day. Bulbs can fry in their shipping carton, even though they're dormant. (It has happened to me.)

EDIBLES

For upper elevations, fall gardening begins this month with cool-season vegetables tucked among the heat-lovers. Meanwhile, zone 8 gardeners will set out the fall crop of tomato family members after mid-month. With all this harvesting and shifting of crops, a plan to follow becomes an important part of being a successful vegetable gardener. You'll need to consider mature height of each crop and sun exposure for germinating seeds.

In zones 10 and 9, the dead of summer is the time to plan and plant a hot-season or monsoon vegetable garden. There are a number of native crops that thrive in triple-digit heat and single-digit humidity. Native Seeds/SEARCH is a good source for native crops and seed of plants that have been grown in the Southwest for centuries. (See Resources.)

Gardeners in zones 8 and 7 can plant potatoes next month, so order seed potatoes now.

In all elevations, as you harvest the current crops, do your soil building. Add either compost or composted steer manure and dig it in. Leave it for two weeks to settle in before planting the next crop.

As you walk around your yard to plan for the future, do you see a site where you need more summer shade? You might dream of a pecan tree, but remember its mature size. A tree that's forty

If you desire herbs with high water use, consider a water garden.

feet tall may produce too much shade for other edibles. Perhaps a smaller almond tree would be a better choice.

If you want to grow high-water-use herbs such as mint or the native yerba mansa, consider a water garden. It can be as small as a kids' wading pool or as large as a stock tank. You'll need to plant the herbs in pots and place them on bricks in the water so only the bottom inch of the pot is in the water. Add inexpensive feeder goldfish to eat any mosquito larvae, and—*voilà*!—you have a water garden. Planting and care of high-water-use plants is discussed under Plant, Perennials.

LAWN

Are you enjoying your lawn to the utmost or has it become a tedious chore? You may decide to downsize or even eliminate lawns from your life. As you drive around town, notice any particularly enticing groundcovers and other lawn alternatives. Take photos and identify them now so you can be ready for planting this autumn.

PERENNIALS

In summer, most of us use our yards more in the evenings than we do in the middle of the day. Enhance that experience with night-blooming plants. In the lower elevations, you can plan where to plant a number of night-blooming succulents this month.

ROSES

Summer-blooming shrubs are so attractive in the garden that you should consider adding shrubby landscape roses that bloom all summer, not just in in spring. Zones 8 and cooler have many options for landscape roses, including the native Woods' rose (*Rosa woodsii*).

SHRUBS

There are so many attractive summer-blooming shrubs! On your drives, notice what does well in your area. Take photos and get identifications now so you can be ready to plant some this autumn or next spring.

Summer-blooming shrubs attract hummingbirds. Along with nectar, they dine on many insect pests.

TREES

Shade is good in the Southwest garden. Too much shade is rarely an issue, but take time to note if any plants under tree canopies are failing to thrive. If so, you could prune the tree to open the canopy and lessen the shade. Do hire a professional arborist for such work. Most landscape maintenance workers are not trained or skilled at proper tree work and can do more harm than good.

Not enough shade? Plan tree placement carefully. Look for a spot where you can passively harvest rainwater to help the tree establish itself. To avoid future problems, large trees should be at least 15 feet away from walls or structures.

VINES, GROUNDCOVERS & ORNAMENTAL GRASSES

If you don't have any, consider adding some vines to your garden. They can take up very little space, yet their blooms can attract hummingbirds in droves. Not only do these tiny flying jewels pollinate plants, but they also eat massive quantities of insects in their quest for high-quality food for their babies.

Groundcovers and ornamental grasses are one way to stabilize banks of rainwater-harvesting berms. Rather than plunking them down here and there, plan their placement so that swaths or swales of them flow across your yard like a living stream.

PLANT

In all elevations, there's not much planting to be done during this hot month unless you have a vegetable garden.

ANNUALS & BULBS

In all but the coolest zones, avoid planting annuals or bulbs. If you absolutely crave color, try heat-lovers such as agastache, amaranth, celosia, creeping zinnia (*Sanvitalia procumbens*), globe amaranth, golden threadleaf (*Dyssodia*), and lisianthus (*Eustoma russellianum*).

Spring bulbs should not be planted this month. However, if you get fall-flowering bulbs, the sooner you get them into the ground, the better.

EDIBLES

Gardeners in zones 6 and cooler can set out transplants of early-ripening cucumbers, green onions, peppers, pumpkins, and squash. Plant a second crop of beans, greens, and members of the cabbage family (broccoli, kohlrabi). Try some of the Asiatic cole vegetables such as bok choy or joy choi.

Gardeners in zones 8 and 7 can plant the Three Sisters: corn, beans, and squash. Not just squash itself, but many members of the family can be planted now, including cucumbers and quickly maturing melons. Avoid blossom end rot problems by planting varieties that grow small fruit such as lemon cucumbers and miniature watermelons. Note the days to maturity of these fruiting crops and make sure you have enough days left before first frost occurs in your area.

For those in zones 10 and 9, the hot-season or monsoon-season vegetable garden can include heat-loving native vegetables and herbs, such as amaranth, short-maturity hard corn, devil's claw, epazote, lemon basil, squash, and tepary beans. You can also plant black-eyed peas, winter squash, okra, pumpkin, sweet corn, and watermelon.

LAWNS

This not a good month to plant a lawn in any elevation. If you have bare spots, buy sod or seed and patch as needed. Be sure to water any newly planted areas more than surrounding lawn to help them become established.

PERENNIALS

Water gardens can be home to any number of perennials, including herbs. Place plants in plastic pots and put them on bricks in the water so only the bottom inch of the pot is in the water. Regular potting soil will generally become waterlogged and drown your plants, so add ample sand to the mix, or use a cactus mix that has added perlite. To help keep soil in the pots and not in the pond, put a section of window screen down in the bottom of the pot before you plant.

Perennials for the water garden include canna, curly sedge (*Carex rupestris*), Japanese sweet flag (*Acorus gramineus*), lady's mantle

Lay a soaker hose after you plant, while plants are still small. You can use landscape staples to hold it in place.

(*Alchemilla mollis*), mint, ruellia, umbrella papyrus (*Cyperus alternifolius*), water iris (*Iris pseudacorus*, *I. kimballii*), and yerba mansa (*Anemopsis californica*).

ROSES

You should avoid planting roses in the ground this month. If you are jonesing for some roses, consider planting miniature roses in containers to enjoy outdoors on the porch. Upper-elevation gardeners will need to bring them inside for winter.

You can find miniature roses in supermarkets but you must take care with such plants. They haven't been kept in ideal growing conditions and may harbor pests such as spider mites. Keep suspect plants in quarantine in an isolated area until you are sure they're safe to bring into contact with your other plants.

SHRUBS

Lower-elevation gardeners can plant the larger cacti and succulents that serve as shrubs in the landscape this month. But even these tough plants need protection from the sun until they're established. To prevent sunscald, orient them in the same direction they were growing previously. Reputable succulent growers mark their pots with a spot of paint, generally on the south-facing side. After planting, cover or wrap the succulent with a piece of shade cloth that you'll leave in place for four to six weeks. Ocotillo do best if you maintain their north/south orientation as well. Failure to do so is why so many ocotillo transplants die or take so long to establish.

Gardeners in the upper elevations shouldn't plant shrubs. It's hard for them to become established unless you're ready to mist them daily and carefully monitor their water. Shade cloth can help as well.

All elevations can start shrubs from seed. (See Here's How to Grow a Woody Plant From Seed.)

TREES

All elevations should not plant container-grown trees this month—but you can start trees from seed. Many trees have a very rapid juvenile growth phase and you can have a nice tree within three to five years. You will need to select a species that is releasing seed at this time of year, such as mesquite, desert willow, hackberry, or catalpa.

VINES, GROUNDCOVERS & ORNAMENTAL GRASSES

Plants in this group are best planted in spring or fall. You can, however, start plants from seed. (See Here's How to Grow a Woody Plant From Seed.)

HERE'S HOW

TO GROW A WOODY PLANT FROM SEED

It is easier than you might think with only three steps: plant, water, cull.

Plant. Collect seed of the desired species and plant a handful in the ground, right where you want your tree or shrub to grow. Bury them twice as deep as their length.

Water often. Even low-water plants need extra water to get growing. Soon you'll have a cluster of seedlings about 6 inches high.

Cull. When they reach 6 to 8 inches high, remove all seedlings but one, using pruners. I advocate clipping rather than pulling the culls, because less root disturbance occurs. Take some time to select the most robust and straightest-growing seedling.

Since you start the seeds in place, there is no transplant shock, no establishment phase, and no broken taproots. I have done this with a number of species, including desert willow, mesquite, loquat, date palms, and jojoba. With all of these species it was a double test, with duplicates grown in containers and transplanted. Within three years, plants started in the yard *far* outperformed their siblings started in pots.

Seed planted in the ground resulted in a jujube tree that grew fast and bore fruit in its third year.

Pinch off spent blooms to encourage continuous bloom.

CARE

July pruning advice is simple: Avoid pruning this month! Pruning is better done in spring or early fall. If you must, remove storm-damaged branches or eliminate hazards to humans or structures.

One exception to the no-pruning advice is the kind ideally done with just your fingers: deadheading and pinching. Deadheading consists of removing spent blooms to help extend the bloom period. Plants that have been pollinated and are starting to set seed generally stop flowering, but by removing spent blooms you encourage them to flower again.

Deadhead by grasping the stem under the spent flower and snapping it where it most readily snaps. Doing this by hand rather than by pruners ensures that the stem is broken at natural abscission areas between cells, allowing a plant to heal more rapidly.

Another important care item in the Southwest garden this month is mulch. Mulch around the bases of your plants (if you haven't already), using organic material, such as leaf litter from trees and shrubs, including pine needles. Vegetative mulch helps retard evaporation. If you have it, used kitty litter made from pine or newspaper can also be used as mulch in our area. Water the top of any organic mulch once you apply it. This helps it mat together and avoid blowing around the yard.

ANNUALS & BULBS

Deadhead annuals and large-flowered summer bulbs, such as gladiolus. Don't take off the entire flower stalk of your gladiolus, just the individual spent blooms. Stake tall flower stalks against summer storm damage.

Mulch your annuals and your bulb beds with a layer 1 to 2 inches deep.

EDIBLES

Do you have tall vegetables such as okra or tomatoes tied to stakes or in cages? If you haven't yet supported them, do this early in the month, before thunder storms arrive. The crashing rain, gusts of wind, and occasional hail that come pounding down can flatten a vegetable garden in no time. If they're already tied, check the ties and add as needed.

If you haven't yet, mulch your garden with straw or pine straw, but never use baled hay, which generally has a wealth of weed seeds in it.

Do you have grafted fruit trees? Remove any water sprouts or suckers that may start growing around the base of the trunk below the graft union. (See Here's How to Remove Water Sprouts.)

Harvest fruit as it ripens. In the lower elevations, this may be grapes and jujube, apricots, and even berry fruits, including blackberry and raspberry.

LAWNS

Mow every 7 to 14 days, depending on species. When you mow, remove no more than one-third of the leaf blade each time. In most cases, set the mower blade height to 2½ to 3 inches. (See June, Here's How to Select the Mowing Height for Your Lawn.)

Some lawns need *no* mowing in summer, which is part of their attraction. Buffalograss stays green, yet is mostly dormant in summer. If you mow it only once or twice a year, it forms a dense, meadow-like cover that looks good and helps retain soil.

If you haven't yet this summer, sharpen your mower blade. Grass is rich in plant compounds that quickly dull blades. Sharp blades will more cleanly cut grass, allowing grass to heal better, without ragged, brown edges. Clean cuts and quick healing mean a lawn uses less water too.

PERENNIALS

Check the mulch over the perennials. A 2- to 3-inch layer of organic mulch, such as cedar bark or pine straw, will help the soil remain cooler and help plants survive summer heat. Building basins

All water sprouts near the graft union should be removed.

HERE'S HOW

TO REMOVE WATER SPROUTS

Water sprouts are upright shoots that arise from the trunk of a tree. They originate from latent buds hidden in the trunk. (They are sometimes called suckers, although that term is more correctly applied to shoots that arise from roots.) Water sprouts often develop in trees in response to sunlight damage or improper pruning.

Water sprouts by their nature are not as strong as regular branches. These shoots are more subject to diseases and pests. Just above the graft union, they generally produce substandard fruit; if they occur below the graft union, they often produce undesirable fruit.

Pruning does not remove the water sprout growth tissue and it will simply resprout.

Your first instinct may be to cut them off, but it's better to remove the latent bud tissue underlying the sprout. If your tree is not drought stressed, this will be easy. Firmly grasp the water sprout as close to the trunk as you can. Twist the sprout as you pull, and it should come out of the trunk with all the latent bud tissue attached in a lump. Your tree should not resprout in the same spot. Note that the twist is circular. Plants develop tissues (flowers, buds, branches) in a helical swirl, thus a twist more effectively removes the underlying bud than a straight pull.

Pull water sprouts when they are small, removing the bud of trunk tissue from which they grow.

If you have a recurring problem with water sprouts, your plant is sending a message that its trunk is getting too much sunlight. You have several options. You can provide shade by planting ornamental grasses or perennials around the lower trunk. Or, you can shade the trunk with paint; use a whitewash, not a latex or enamel house paint. Finally, you could loosely wrap the trunk with a piece of shade cloth or even window screen. Loosen and rewrap this cover twice a year so the tree doesn't grow over it. To prevent such problems, try to let trees grow in their natural form. Olives and citrus, especially, have arching canopies that shades their trunk.

or plant wells around perennials helps keep the mulch in place, plus helps catch rainwater.

ROSES

Deadhead any roses still blooming. No other pruning is required; in fact, most roses don't respond well to summer pruning in the Southwest.

Landscape roses may be overgrowing their space and impinging on walkways. Since this is a safety issue, you can prune those back. But don't simply cut them back equal to the edge of the walkway; cut them at least half a foot farther back to give them some space to grow into.

SHRUBS & TREES

There is no major pruning of shrubs or trees during this hot summer month. You can remove dead and damaged limbs as you notice them. Remove any water sprouts or suckers that may start growing around the base of the tree. (See Here's How to Remove Water Sprouts.)

Mulch over the roots of trees and shrubs if you haven't yet, with a 2- to 3-inch layer of organic mulch.

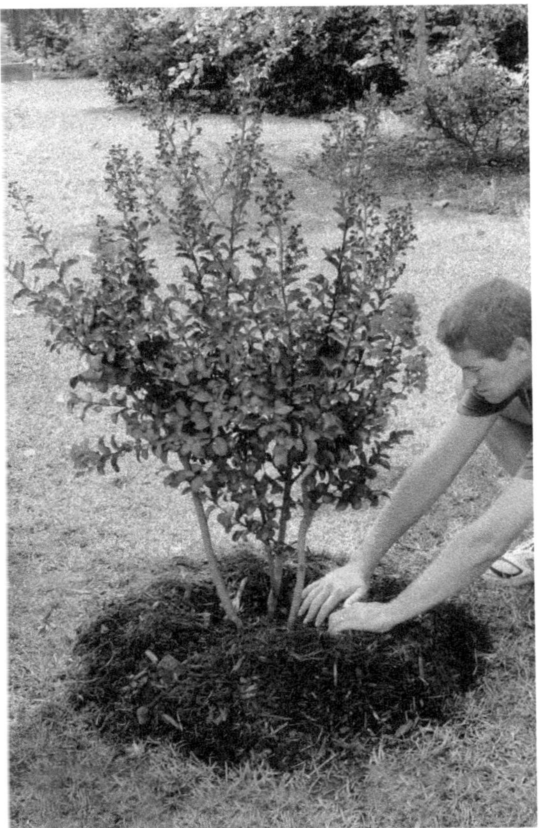

To avoid disease and pests, don't make mulch volcanoes with your plants erupting out of the center. Pull mulch away from stems.

VINES, GROUNDCOVERS & ORNAMENTAL GRASSES

Vigorous summer vines may need pruning so that you can use your yard. If they're overtaking the space, then prune them. If they're not, it's better to leave them unpruned in the heat. Tie up vines that may need it. This will help avoid breakage in summer storms.

Many heat-loving groundcovers are aggressive growers in summer, and lantana is one of the worst culprits. You may want to hack the cursed thing to the ground, but leave aggressive pruning for spring rejuvenation pruning. In summer, merely cut it back enough to control growth, otherwise you risk sunscald.

Now is not the time to prune ornamental grasses.

WATER

All plants, even drought-adapted natives, need extra water during periods of higher temperatures. Ever notice how widely spaced plants naturally are in the Southwest? Since we plant them closer together in the yard, they need more water than their wild relatives.

Water at dawn to conserve water, discourage fungus, and give plants the water they need as they wake up for the new day. Apply enough water so it sinks deeply into the ground. Roots need encouragement to grow deep underground where it's cooler. Trees need to be encouraged to anchor themselves well, so apply their water at the drip line, away from the trunk.

Water is especially critical for plants held captive in containers. Protect container plants from excessive sun. Depending on species, sun exposure, and the type of container, you may need to water every day. Many succulents can't take full sun without extra water.

The irrigation system maintenance this month is to check irrigation controller settings after every power outage. Manually turn the system off if you get a heavy rain. Consider adding a rain sensor that will do this for you.

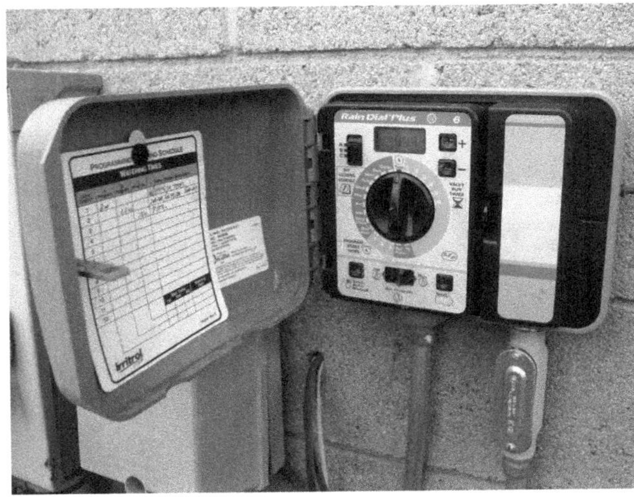

Once you have done it a few times, programming your irrigation controller becomes quite easy.

HERE'S HOW

TO COLLECT WATER INSIDE THE HOUSE

If water restrictions are in place in your area, consider a greywater system to collect nontoilet water from inside your home for use in the garden. If this sounds like too much work, start by collecting the clean "white" water you otherwise send down the drain.

Keep some 5-gallon buckets beside the shower. As you wait for the warm water to reach the tap, fill the buckets with this clean water. Hauling water out to the plants will remind you that "a pint is a pound the world around." In our house, we only fill each bucket halfway to avoid sloshing and to balance the weight.

A large watering can beside the kitchen sink can catch that water; it will be easier to carry and apply.

ANNUALS & BULBS

When it comes to water, annuals will need you to keep it coming! Even mulched and summer-tough annuals may need daily water when temperatures are at 90°F and beyond.

Do you have fall-flowering bulbs? If you're like me, you may forget exactly where in the yard they're planted and need to refer to your journal. They need water now to encourage them to emerge on schedule.

EDIBLES

Water harvesting is not a new idea. Long ago, area natives taught the Europeans that here in the Southwest a sunken garden is the best way to grow a crop when there's little rainfall. This was called *ak chin* by the O'odham peoples, who would sink their growing space in an area near a wash and divert rain runoff into it. The urban equivalent is the downspout off your roof. Divert it to a sunken garden, and if you plant drought-adapted Southwest heirlooms, two or three rains may be sufficient for a healthy crop of vegetables.

In all elevations, fruit and nut crops—including apple, citrus, and walnut—should be watered on a regular basis. Basins and berms to catch rainwater can reduce the amount of water you need to pay for. Avoid overwatering; roots can rot if the soil doesn't dry out somewhat between waterings.

Many perennial herbs slow their growth in the hottest part of the year. Check *before* you water; drought-tolerant species may only need irrigation every 10 to 21 days. Annual herbs have shallow roots and need more frequent water.

LAWNS

Water lawns every 5 to 10 days, depending on your soil type, prevailing winds, and any rainfall. When you water, apply enough to penetrate the soil to 2 feet deep. Don't let a lawn become bone-dry; that makes it difficult for water to penetrate the soil.

PERENNIALS

When it comes to water for succulents, water needs depend on where they are native to. Sonoran and Chihuahuan Desert natives of New Mexico and Arizona are genetically programmed to grow in the hot months of summer and with the summer rains. If it doesn't rain, plan on watering succulents such as golden barrel and soaptree yucca (*Yucca elata*) two or even three times this month. If you live in Nevada or northern Arizona and have Mojave Desert succulents, such as beavertail prickly pear and Joshua tree, you need not water them. They grow with the winter rains. Don't despair if you don't know where your succulents are native to! As long as you let the soil dry out between watering, the summer dormant plants will not be harmed by water in the summer.

ROSES

If your roses are blooming, be sure to provide sufficient moisture to help them continue flowering. Soaker hoses and drip systems are ideal for this. If you haven't yet, consider forming a berm or plant basin around your roses. Make it as wide as the canopy of your roses. Filled with mulch to prevent evaporation; this will help deliver the moisture right where it is needed.

Rainwater harvest systems in the Southwest should be large enough to capture the infrequent summer rains that often dump the rain supply for an entire month in a single hour.

SHRUBS

Drought adapted or not, summer-flowering shrubs such as cordia or abelia, as well as those currently producing berries, such as pyracantha or viburnum, will need extra water to prevent drought stress. Monitor their needs carefully; you may need to water them more often than the guidelines listed in Here's How Often to Water Your Landscape (in April).

TREES

Growing in the wild, trees make do with whatever rain falls on them. In our yards, we planted those trees for a purpose, and to help them meet our expectations we should provide them with water before they become drought stressed.

It can take as long as three years to establish a tree. Be sure to monitor moisture levels in the soil below the drip line and *do not* be stingy about water during this establishment phase. Trees need to be encouraged to anchor themselves well, so apply their water well away from the trunk, at the canopy drip line. You may have to move your drip emitters, and even add new ones several times in the first few years of a tree's growth.

VINES, GROUNDCOVERS & ORNAMENTAL GRASSES

Any plants in this category planted this spring, or even last autumn, may still be establishing their root systems. If you don't have a drip system or use soaker hoses, consider adding large berms (plant wells) around the plants, and fill them with water. Let it soak in for 30 minutes, and then water again until you've wet the soil to a depth of 2 feet. (See March, Here's How to Gauge How Deep Irrigation Goes.)

FERTILIZE

If you fertilize according to the holidays (see April, Here's How to Fertilize the Forgetful Gardener's Way), Fourth of July is this month, and it's time for this garden task! But not if you live in zones 10 or 9. These hottest zones should avoid fertilizing this month. (But, of course, there are just a *few* exceptions.)

Beds and soil covered with organic or vegetative mulches need less fertilizer than areas of open soil, because the mulch is slowly breaking down, releasing nutrients into the soil. You could skip fertilizer this month if you practice good mulching.

ANNUALS & BULBS

In all zones but 10 and 9, fertilize annuals with a bloom fertilizer early in the month. Do not use a nitrogen-rich or general-purpose fertilizer; these promote foliage growth (you planted annuals for their blooms, not foliage). Avoid fertilizing annuals if they're wilting or showing other signs of heat stress.

Summer-blooming bulbs need fertilizer this month in any zone. Apply a bloom fertilizer early in the month.

The first number on a fertilizer package represents the percent by weight of nitrogen, the second of phosphorus, and the third of potassium.

EDIBLES

Gardeners in all zones will fertilize the vegetable garden at least once this month. Read and follow the recommended dose on the fertilizer label, but less than the recommendation can't hurt, especially as many plants slow their growth in summer heat. Excessive nitrogen fertilizer in the vegetable garden can cause plants to produce more leaves and fewer of the vegetables classified as fruits—such as tomatoes and melons. (If they contain seeds, they are a fruit.) Use a bloom or fruiting fertilizer high in phosphorus, with a nutrient ratio such as 6-12-6.

Avoid fertilizing corn with a high-nitrogen fertilizer within two weeks of tasseling. How to know when that is? Err on the side of caution, and use nitrogen-rich fertilizer during the first month of growth, then switch to bloom fertilizer.

Fertilize date palms and grapes with a nitrogen-rich fertilizer. Fertilizer is applied to grapes once fruit has been harvested. This helps them grow well and store ample energy for an even better harvest next year. Since you want to encourage foliage growth at this stage, use a nitrogen-rich fertilizer.

Pecan trees may turn chlorotic due to zinc deficiency, not iron deficiency. Look for a bronze color in the chlorotic areas. In most cases, acidifying the soil will help plants recover. Switch to a high-nitrogen fertilizer, because the phosphorus in bloom fertilizer competes with zinc in the soil.

LAWNS

All elevations should avoid fertilizing lawns in July. If your lawn is not irrigated or is growing a semidormant species such as buffalograss, it doesn't need fertilizer in any summer month; fertilizer will damage, even kill, a dormant lawn.

PERENNIALS

In zones 8 and cooler, fertilize summer- and fall-blooming perennials with a bloom fertilizer this month. Spring-blooming perennials should be treated with a high-nitrogen fertilizer. If you wish to use a slow-release, granular fertilizer, push aside the mulch and sprinkle it onto the soil. Reapply the mulch, then water.

Succulents grown in containers will do well fertilized during their summer growth phase. If they're a flowering succulent such as crown of thorns or desert rose, use a bloom fertilizer at half-strength. Treat nonbloomers, such as many of the euphorbias, with general-purpose fertilizer at half strength.

ROSES

All zones except zones 5 and 4 should avoid fertilizing roses in July. This is especially true if you applied a slow-release fertilizer earlier in the season.

SHRUBS

In zones 8 and cooler, fertilize any summer- and fall-blooming shrubs with a bloom fertilizer this month to promote bloom. If you wish to, skip fertilizer on spring-blooming shrubs during this hot month, or apply a slow-release, granular fertilizer.

TREES

In zones 5 and 4, fertilize trees that were planted last fall or this spring with a general-purpose fertilizer. In all elevations, there's no need to fertilize established trees this month.

VINES, GROUNDCOVERS & ORNAMENTAL GRASSES

Plants in this category that were planted last fall or this spring should get a dose of general-purpose fertilizer. Established plants in this category don't *need* fertilizer this month, but if you wish, summer-flowering vines and groundcovers benefit from a bloom fertilizer this month.

Ornamental grasses in zone 8 and cooler can be fertilized this month with a general-purpose or high-nitrogen fertilizer.

PROBLEM-SOLVE

Alkaline-induced iron chlorosis commonly rears its ugly head in the hotter months of summer. Leaves turn yellow between veins, while the veins stay green. Textbooks call this iron chlorosis and recommend adding iron. While necessary in iron-poor soils elsewhere, this is not the treatment in iron-rich Southwest soils. Plants exhibit chlorosis because they can't absorb the iron they need out of our alkaline soils. Acidify the soil as discussed in June, Here's How to Know & Treat Chlorosis.

Four-legged pests increase their numbers in summer. The living is easy in your nice, lush yard, so mice, ground squirrels, and packrats all multiply. As if eating your plants isn't annoying enough, their predators pose a real threat to life and limb, even in urban areas. I mean rattlesnakes. Just remember, in the Southwest never put your hands or feet anywhere you cannot see. Snakes have incredibly good camouflage. Timber rattlers are active throughout the uppermost elevations, and the rest of the Southwest has an ample share of other species.

Scorpions are another reason never to put your hands anywhere you can't see. I have found them inside stacks of flowerpots, under pots on benches, and in the bark of living trees. An entomologist explained to me that they will only sting if they feel threatened, and even then the sting may be a dry one—in other words, they may not inject their venom. They may also pinch you with their lobster-like claws. In general, they want to be left alone, and I, for one, am more than happy to do so. Scorpions eat insects, so if you regularly find them inside your home, you may want to spray against roaches.

ANNUALS & BULBS

Aphids were found earlier in the year; now it's spider mite season. Look for signs of fine webbing or a salt-and-pepper appearance on plants. A daily jet of water from the hose will get rid of them. If you must, use a soapy spray, but be aware that such sprays drown pests and predators alike.

Thrips may block bulb buds from becoming blossoms. Green lacewings are an effective natural predator and can be purchased from retailers that offer IPM supplies.

Use your journal. Note these pests and their preferred food, and use this information next year. For annuals, select a different variety or an entirely different species and see if you have fewer problems. For thrips on bulbs, you may want to order IPM supplies earlier in the season.

EDIBLES

In all elevations, the vegetable garden has a whole host of pests that show up now to munch. Watch for cucumber beetles, stink bugs, spider mites, and caterpillars, and treat them early. See the various Here's How sidebars in this section for signs and treatments.

Rodent pests leave scent trails that their predators follow. Eliminate rodents to eliminate the danger of rattlesnakes in your garden.

HERE'S HOW

TO KNOW & TREAT HORNWORMS

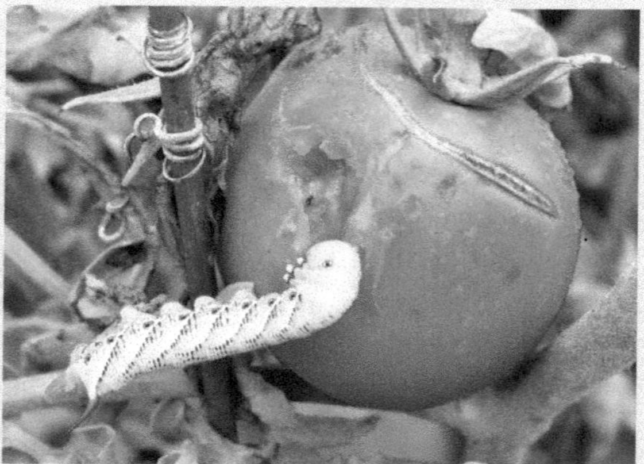

Hornworms are voracious caterpillars, munching entire leaves, small stems, and even parts of immature fruit of all tomato family plants, including eggplants, peppers, and potato leaves. You will generally see damage before you see the hornworms, because they are so well camouflaged. You may see their dark frass on foliage and around the base of a plant. A single hornworm can denude a plant in a matter of days, but if they're detected and removed early, the plant will recover just fine.

Identify. Tomato hornworm (*Manduca quinquemaculata*) and its cousin the tobacco hornworm (*M. sexta*) attack members of the tomato family. Both species reach 3 to 4 inches long and are green with white marks along the sides. They get their name from the black or red horn projecting from their rear.

Treat. Because a hornworm is so large, the easiest and most effective way to get rid of it is to pick it off plants and either squash it or toss it into a bucket of soapy water.

If you find a hornworm covered with white egg sacs, leave it. The egg sacs are those of parasitic braconid wasps. Let the eggs hatch, and you'll have plenty of tiny wasps to defend your garden against many species of caterpillar pests.

A severe infestation of hornworms can be treated by applying Bt (*Bacillus thuringiensis*). This is most effective when the larvae are small. Use with care, because it kills *all* butterflies and moths, even the ones you wish to attract to your garden.

Prevent. Take these steps in future years:

- Turn over garden soil before planting. Hornworms overwinter in the soil in a large, dark brown chrysalis, then emerge and mate in late spring.
- Companion plants are useful. Next year, plant a confusing companion plant next to your tomato family members. Dill, borage, and epazote are all good at confusing mama moth when she is looking for a place to lay her eggs.
- Trap crops. I plant the hornworms' native food source, datura. I scatter seed of this summer wildflower in the alley and along my fence. Mama moth pollinates and lays her eggs on this plant, not on my tomatoes. The few times I've found hornworms in the vegetable garden I have successfully moved them to this native.

HERE'S HOW

TO TREAT CUCUMBER BEETLES

There are six species of cucumber beetle. The one in your area may look different. Your local cooperative extension can help you ID this pest.

There are six species of cucumber beetles in our region, and they can produce two to three generations per year. Cucumber beetles damage all members of the cucumber family, including squashes, melons, pumpkin, and gourds. If consuming your plants wasn't bad enough, these beetles also transmit bacterial wilt.

Cucumber beetles cause damage in all active stages of their life cycle. Overwintered adults feed on emerging seedlings; larvae tunnel into the soil and feed on plant roots; adults feed on foliage, flowers, stems, and can even damage the fruit. But the greatest threat posed is their transmission of bacterial wilt caused by *Erwinia tracheiphila*, which is stored in the intestinal tract of adult cucumber beetles. Once a plant is infected, the bacteria spreads rapidly, causing the plant to wilt and die within 7 to 10 days.

TREAT:

- **Floating row covers.** Place these when you plant your seedlings. Remove row covers at the onset of flowering to allow pollination. Most cucumber beetles will have moved on by then.
- **Sticky traps,** either purchased or homemade. For added effect, attach a cotton swab soaked in oil of clove, cinnamon, cassia, or allspice—all of which act as a powerful attractant.
- **Chemical sprays.** There are several chemical sprays rated for this pest, including insecticidal soap.

PREVENT:

- **Delay planting.** If you have enough days before first frost, simply delay the planting of summer cucurbits by a few weeks. Gardeners in the lower elevations can elect to skip summer cucurbits altogether, planting in time for a fall harvest when beetles are much less of an issue.
- **Culture.** Cucumber beetles overwinter in old vines and roots. It's important to practice clean and thorough cultivation after harvest. Cover cropping with buckwheat or crimson clover can help as well.
- **Mulch.** Using straw, hay, plastic, or fabric as mulch can deter cucumber beetles from laying eggs in the ground near the plants.

LAWNS

Sod webworm damage may show up in July. These caterpillars eat the leaves of lawn grasses. While the damage is unsightly it isn't deadly to a lawn, since they eat only blades, not the crown (core) of a grass plant. In closely mown lawns, damage is more severe than in taller turf. Lawns generally recover without specific care. If you have a serious infestation, predators of sod webworms generally appear. Birds, including our state birds (cactus wrens, bluebirds, and roadrunners), eat the caterpillars. There are a number of other predators, including ground beetles, robber flies, and predatory wasps. If nature isn't ridding you of a webworm infestation, consider IPM methods, which include parasitic fungi or parasitic nematodes.

PERENNIALS

The main pests on most perennials this month are whiteflies, spider mites, and the occasional caterpillar. Caterpillars can be picked off by hand or left in place if they are doing little or tolerable harm to your plants. Knock spider mites and immature whiteflies off with a jet of water, and/or spray with soapy spray. A persistent problem with these pests throughout your garden is a strong indicator that you need to change your cultural practices, and maybe change the source of your nursery stock.

Summer hail can damage succulents. It's most noticeable on agave, aloe, yucca, manfreda, and similar fleshy-leaved species. It may look like thousands of white spots all over your plants, but search as you might, there's no frass and no bugs about. There is no cure for this bruising and freezing damage—just time. The new leaves the plant produces will be unscarred.

Know your neighbor. Silk moth caterpillars (shown here) do nowhere near the damage that hornworms do. Learn to identify the pests so you can leave the nonpests to live in your garden.

ROSES

Spider mites are the main summer pest of roses in the Southwest. Look for signs of fine webbing or a salt-and-pepper appearance on plants. A daily jet of water from the hose will get rid of them. Avoid recurrence by keeping the soil under roses free of leafy debris. Cedar bark mulch also appears to help keep the numbers of this pest in check.

Cedar mulch contains natural oils that help keep a number of insect pests at bay.

SHRUBS

Around 25 species of moths known as silk moths live throughout the Southwest in all zones, feeding on a number of native shrubs and happily munching on some of the imported species as well. This family includes the glorious luna and cerocropia moths also found back East.

The silk moth caterpillar is generally a dull green with no hairs or spots at all. It eats and molts its way through summer to an eventual length of 3 to 4 inches, developing silvery or tan, thorn-like protuberances on its back in its last stages. Then comes the silk moth cocoon. About the size and shape of a small chicken egg and made of tough silk, you can spot them in bare branches of shrubs in winter. The silken armor of the cocoon is very strong, and yet they have numerous predators even at this stage. Woodpeckers and jays can punch through the tough silk; and deer mice, other rodents, ichneumon flies with long ovipositors, and even ants, all take a toll. I have kept an eye on these caterpillars as they munched on several different species of shrubs and trees in my yard. They never did excessive harm. I let them alone to feed and be fed upon.

TREES

A number of species of blister beetles may appear in hungry hoards to feed on trees, as well as on your vegetable garden. You can easily get rid of them. Put on disposable latex gloves, knock them to the ground with a jet of water, pick them up, and toss them into a bucket of soapy water. It's easy to pick up blister beetles, because all members of the family drop to the ground and play dead when disturbed. Throw away your gloves when done. The "blister" part of their name is a warning—these beetles can cause a severe skin reaction.

Next year, plant calendula and amaranth, which are trap crops for blister beetles. Alternatively, there are IPM sprays made by fermenting naturally occurring soil-borne bacteria. Spray this on the foliage and fruit of the plants under attack, and the beetles stop feeding soon after they eat treated leaves. This is a handy spray because non-leaf-eating beneficial insects will not be affected.

VINES, GROUNDCOVERS & ORNAMENTAL GRASSES

In the lower elevations, caterpillars of the queen butterfly can eat a passionflower vine to the ground, seemingly overnight. Plants generally resprout, but you'll lose this year's fruit crop. When you first spot the orange caterpillars with punk-looking black spikes on their back, you have to decide if you want to keep the plant or keep the butterfly. If you want the plant (and its delicious fruit) then don latex gloves, handpick the caterpillars, and toss them into a bucket of soapy water. Leave any caterpillars that have white knobs among their black spikes. Those knobs are the eggs of tiny parasitic wasps, and those caterpillars are living-but-doomed nurseries for some homegrown IPM. Wear disposable gloves when handling queen caterpillars, because the black hairs are irritating to sensitive skin.

Watch for ants in groundcovers. Leafcutter ants may denude a patch in just a few days. Place a wide line of diatomaceous earth around the attacked plant. Pool filter sand is not quite the same thing, but a 1-inch-deep layer of this type of sand under an affected plant will discourage the ants.

In the upper elevations, creeping junipers and Virginia creeper may be attacked by spider mites. A strong jet of water from the hose knocks the young off a plant and disrupts their life cycle. You must hose down plants every two to three days for three weeks to knock back their numbers. Insecticidal soap is effective on deciduous plants, but do not use on junipers, because it removes the waxy coating they need for winter protection. Note this infestation in your journal, and be sure to fertilize these plants next year. Healthy, fertilized plants tend to tolerate spider mite feeding.

Ornamental grasses don't have problems this month.

Do wear disposable gloves when dealing with blister beetles; they are an aptly named pest.

August

August is the month when harvest begins in many parts of the world, including here in the Southwest. You may have been harvesting vegetables and fruit from your garden for the last few months, but August is the time when there begins to be a bona fide bounty, even a glorious glut.

August 8 is a little-known national holiday—National Sneak Some Zucchini onto Your Neighbor's Porch Day. Hopefully, you will have some to share! If your neighbors have zucchini of their own, contact your local food bank and see if they would be willing to take some off your hands. Next year you and your neighbors could "Plant a Row for the Hungry." This program was started in 1995 by the Garden Writers Association to encourage gardeners to share healthy food with their community. Since then over 20 million pounds of produce providing over 80 million meals have been donated by American gardeners. All of this has been achieved without government subsidy or bureaucratic red tape—just people helping people.

If you have a number of native songbirds in your area, you may notice an interesting phenomenon. The day after the full moon of August they are silent. They have spent spring and half the summer flitting about and chattering with their friends, but overnight that all changes. They get quiet. These birds are not less busy—if anything, they're more so. They are silently intent on gathering enough food to get fat enough for their migrations, or to overwinter in place. Just like us, birds are harvesting now. It may not be a seed harvest either; insectivorous birds are rounding up the last of the summer bugs.

All species are harvesting food to get fat for the winter ahead. Bugs will try to eat your plants, or maybe other bugs. Lizards will scurry through the garden, looking for bugs to bulk up on. Rodents will make a run at your garden, and many species of rodent cheerfully snack on protein rich insects. Meanwhile rodents have predators, "and so on and so on, *ad infinitum*."

Every garden contains a slice of the universe.

PLAN

Rock mulches are popular throughout the Southwest, and Home Owner Associations (HOAs) adore them. But rocks make terrible mulch for plants. The wind blows constantly in the Southwest, bringing dust to fill space between the rocks. Plants drop leaves, adding to debris buildup, and rock mulches are hard to clean. Weed seeds are brought in by the wind and can quickly grow. Worst of all, rock mulches heat up during the day and take a long time to cool at night, increasing heat stress on plants. If all that weren't enough, native wildlife such quail and lizards avoid walking on rock mulch, thus you lose some pest predators.

It's not too late to replace rock mulch with plant-friendly material. Organically based mulch, such as cedar bark or pine needles, helps keep moisture in the soil, and shades and cools the soil; any leaf litter is easily removed or left in place to decompose and fertilize plants. Moisture-retaining plant wells or basins, also called berms, can be built around shrubs, trees—even flower beds—and filled with organic mulches. These wells can be planted with groundcovers to hide this mulch from disapproving HOAs.

*A plant well or basin filled with organic mulch and evergreen groundcovers such as these rain lilies (*Zephyranthes*) saves water and many cleanup chores. Ideally, increase the size of the basin as the trees grow larger.*

ANNUALS & BULBS

An August chore to do indoors is to plan (but not plant) a spring wildflower garden. Consider color options, bloom times, and overall heights as you select the seed you want for autumn planting.

Bulbs should be planted in autumn for spring blooming. This means you'll need to consider what you might want and order them now. As you drool over catalogs, check the final height of the plants and their blooms. Plan on taller-flowering bulbs for the back of your garden bed and shorter ones in front. Look at staggering bloom times as well—it's nice to have early, mid-, and late-spring bloomers for long-lasting spring color. Some bulbs, such as early crocus, can be planted under lawns because they tolerate being mown later in the season. Most tulips would never stand for such treatment!

If you wish to have flowering bulbs indoors for holiday cheer, you'll need to purchase them now to begin the forcing process. For most species, it will take 18 weeks to bloom.

EDIBLES

Cool-season autumn vegetables and herbs can be planted in September in lower elevations. In some cases, you can start the seed indoors in August. But in any case, order seed if you haven't already.

LAWNS

In the upper elevations, temperatures start to drop and lawns start to recover from summer's heat. Plan to aerate if it's been longer than two years since it was last performed. If your lawn doesn't get much traffic, you may be able to skip this task for one more year.

In the lower elevations, you can start to plan fall lawn chores and possible overseeding, but work does not begin until late September or (in the lowest elevations) October.

PERENNIALS

Drought has been the hot topic in the Southwest for a number of years. Plan on replacing some non-drought-adapted perennials with low-water species. There's a vast array from which to choose, and with judicious selection, you could have flowers in

Consider replacing lawn with synthetic turf. The relief from chores can be worth it.

your garden for months. Depending on elevation, you could have an ever-changing display of color in the garden all year.

ROSES

Roses have a place in the oasis zone of a xeriscape garden, so there's no need to get rid of them as you plan the low-water replacements—unless you want to lessen your garden chores.

SHRUBS

As the days get shorter, fall-blooming shrubs start to strut their stuff. If you don't have much autumn color in your yard, consider adding some of these plants in the weeks ahead.

In the upper elevations, garden centers will start their fall sales, trying to clear the lot before winter. Plan where you might want to add some discounted shrubs to your landscape.

TREES

Sometimes the tree common to your neighborhood is not the best tree for your area. Visit a botanical garden or arboretum for some ideas on recently introduced trees that may perform better in your landscape.

VINES, GROUNDCOVERS & ORNAMENTAL GRASSES

You can have autumn color, even in the lowest elevations. Virginia creeper is either a vine or a groundcover, depending on how it's planted. There are various cultivars for lowest and highest elevations, some with leaves that turn crimson in fall. Plan where you might add either groundcovers or vines this fall.

Ornamental grasses are great at providing fall color. Grasses such as 'Autumn Glow' and 'Regal Mist' are two traffic stoppers. They are warm-season growers, so consider where you could add them to your yard this month.

PLANT

In the lower elevations, August is still warm enough to plant succulents and palms. These establish themselves better in summer's heat. Meanwhile, it's still too hot to plant most other plants. You can prepare for fall planting by digging any needed planting holes. If you get summer rain, digging holes in rain-softened soil is a cinch compared to digging in dry soil.

In the upper elevations, summer heat is lessening, and some fall planting can occur after mid-month. Wet the soil 24 hours before digging to make the task easier. In the uppermost elevations, most planting can be done throughout this month.

Versatile Virginia creeper comes in a number of cultivars. Select one for your zone.

ANNUALS & BULBS

After mid-month, gardeners in the upper elevations can start to plant cool-season annuals. In the lower elevations, it's still too hot to plant next season's annuals.

Those in zones 6 and cooler can start to plant spring-flowering bulbs now. Those in other zones should wait until next month (or later).

EDIBLES

For gardeners in zones 6 and cooler, sow seeds of arugula, short-season beans, half-long carrots, lettuce, microgreens, chard, radish, spinach, and turnips. You can set out transplants of cole crops (cabbage, broccoli). It's time to plant onion family members, including winter onions and garlic bulbs.

In zones 8 and 7, sow short-season varieties of the Three Sisters (corn, beans, and squash). Set out transplants of cabbage family members, spinach, chard, and I'itoi onions. You can plant potatoes now.

In zones 10 and 9, sow bush beans, carrots, collards, green onions, summer squash, turnips, and short-season corn.

Gardeners in the upper elevations can plant container-grown fruit and nut trees and shrubs. Avoid planting balled-and-burlapped plants until next month.

Lower-elevation gardeners should avoid planting temperate or deciduous fruiting trees and shrubs from containers this month. Tropicals such as date palms, cherimoya, and jaboticaba should be planted now.

A number of herbs and edible flowers can be planted now. In the upper elevations, plant transplants of calendula, chives, marjoram, oregano, and garlic chives. In the lower elevations, plant transplants of lemon balm, pineapple sage, garlic chives, and nasturtiums.

LAWNS

August is an in-between month for most lawn plantings. One exception is to sod bare spots in any lawn.

In the upper elevations, you can seed a cool-season lawn after temperatures are no longer above 90°F. Seeding a new lawn now lets young grass plants establish well before winter. Consider some of the newer cultivars of buffalograss or use turf-type fescue, perennial ryegrass, or a Kentucky bluegrass rated for your area.

PERENNIALS

In zones 5 and 4, you can plant most perennials until the end of the month. Those in zones 7 and 6 should start after mid-month. At lower elevations, wait until September for most perennials; the exception is succulent perennials, which can be planted now.

ROSES

In all elevations except zone 4, it's still too hot to plant roses. This doesn't mean you can't window shop. Garden centers may put leftover roses on a back-to-school special. If plants are healthy and don't harbor pests, take advantage of this offer. You can plant them next month. But, fair warning: plants that have hung out in a nursery all summer may be pot bound. You will need to deal with this as you plant them.

SHRUBS

Gardeners in the lower elevations can still plant the large succulents that serve as shrubs in the landscape. To prevent sunscald, remember to orient them in the same direction they were growing previously. Other shrubs should not be planted this month.

Upper-elevation gardeners shouldn't plant shrubs until after mid-month. Even then it will be hard for shrubs to establish themselves, but those garden center sales are just so tempting I had to give you permission.

TREES

Those in the lower elevations should not plant container-grown trees this month.

Those in the upper elevations can plant container-grown trees after mid-month. Prepare the soil well so your new plants will thrive, not merely survive. (See October, Here's How to Dig a Hundred-Dollar Hole.)

HERE'S HOW

TO TREAT POT-BOUND PLANTS

Pot bound is also called root bound; whatever you call it, the roots are all bound up into a tangled, matted mass. Worse, they may be growing in circles. Unless you prune the roots, they'll continue to circle the plant rather than spread out as they should, and the plants will fail to thrive.

Once you are ready to plant, take your pruners and cut 1 inch into the root tangle from the top of the pot to the base. Do this in two or three places around the sides of the rootball. Note you are not sectioning the rootball into separate parts, but merely slicing it open slightly. At this point, you can dust these wounds with rooting compound or fungicidal powder.

As you plant in the prepared hole, wedge some soil between the sliced sections to ensure they don't simply close up and heal back together.

After planting, water so the soil settles into any gaps and eliminates large air pockets that might slow the healing of the roots. To cut down on fungal infections, don't fertilize such root-pruned transplants for at least two weeks after planting.

A plant living too long in a container will need some help so its roots don't just keep growing in circles. Use clippers, or tease the rootball open with your fingers.

VINES, GROUNDCOVERS & ORNAMENTAL GRASSES

In the upper elevations, you can plant after mid-month. Prepare the hundred-dollar hole for plants. By the time you factor in the true costs of planting and nurturing a plant until it's established, that hole will have paid for itself.

CARE

In all elevations, check plant mulch over roots. It naturally breaks down, the wind blows, and summer storms may have washed some away; replace as needed. In the lower elevations it's still hot out and the roots will benefit from the protection. In upper elevations you're getting a jump on winter chores.

ANNUALS & BULBS

Deadhead spent blooms on annuals and summer bulbs that might still be blooming. Clip the brown leaves off bulbs that have completed blooming.

EDIBLES

In all elevations, check vegetable garden mulch. Add as needed to maintain soil moisture and suppress weed growth. Mulch around tomatoes and peppers to keep the fruit from touching the ground and rotting. Cucumber-family fruits, such as pumpkins, winter squash, and melons, should also be protected from moist soil. These heavy fruits need more than mulch. Cedar shakes are ideal, or you could also use a patch of outdoor carpet, a landscape paver, or a sheet of Styrofoam from a supermarket meat tray. Avoid anything that traps water, such as a pie tin.

If temperatures are in the upper 90s (or greater), tomatoes will not be producing in the heat. In all zones where this is the case, rejuvenate the plants by cutting them back at least one-third. In zones 10 and 9, cut them down to 1 foot tall. They'll branch after this pruning, and produce again as temperatures drop below 90°F.

Harvest fruit as it ripens, including early apples and their kin, such as pears and quince. Watch berry fruits for readiness, including black- and

Stake vegetables to protect them from damage in summer winds and storms.

raspberry, aronia, and goji. You may have to use bird netting to protect fruit. Don't let fallen fruit sit on the ground; it'll attract pests such as yellow jackets and rodents.

Harvest herbs in the cool of morning. (See Here's How to Harvest & Preserve Herbs for tips.)

LAWNS

In all elevations, continue to mow at the maximum recommend height for your type of lawn to maintain a lawn's ability to tolerate heat stress.

Sharpen mower blades if you didn't last month. Sharp blades cut cleaner, which means grass will have less brown scarring of its leaf edges.

Dethatch and aerate your lawn, especially if you have not done it in the last three years. Aeration and dethatching helps a lawn survive winter, recover quicker in spring, and use less water. In the upper elevations, do this no later than the end of this month. In the lower elevations, you can start after mid-month and continue until the end of September.

PERENNIALS

Deadheading is always appropriate. It helps the summer garden look less bedraggled.

Taller perennials such as ruellia and Mexican bush sage (*Salvia leucantha*) need to be staked or placed in tomato cages to prevent them from toppling when they get top heavy with flowers.

Check mulch depth. A 2- to 3-inch layer of organic mulch helps plants survive lower-elevation heat and gets upper-elevation plants ready for winter.

ROSES

Maintain rose mulch. A uniform 2- to 3-inch layer of clean, organic mulch such as cedar bark or pine straw will give a tidy appearance to the rose bed—but more importantly, it makes it easy to see the fallen rose leaves that should always be removed.

Tie roses to their arbors so the canes do not break in the summer storms.

HERE'S HOW

TO HARVEST & PRESERVE HERBS

HARVEST

- Select clean, healthy, pest-free material.
- Herbs are best harvested when they are unstressed, in the morning, not at the end of a long, hot day.
- Rinse herbs well with a hose while they're still on the plant, or under the tap after you cut them off the plant.
- Shake well or gently pat with a towel to remove excess water.
- If you're harvesting seed, simply cut the stalks into a paper bag for drying.

DRY

Dry leafy herbs out of direct sunlight, and in such a manner as to allow air movement. This prevents discoloration of the foliage and oxidation of essential oils.

- Tie herbs into small bundles and hang them from a ceiling.
- Place a single layer of herbs flat on an old window screen that's propped up so air can flow under the herbs.
- Place herbs in a single layer in a large, unglazed terra cotta plant saucer.
- Use a dehydrator, as long as the temperature remains low enough and the leaves stay green. (Most dehydrators are designed for fleshy fruits and vegetables.)

Once dried, store herbs in a dark glass jar or other opaque container, out of direct sunlight. Date the container with the date of harvest and ideally use herbs within 12 to 18 months for best flavor.

FREEZE

Many culinary herbs don't dry with any subsequent flavor. Luckily, a number can be frozen. Herbs remain tasty in the freezer for at least six months if they're sealed well. Cut harvested herbs into the size you desire. Cilantro, for example, is generally chopped into small pieces. Place herbs in a plastic bag or freezer container from which usable amounts can be removed, label the contents, date, and freeze.

INFUSE

The flavorful or medicinal qualities of herbs can be infused into liquids. Fresh herbs can be infused into a suitably bactericidal liquid, such as vinegar, brine, or alcohol. Herbs can be infused into honey or oil, but due to the lack of acidity of these last two substances, these herbs must—*absolutely must*—be dried first to kill any potential harmful fungi or bacteria, such as *Clostridium botulism*, which causes botulism and can kill you.

HERB SEED

Some herbs are seeds, such as coriander or dill seed. Harvest seed by cutting the seed stalks and tipping the entire mass into a large paper bag. Let seed dry for several weeks. Ideally, hang the bag for air circulation—say from the garage rafters. Once dry, crumble to release the seed and winnow out the chaff. A kitchen colander or sieve works well for winnowing—simply let the chaff fall through the holes and the colander will retain the seed.

Rambling and climbing roses may be climbing past their supports. Add ties as needed so that the new growth is securely fastened and will not break in summer wind and thundershowers. You may want to increase the size of your rose arbor. If you've never seen the Lady Banks rose living in Tombstone, Arizona, you owe yourself a visit. It covers more than an acre!

Check hybrid tea roses for sucker growth emerging below the graft union. Technically, these are water sprouts, but rosarians call them suckers. (See July, Here's How to Remove Water Sprouts for removal tips.)

Some vines need to be tied to their trellises. Check their ties at least once this summer and add any as needed.

SHRUBS

In all elevations, shrubs need minimal care this month. Especially avoid pruning any fall-flowering shrubs, as you'll remove the flower buds.

TREES

Avoid excessive pruning of trees; it's too hot in the lower elevations, too late in the upper elevations. It's always appropriate to prune storm damage, and remove dead or diseased branches. If your tree is grafted, remove any water sprouts.

VINES, GROUNDCOVERS & ORNAMENTAL GRASSES

Continue to tie up vines as they need it and to cut back faster-growing species that may be overgrowing their space.

In all elevations, tidy up groundcovers overgrowing their space. Cut them at least 6 inches back beyond the edges of the space where you want them.

Now is not the time to prune ornamental grasses, although you could check their mulch and add some if needed.

WATER

Although the days are getting shorter this month, summer is still here. Months of high temperatures take their toll on plants, and they become stressed and more susceptible to disease as summer drags on. Also, winds may sweep through our area as the season shifts (or they simply never stop in eastern New Mexico); either way the garden needs extra attention in such windy, drying conditions. Monitor water needs carefully this month.

Days are getting shorter, but the temperatures still soar. The temptation is to water late in the day when you come home from work, but this is generally the worst time to water. In our region of ample sunlight, most plants use water early in the morning to make more than enough sugars for the day, then take a biological siesta for the rest of the day. Early morning water is ideal.

Water applied regularly in late summer and into fall helps pecans and other nuts fill their shells with plump kernels.

If you started a passive water-harvesting system, think of it as part of your irrigation system. Check berms after big thunderstorms; washouts can happen. If an individual berm washes out repeatedly, you are getting more water there than you think. It's time to add extra berms on the upslope side.

Irrigation system maintenance this month is to move emitters out to the drip line or edge of trees and shrubs after their summer growth.

ANNUALS & BULBS

Many annuals are not very drought tolerant. Irrigate early in the morning to help them get through the day. Annuals in pots especially may need daily water this month.

Irrigate summer-blooming bulbs, even if they are done blooming; the leaves need to remain green for as long as possible and translocate ample nutrients into the plant's storage organ. Encourage your fall bulbs. They are beneath the soil and need moisture now to break dormancy and start to emerge.

EDIBLES

Keep monitoring the moisture needs of your edibles. Hot weather and drought stress can rob plants of the energy they need to produce well. A good layer of organic mulch can reduce how often you need to irrigate, but it pays to check under the mulch every three to seven days to see if the soil is drying out.

If you have newly planted seeds or seedlings in the vegetable garden, keep them moist to ensure a strong, healthy root system. Especially at first, you may have to water twice a day. Don't let the soil become bone-dry; newly germinated plants and tiny seedlings will die.

LAWNS

Especially when it is still above 90°F, monitor your lawn for water needs. Ideally, you have trained it earlier in the summer to grow deep roots, and thus, depending on your soil type, you should only need to water every 6 to 10 days—less often if it rains. (See Here's How to Identify Water Stress in Your Lawn.)

PERENNIALS

Monitor your leafy perennials carefully during these hot, difficult dog days of summer, and water once the soil is dry below 2 inches deep.

Chihuahuan and Sonoran Desert succulents of Arizona and New Mexico need water when it is so hot out. If you get ample rain, you won't need to water, but otherwise, water them at least twice this month. If you live in northern Arizona or Nevada but aren't sure if your succulents are native to the

A broken sprinkler head can lead to a patch of soaked lawn. Periodic checks of your system are a good idea.

Mojave, water all succulents twice this month. Water any container-grown succulents at least weekly this month.

ROSES

It is hot for roses this month, and they may wilt or even drop leaves to signal that they are thirsty. Especially monitor any roses planted earlier this year. This is their first summer in their new home, and they may not be fully established. Container roses should be watered once their potting soil is dry 1 inch below the surface, which may be every day, especially in windy sites.

SHRUBS

Did monsoon rain fall in your yard? It is still worthwhile to check the soil under the drip line. Often, far less water reaches the root zone than we imagine. This is why basins and berms come in handy. They trap the water and help it sink in where it is needed. Any shrubs you planted within the last year will need careful monitoring and extra water through the dog days of summer, so they can head into autumn unstressed.

Tall succulents, such as saguaros and yucca, grow more quickly if you water them every 14 to 21 days. Water to 6 inches deep, at a distance roughly equal to the height of the plant in a radius around the plant. If ocotillos have leafed out in response to rain, water them as well to keep them growing vigorously and encourage bloom.

TREES

Are your native trees mature yet? If so, they may need no water at all, especially if you get rain. Trees have roots 3 feet deep and they may be getting water that has sunk below the roots of the smaller plants in your garden, such as roses or perennials.

Recently planted trees will need water more frequently until they become fully established. (See April, Here's How to Often to Water Your Landscape.) Establishment may take up to three years. Immature trees (those less than seven years old) will also need extra water until they reach their mature size.

Simply standing with a hose will not provide enough water for a tree, nor will simply filling the tree well or basin with water. Instead, lay the hose on the ground with a trickle coming out and move it all the way around the drip line of the tree over the course of several hours. Of course, it is easier to use a soaker hose or irrigation system.

VINES, GROUNDCOVERS & ORNAMENTAL GRASSES

Depending on how much sun they get, what is planted nearby, your soil, and your mulch, you may need to water these plants often or scarcely at all. (See April, Here's How Often to Water Your Landscape.)

HERE'S HOW

TO IDENTIFY WATER STRESS IN YOUR LAWN

Summer is hard on lawns, even heat-tolerant varieties. Keep an eye out for these problems and treat them by either increasing or decreasing irrigation frequency.

TOO LITTLE WATER

- The grass plants do not spring back quickly when pressure is applied.
- The lawn may feel hot to the touch early in the morning.
- Leaf blades curl more than normal to reduce evapotranspiration (water loss).
- The color is wrong—Bermudagrass and St. Augustine are both normally bright green; they gain a blue to blue-gray tint when drought stressed.

TOO MUCH WATER

- Puddles or standing water that does not rapidly disappear
- A musty odor
- Soft or mushy soil when pressure is applied
- The growth of algae or mushrooms

FERTILIZE

The national holiday Sneak Some Zucchini onto Your Neighbor's Porch Day, on August 8, is the signal to fertilize your garden in most zones. For zones 6 and cooler, this is the last time you should fertilize for the year, because it's not a good idea to stimulate new growth too close to first frost day.

Those in the lower elevations do not *need* to fertilize this month. If you spend a lot of time in your yard or if you're growing edibles, then fertilize; but if you spend August hibernating in air conditioning, avoid spending time and money fertilizing your garden when you aren't going outside to enjoy it.

ANNUALS & BULBS

Warm-season annuals produce a nice end-of-season display if fertilized now. In the upper elevations, use a bloom fertilizer. In the lower elevations, you can add a granular slow-release product because it lasts 8 to 12 weeks, depleting about the same time first frost arrives. In all elevations, the nutrients for plants in containers wash away faster than plants in the ground. Use half-strength, general-purpose fertilizer every other watering from now until two weeks before first frost.

If you're preparing bulb beds for spring-flowering bulbs and they're currently devoid of plants, add a 2-inch layer of composted steer manure and dig it into the soil, then plant your bulbs. It takes months for soil organisms to blend the nitrogen-rich material with inert components of the soil, thus the nitrogen will be there as the bulbs begin to grow. Slow-release granular fertilizer doesn't last in the soil long enough to be used by spring bulbs.

EDIBLES

The vegetable garden is awash in crops in various stages—fruiting, leafing, or just starting out. Fertilizer is problematic to add in such cases, and sidedressing is useful. (See Here's How to Sidedress Fertilizer.) Younger crops and the seedlings you set out two weeks ago are your target audience here.

HERE'S HOW

TO SIDEDRESS FERTILIZER

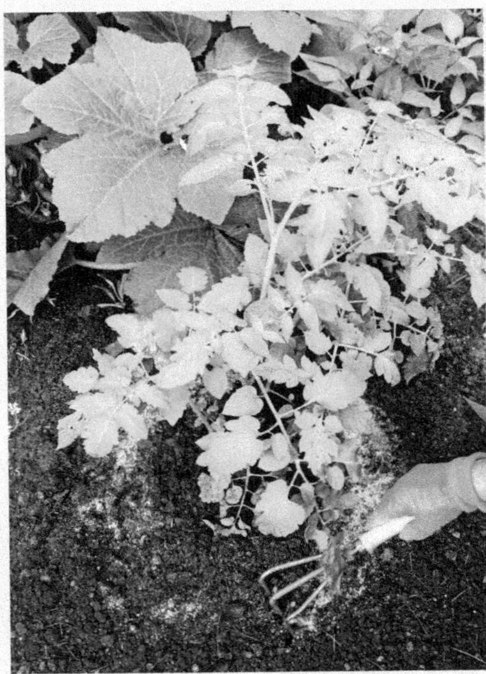

Sidedressing is a process of applying fertilizer to a single established plant. Sprinkle fertilizer granules around the plant, being careful not to get granules on plant leaves; it can burn them. Gently scratch the fertilizer into the soil, being careful not to damage roots. Water well so that fertilizer soaks into the soil.

Fertilize fruit and nut crops to ensure good fruit or nut size. At this stage of growth, the fruit is well set and has lasted past June drop, so the goal is to provide the elements that leaves need to do their job—make the sugars grow large, sweet fruit. Leaves need nitrogen. A palm or lawn fertilizer would work (20-0-0), generally 1 pound for every 10 feet of tree height.

Fertilize grapes and other fruits, such as quince and jujube, once fruit has been harvested. This helps plants grow well for the rest of the season and store ample energy for an even better harvest next year.

Since you want to encourage foliage growth now, use a nitrogen-rich fertilizer.

Perennial herbs benefit from some fertilizer. In the upper elevations, it will help strengthen them for winter and should be applied before mid-month. In the lower elevations, it will help them recover from summer's heat and thrive this fall. Use general-purpose or slow-release granular fertilizer in all elevations. Annual herbs should not be fertilized; it stimulates plants with lush growth but little flavor.

LAWNS

For a healthy, luxuriant, warm-season lawn, you can fertilize with a nitrogen-rich fertilizer once per month through the growing season, and up to four weeks prior to first frost in your area. If you prefer a slower-growing lawn, skip the August fertilizer application. Here is your official and scientifically backed excuse for the spouse: "Chemical burning of the lawn with excessive fertilizer is a distinct possibility in the hottest time of year."

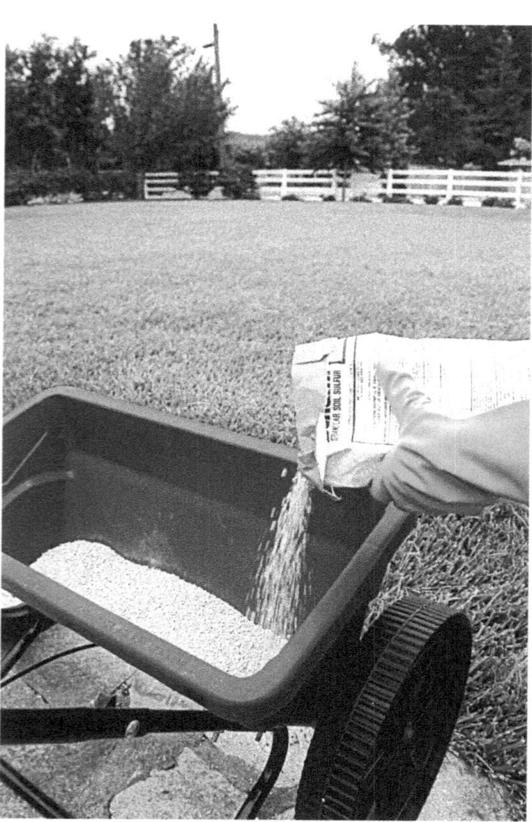

Fill a drop spreader on a hard surface where you can sweep up any spills. This way, excess fertilizer won't fall onto the lawn and chemically burn the grass.

In all elevations, fertilize the cool-season lawn next month.

PERENNIALS

In lower elevations, fall-flowering perennials could get a bloom fertilizer. Consider a slow-release fertilizer for most plants—but *not* for succulents. Succulents should not get a slow-release fertilizer within 12 weeks of first frost, because it will stimulate tender growth that would be harmed by the lower temperatures.

In the upper elevations, fertilize perennials before mid-month to help them recover from summer heat and bolster plants heading for winter dormancy. Fall-flowering perennials could get a bloom fertilizer. Avoid using slow-release fertilizers at this stage of the garden year.

ROSES

In the lower elevations, don't fertilize roses yet, but now is a good time to acidify the soil to head off chlorosis. In the upper elevations, fertilize all roses with a general-purpose fertilizer before mid-month. This will help strengthen rose bushes for winter dormancy. Avoid the use of slow-release fertilizers at this stage of rose growth.

SHRUBS

In the lower elevations, a bloom fertilizer will benefit fall-blooming shrubs now. In the upper elevations, fertilize all shrubs with a general-purpose fertilizer before mid-month to help strengthen your shrubs for winter dormancy. Avoid the use of slow-release fertilizers at this growth stage. Evergreens that had pest issues over summer could especially benefit from fertilizer now.

TREES

In the upper elevations, avoid fertilizing trees within eight weeks of first frost in your area. You

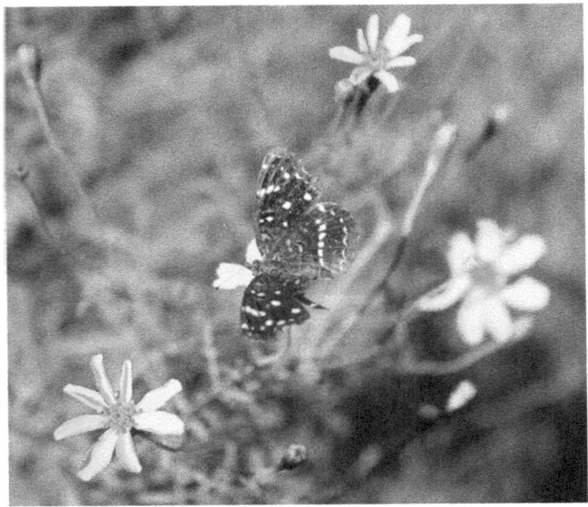

Fertilize fall- and winter-blooming shrubs now for prolific bloom and increased chances to watch the butterflies cavort.

can start preparing them for winter with a fresh application of organic mulch or compost around the root zone. This will renew the decaying mulch applied in spring.

VINES, GROUNDCOVERS & ORNAMENTAL GRASSES

In the upper elevations, avoid fertilizing vines, groundcovers, and ornamental grasses within eight weeks of first frost in your area.

Ornamental grasses require relatively low levels of fertility. In fact, excessive use of fertilizer can cause them to flop over. The fertilizer applied in spring should last through to winter dormancy. If desired, zone 7 gardeners can sidedress ornamental grasses with fertilizer to increase their fall display, but those in the uppermost zones should avoid doing so.

PROBLEM-SOLVE

Weeds in our region are very well adapted to living here, and can start to make seeds with only a single rainfall when they're as young as three weeks. Get into the habit of pulling them right after a rain or after you water, when they're easily pulled from the moist soil—roots and all. Be sure to remove the slain bodies from the battlefield before they translocate their death throes into producing seeds and leaving them behind. (Heed my sad voice of experience!) Most weed killers don't work well if they are applied after 10:00 a.m. in our area. Many plants only open their pores early in the morning and are inactive the rest of the day. If inactive, they do not absorb the full killing dose.

Encourage beneficial insects to call your yard their home, and let them keep the insect pests under control. You can purchase ladybugs and preying mantids at your local garden center. I have even seen them sold in net bags in hardware stores in remote Southwest towns. Other IPM insects, such as green lacewings, can be ordered over the Internet.

Don't forget your friends that have eight, four, and two legs, rather than six. Hunting spiders are great in the garden. They come in thousands of sizes and colors, from no bigger than a pinprick to silver-dollar-sized wolf spiders. Lizards are our friends. In all but the coolest zones they run around our yards eating all manner of insects. Countless native birds will also eat insect pests.

With eight eyes plus eight legs, even the tiniest hunting spiders are efficient at spotting their prey and leaping upon it. They consume vast numbers of pesky garden insects.

HERE'S HOW

TO IDENTIFY & TREAT POWDERY MILDEW

August brings powdery mildew across much of the Southwest, even in our relatively low humidity. August conditions that favor powdery mildew formation include dry foliage, (relative) high humidity, lower levels of light, and warm days with cool nights. In the lower elevations the fungus may not appear until September or October.

Powdery mildew can affect many species of plants.

One of the easiest problems to diagnose, powdery mildew appears as white or gray powdery spots covering part or all of leaf surfaces. It is found on stems, flowers, and even fruit. The good news is that it looks worse than it is. Powdery mildew is rarely fatal to the plant, but it does decrease flower and fruit production. Powdery mildew is host specific, meaning it will appear only on its host species. It may *seem* to spread to other plants, but that's because there is a powdery mildew species for almost every species of plant.

CONTROL

It's important to start a control program at the earliest sign of mildew. Once an entire plant is covered, it's too late. These treatments do not eliminate the fungus—they merely control the spread of it.

- **Retail fungicides.** Use products specifically for treating powdery mildew. All generally contain chlorothalonil. A side effect is a white, milky film on the leaves.
- **Water.** Wash spores off leaves before they have time to embed. Do this early in the day so foliage has time to dry out quickly. Do it every three days.
- **Baking soda (sodium bicarbonate).** Mix 1 tablespoon baking soda with 1 teaspoon dormant oil and 1 teaspoon insecticidal or liquid soap in 1 gallon of water. Spray on plants every 7 to 10 days.
- **Potassium bicarbonate.** This is a contact fungicide that kills powdery mildew spores quickly. It's approved for use in organic growing.
- **Mouthwash.** Use one part ethanol-based mouthwash to three parts water in a spray bottle. New foliage will be burned by this solution.
- **Vinegar (acetic acid).** Mix 1 teaspoon of white or apple cider vinegar in 1 quart of water. Be careful: too much vinegar can burn plants.

ANNUALS & BULBS

Watch for powdery mildew and treat early. Zinnia, phlox, and petunias seem to be the most susceptible species. Note the fungus in your journal, and consider selecting different species next year. Some gardeners discard infected plants as soon as they are noticed.

Bulbs are not much bothered by powdery mildew, but if you see it, cut off and discard affected leaves.

EDIBLES

In the upper elevations, I can almost guarantee powdery mildew in the vegetable garden. You can leave it or treat it on plants nearing the end of

- **Milk.** It is not clear why it works, but it's believed that milk compounds combat fungus growth. Spray once a week with one part whole milk to two parts water.
- **Sulfur.** Sulfur prevents fungal spores from developing. Mixed with hydrated lime, the solution penetrates leaves for greater effectiveness. The best-known and widely available version is Bordeaux mix, which includes copper sulfate and hydrated lime. Sulfur and copper both can burn plant tissue, damage microorganisms in the soil, and are harmful to beneficial insects. These compounds also are considered moderately toxic to mammals and humans. Use sparingly and with caution.

PREVENTION

Take these steps to avoid or minimize powdery mildew in your yard:

- Look for disease-resistant varieties of annuals and vegetables. Contact your local extension service for named varieties and cultivars for your area.
- Provide adequate air circulation by not crowding plants.
- Place plants where they get sufficient light. For most species this is six hours or more each day.
- Avoid overfertilization. New growth is more susceptible.

their life cycle, but definitely deal with it on newly planted vegetables.

In all elevations, problems in the vegetable garden include weeds, spider mites, and whiteflies. Yank the weeds. Blast the spider mites and whiteflies off foliage with water or soapy spray.

In all elevations, be on the watch for virus in tomato-family plants. There are a number of viral infections with numerous and varied symptoms. Most viruses manifest as a plant's failure to thrive, often with a checkerboard appearance or discolored spots on leaves. Affected leaves may wilt, while other leaves are fine. The only treatment is to eliminate the plants at the first sign of virus. Viruses can persist in root fragments in the soil over winter and reinfect plants next year. Most viruses are spread by sap-sucking insects, especially thrips and leafhoppers. Prevention includes planting resistant varieties, rotating the locations of specific crops each year, and controlling sap-sucking insects.

In the lower elevations, you may not have powdery mildew yet, but the caterpillars discussed in July still abound. Watch for hornworms and deal with them before they consume plants.

Upper-elevation gardeners should watch for powdery mildew in rose family fruit trees, including apple, apricot, and peach. If you see it on a few leaves, treat the entire tree and all trees of that type in your garden. While it's not fatal, powdery mildew reduces a tree's ability to produce sugars for ripening fruit.

In all elevations, don't forget to pull weeds before they go to seed.

Lizards come in many different sizes and colors and eat many different garden pests.

LAWNS

There are a number of noninfectious lawn diseases that are revealed in the heat of summer. You may notice bald or dying patches developing in your lawn. Once you rule out irrigation issues, consider these:

- **Pet waste.** Urine left on a lawn in the heat of summer causes chemical burns on the lawn. Consider training your pooch to use a different area of the yard. Alternatively, hose down the lawn area used on a daily basis.
- **Compaction.** Is it a heavy traffic area? Regular aeration of the soil helps relieve this issue.
- **Thatch.** When is the last time you dethatched your lawn? A bald patch may simply be the result of a clump of old lawn clippings preventing water infiltration.
- **Buried debris.** A thin layer of soil over rocks, old construction debris, or tree stumps will prevent lawns from getting ample moisture. Use a probe such as a knitting needle or screwdriver, determine if this is the problem. Dig out and remove the cause, fill the area with good topsoil, tamp it firmly, and re-lay the sod.
- **Scalping.** You may have a high spot in the lawn that's being scalped by the mower. If the spot is not due to buried debris, peel back the sod, remove some excess soil, and lay the sod back down.

PERENNIALS

Watch for powdery mildew and treat early. While it doesn't kill the plants it grows on, it's unsightly. Some gardeners toss infected plants as soon as they're noticed. Other issues this month include weeds, whiteflies, and spider mites. Yank the weeds. Blast the whiteflies and spider mites off the foliage with water or soapy spray.

ROSES

Spider mites love roses. Look for signs of the fine webbing by which they move from leaf to leaf, or a salt-and-pepper appearance to leaves. A jet of water from the hose every day or two for at least three weeks will disrupt their life cycle. Insecticidal soap also works. In the lower elevations, you should get rid of spider mites now so plants can bloom robustly this fall. Gardeners in the upper elevations should eliminate them so plants can be healthy for overwintering.

Know your neighbors. Spider mites are mites, not spiders. They got their name from the webs they use to travel around so they can suck sap, not to catch prey.

In the upper elevations, watch for powdery mildew on roses. Treat as discussed in Here's How to Identify & Treat Powdery Mildew. Note in your journal which plants are afflicted. If one particular plant is affected every year, it's time for some shovel pruning. In lower elevations, powdery mildew generally shows up on roses in September.

SHRUBS

Check oleanders if you have them. Oleander gall shows up as rough-barked, knotted lumps on stems in hot weather. It's caused by bacteria spread by sucking insects. Left unchecked, it causes first malformed flowers, later split branches, and ultimately it kills the plant.

Start elimination of this problem by removing any oleander leaves beneath the plants and discarding them in the trash (this gets rid of a potential source of reinfection). Next, cut off affected branches at least 1 foot below the galls, and throw these branches in the trash. Sterilize your clippers in a bleach solution (¼ cup bleach in 2½ cups water) or 70 percent isopropyl alcohol after every single cut. Oil clippers when you are done to prevent rust.

Alternatively, simply eliminate poisonous oleanders entirely. There are a number of lovely native shrubs, such as drought-tolerant Arizona rosewood (*Vauquelinia californica*). It has fragrant white flowers, slender glossy green leaves, and sheds far less than oleander.

TREES

In all elevations, all trees—but especially evergreens—can suffer an outbreak of spider mites in August. Symptoms of an infestation include a salt-and-pepper appearance or a bronzy cast to the foliage. A jet of water from the hose every two to three days will help knock back their numbers. Do not spray evergreens with insecticidal soap; it removes the waxy coating they need for winter protection. Note this infestation in your journal, and be sure to fertilize your trees early in the season next year. Plants with healthy foliage are better able to fight off this pest on their own.

In upper elevations, check aspens and poplar for cercospora leaf spot, a fungal disease that causes distinct sunken brown spots on leaves. Leaves will turn brown or yellow and then fall off. Some of this fungus is normal in the population, but if it affects many trees, rake up and discard the leaves—don't compost them. Treatment is to maintain good air circulation between the trees, which may require some pruning or thinning. Cercospora leaf spot can also appear on a number of other garden plants, but it is host specific and will not spread from one species to another. In all cases treatment is based on good air circulation. There are some IPM fungicidal sprays that are effective.

VINES, GROUNDCOVERS & ORNAMENTAL GRASSES

In all elevations, vines and groundcovers may be attacked by spider mites. A strong jet of water from the hose knocks the young off the plants and disrupts their life cycle. You must hose down your plants every two to three days for three weeks to knock back their numbers.

Ornamental grasses do not have significant problems this month.

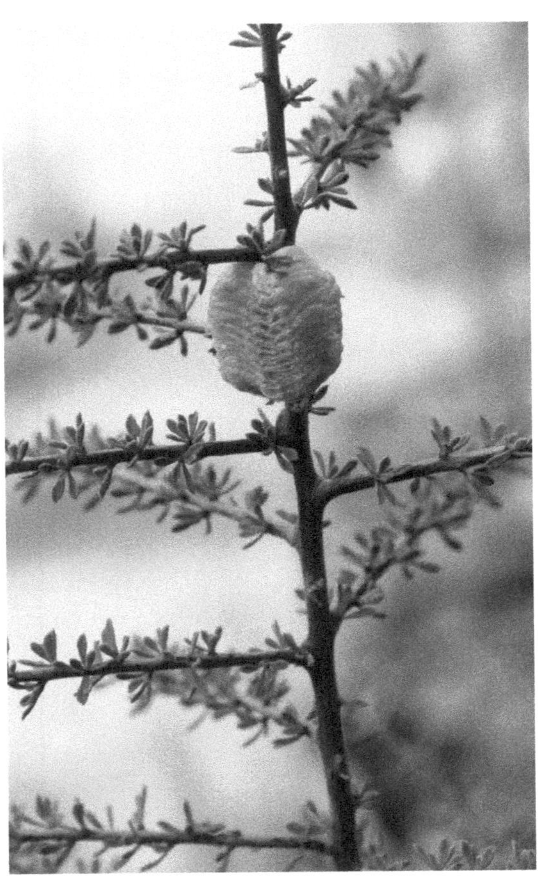

Know your neighbors. If you find a praying mantis egg case, keep an eye on it. You may get to see the tiny babies emerge.

September

Depending on where you live in the Southwest, September is either the time to wind down for the year or the time to crank it up after summer "hibernation." Either way, the nights are getting longer and cooler. Plants physically sense these longer hours of darkness and their "winter is coming" genes kick in. Some plants start to flower, others set seed or ripen fruit, and yet others start to transfer energy out of their leaves and send it to the roots for storage.

Late summer into fall is a good time for planting. The exception to this statement are plants that have tropical genes, such as palms, citrus, and most succulents. Also, at the higher elevations, it's recommended to plant evergreen shrubs in spring instead of fall. In all areas, fall planting should be completed by two weeks before your first-frost date.

Whether you live at a higher elevation or a lower one, September is a wonderful time of year simply to enjoy the garden. Along with a new school year, autumn begins a new garden year. September is an ideal time to reflect back on the garden year past, remember any mistakes and triumphs, plus plan for the garden year ahead. Keeping a notebook or journal makes this task easier. It is never too late to start one.

Enjoy your garden in the cooler days of September. Enjoy the colorful flowers that bloom now, as well as the plants that rebloom after the summer heat. Savor the fruits and vegetables you harvest this month. Delight in the autumn leaves changing color. Enjoy the flitting butterflies that are getting their last feeding before winter. Relish the sight of birds busily sipping nectar or foraging for seed and storing energy for winter. September is a time when Southwest gardens are filled with life.

PLAN

Take a stroll around your yard to see how various plants fared over summer. Write this down in your garden journal, and especially note the vegetable selections. This will aid you to select seed and seedling varieties for next year.

Notice how the sun's arc is shifting southward in the sky. Does this expose shade-loving plants to too much light? Or does it highlight a spot in the garden that might be the perfect one to add some autumn-flowering plants?

Do herbivore pests visit your garden? While no plant is 100 percent rabbit-, javelina-, or deer-proof, there are many varieties upon which these critters are highly unlikely to browse. Plan for animal-resistant plants you can add. Aromatic plants, those with oils in their stems and leaves, release scent when bent or crushed. These scents, while often pleasant for the gardener, are distasteful to many herbivores. Culinary herbs, such as sage, thyme, or rosemary, are great choices for animal-resistant plants, because you can also use them for cooking. Other plants well adapted with a strong scent to deter herbivores include yarrow, tansy, echinacea, agastache (hummingbird mint), and monarda.

ANNUALS & BULBS

Nights are cooling off. In the higher elevations, consider rooting some annuals to overwinter indoors. Geraniums, coleus, begonias, and others can be rooted in sterile potting mix. In lower elevation areas where there is little frost, these annuals can overwinter outdoors just fine.

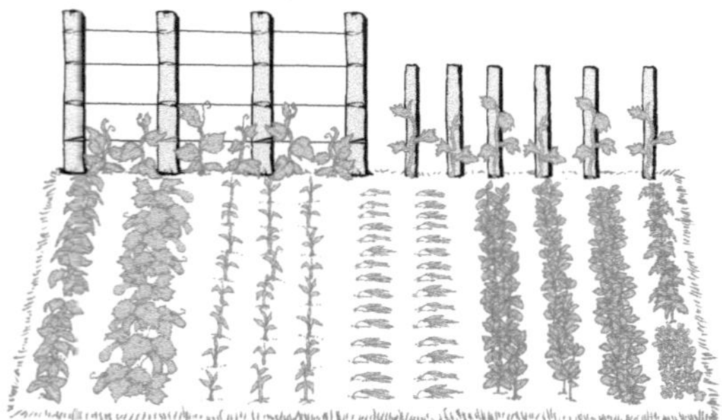

■ *Plan the vegetable garden so that cole crops are rotated to a new area of the garden each season. This helps deter a number of crop pests.*

Don't overlook spring bulbs when choosing plants for deer resistance. Daffodils, bearded iris, hyacinths, and muscari offer bright color and delightful fragrance, but are rarely browsed by deer.

Where do you want some blooms next spring? How about a patch near your front door or along the driveway? Hopefully you ordered bulbs last month, but if not, shop your local nurseries now for bulbs to plant this month.

EDIBLES

Even more than August, September is for harvesting. Canning jars, seed harvesting bags, and a method for drying herbs and/or fruits should all be on hand. If you have a root cellar, be sure it's cleaned out and ready for the new harvest.

In the lower elevations, September is the time to plant cool-season vegetables and herbs. Hotter and low-frost areas should wait until after mid-month. Certain crops, such as the members of the cabbage family, need to be planted in new soil each year. Plan your planting before you plant your plan!

In the lower elevations, fall is for planting, especially fruiting trees, shrubs, and vines. You want them to be well-established long before next summer's heat and drought come along. Consider where you can add a fruit tree or other edible to your landscape. Start small—replace one purely ornamental flowering shrub with a plant such as elderberry. You'll still have a flowering shrub, but you will also get fruit you can enjoy.

In the upper elevations, plan on bringing frost-tender perennial herbs indoors. (See Here's How to Overwinter Frost-Tender Tropicals.)

LAWNS

To overseed or not to overseed, that is the question for the lower elevations. September into October is the time to do the work. If your lawn

Replant steeply sloping lawns with ornamental grasses and perennials now to erase future mowing headaches.

had a hard summer due to drought, disease, or irrigation issues, give it a rest this winter and do not overseed.

Also consider this—has your lifestyle changed so that perhaps you don't use your lawn so much? One friend downsized his lawn when his children went away to college, putting in a new perennial bed and a clump of berry bushes. September is an ideal time for such work in lower elevations. If you don't replace your whole lawn, then at least deal with problem areas, such as under trees or on steep slopes. Once reworked, you will no longer have a headache to mow all summer long—just an area that gets occasional pruning.

PERENNIALS

Many perennials require dividing every three to five years, and now is the time to do it. Take a walk around your property *before* you divide, and determine where you will put the divisions.

ROSES

Evaluate roses after the heat of summer. Plants that lost more than half their canes may need a shadier or cooler location. Also consider their age. Many modern hybrids only last about a decade before they decline. Those in zones 10 to 7 can consider a shrub rose such as the Lady Banks rose (*Rosa banksia*). Originally from an arid area of China, a cutting was brought to Tombstone, Arizona, in 1885. That same plant is still thriving today and is listed in the Guinness Book of Records as the world's largest rose bush. In upper elevations, gardeners can plant the native Woods' rose (*Rosa woodsii*) instead.

SHRUBS

Take time to walk around your neighborhood or visit a nearby botanical garden. There are a number of native and fruit-bearing shrubs that provide stunning autumn color. Consider some of these for your garden to broaden your landscape's color palette.

TREES

In the upper elevations, deciduous trees will be shedding their leaves. Leaves make wonderful organic mulch in beds or under trees and shrubs; or, you can add them to your compost pile. If you don't have a compost pile, leaves are an easy way to start. (See January, Here's How to Compost in the Southwest.)

VINES, GROUNDCOVERS & ORNAMENTAL GRASSES

All vines feel the cool breath of winter approaching. Some, such as bougainvillea, put on a last frenzy of bloom, while others, such as queen's wreath or wisteria, lose their leaves. Get the rake or broom ready for cleanup.

Use the microclimates around your home to place plants that do best with certain conditions, such as morning sun and afternoon shade.

Gravel mulch is popular in the Southwest, but it can increase the heat load on surrounding plants. Low-water native groundcovers offer cooling vegetation plus blooms for butterflies. In the lower elevations, this is an ideal month to remove gravel and add groundcovers to your yard.

Many ornamental grasses bloom in autumn. Plan to harvest some seedheads for indoor arrangements, or enjoy them backlit by the autumn sun.

PLANT

Cooler weather in September is great for planting just about everything, but it is always best to get plants into the ground at least two weeks before the first frost date for your area.

ANNUALS & BULBS

In the lower elevations, set out seedlings of cool-season annuals after mid-month. This includes calendula, feverfew, pansy, petunia, stock, sweet alyssum, and violets.

In the upper elevations, sow seed of spring-flowering, cold-tolerant annuals such as calendula, cornflower, larkspur, nemissa (buffalo flower), and poppies. These will overwinter and plants will appear in early spring.

HERE'S HOW

TO SCREEN BULBS FROM PREDATORS

Bulbs are tasty treats for gophers, ground squirrels, and other digging mammals. If they have been pests in prior years, purchase hardware cloth, a type of welded metal mesh. Lay a sheet over your bulbs after planting and before you cover them with soil. The bulb leaves will grow through the holes in the mesh, but the animals can't dig through it. If animals dig around the mesh, which occasionally happens, then next year you will have to build a bulb cage out of hardware cloth and entirely enclose your bulbs.

Plant seed of our showy Southwestern spring wildflowers from seed now. A wide variety grace the Great Basin, Mojave, and Sonoran Deserts following winter rains off the Pacific Ocean. You can also plant spring wildflowers in New Mexico, but plan on watering them through the winter. (See Here's How to Grow Southwestern Wildflowers.)

Those in the lower elevations should select spring-flowering bulb varieties that don't require chilling. These include amaryllis, crocosmia, narcissus, iris, freesia, ranunculus, sparaxis, species tulips (not hybrid tulips), spider lily (*Hymenocallis*), tritonia, and watsonia. Anenomes and hyacinths produce in zone 8 but aren't good performers in hotter zones.

Spring-flowering bulbs for the higher elevations include daffodils, narcissus, iris, freesia, ranunculus, hybrid tulips, anenomes, muscari, and hyacinths. If browsing deer and elk are an issue, consider the less palatable species: daffodils, narcissus, bearded iris, and hyacinths.

If you want something unique, consider the durable heirloom bulbs from around the globe and popular in previous centuries, including Spanish bluebell, German flowering garlic, and Turkish glory-of-the-snow.

Bulbs are ideally fertilized at planting, but not with fertilizer—instead, add compost to their soil as you plant. Do not sprinkle fertilizer over the bulbs as older books demonstrate, because fertilizer (even organic types) can harm bulbs when in direct contact with bulb tissues. Slow-release fertilizer is mostly degraded by the time spring bulbs start to grow, so save your money.

EDIBLES

In the upper elevations, it's time to put the vegetable garden to bed for winter. If you wish, you can plant cover crops such as buckwheat or crimson clover. Ideally, plant these four to six weeks before first frost, so the seeds can germinate. (See October, Here's How to Use Cover Crops to Help a Dormant Garden.)

HERE'S HOW

TO GROW SOUTHWESTERN WILDFLOWERS

In all elevations, sow seed of native spring wildflowers in September, before the winter rains begin. Loosen the soil to a depth of 4 inches to help tiny roots grow into hard desert soil. Scatter the seed, not too densely, over the area. Cover the seed with ¼ inch of playground sand. (Unlike construction sand, playground sand is washed to remove weed seeds.) Some people say to simply rake the seed into the soil, but I've had poor results doing that; raking just seems to make it easier for seed-eating birds and rodents to find your seed.

If you have many seed eaters in your area, you may need to lay a piece of chicken wire flat on the ground over your wildflower bed. Birds and rodents will not walk on the wire, and the growing plants will eventually hide it from view.

Seed-eating birds will be delighted that you spread wildflower seed for them. Hide it under sand or deter them with some chicken wire.

In the lower elevations, it's time for the cool-season vegetable garden featuring all the green leafy crops as well as root vegetables, including artichoke, arugula, beets, bok choy, broccoli, brussels sprouts, cabbage, carrots, cauliflower, chives, collard greens, endive, garlic, horseradish, jicima, kale, kohlrabi, leeks, lettuce (head and leaf types), mesclun mix, mizuma, mustard greens, onion, pak choy, parsnip, radish, radiccio, scallion, shallots, spinach, Swiss chard, and turnip.

Lower-elevation gardeners can plant seed of cool-season herbs. These are primarily members of the carrot family, such as anise, caraway, cilantro, cumin, dill, fennel, and parsley. Other cool-season herbs come to us from northern Europe, including calendula, feverfew, and German chamomile.

Do you like garlic? In the upper elevations, you can plant garlic seed now. It will overwinter in the soil and grow in spring. Lower-elevation gardeners should wait until January. Gardeners in the lower elevations can plant two perennial plants

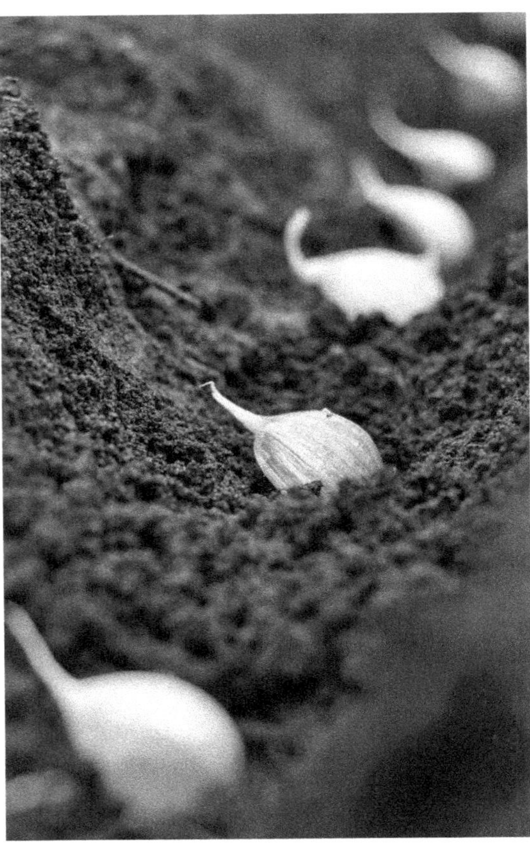

Upper-elevation gardeners can plant garlic now for harvest next summer.

with garlic-flavored leaves: garlic chives (*Allium tuberosum*) or society garlic (*Tulbaghia violacea*). Both form charming clumps of bright green leaves, and tend to bloom in the cooler weather of autumn. When choosing which to plant, know that society garlic, originally from South Africa, doesn't tolerate temperatures much below 28°F.

Some fruiting shrubs tolerate September planting in upper elevations. The bush cherries do well in our soil. Select either Nanking cherry (*Prunus tomentosa*) or the somewhat more drought tolerant sand cherry (*P. besseyi*). Both make tasty jellies, and taller varieties can serve as a windbreak.

Those in the lower elevations can consider adding pomegranate or almond—both can be grown as small trees or large shrubs. The exceptions to planting edibles now are the tropical edibles, such as citrus, date, dragonfruit, jaboticaba, and Peruvian apple cactus. It's better to wait until spring to plant these frost-tender plants.

LAWNS

In the cooler areas of the lower elevations, start overseeding lawns after mid-month. Those in the hotter areas should wait until October.

PERENNIALS

Native fall-blooming perennials suited for almost all Southwest gardens include a number that also bloom in spring, including blanket flower (*Gaillardia*), evening primrose (*Oenothera*), scarlet betony or Texas hedgenettle (*Stachys coccinea*), and hummingbird mint (*Agastache*). These showy bloomers often appear in garden centers once they begin to flower, but experienced gardeners know that all plants transplant better when their energy is not focused on blooming. Consider starting any of these from seed. Plant their seed in autumn—logical if you think about it, since that's when these species flower and scatter their seed.

In the upper elevations, plant columbine from containers. Sow seed of carnation, columbine, feverfew, hardy asters, statice, and yarrow.

ROSES

Those in the lower elevations can plant container-grown roses. The days are still hot, however, so plan on watering them often until they establish.

Upper-elevation gardeners can plant shrub and heirloom roses in the first part of the month, but plant hybrids (even from containers) and all bare-root roses in spring.

SHRUBS

In all elevations, you can plant any shrub that's not cold sensitive up to two weeks before first frost. Consider shrubs with a long history of use as herbs, such as aloysia and myrtle. These look good in the landscape, can be used as herbs, and do well in cut-flower arrangements.

TREES

In the lower elevations, plant any trees that aren't frost-tender in September. In the upper elevations, wait until spring to plant trees, especially evergreens such as pinyon pine.

Plant Joshua tree (*Yucca brevifolia*), a native of the Mojave Desert in Arizona and Nevada, now or in October as it breaks summer dormancy.

VINES, GROUNDCOVERS & ORNAMENTAL GRASSES

Some vines, such as native passionflower and clematis, can be planted up to two weeks before first frost. Passionflowers usually bloom (and produce fruit) their first year, but clematis may take a year or two to establish. Arizona honeysuckle vine (*Lonicera arizonica*) is a charming native vine that does well in alkaline soils in zones 9 to 6. You can plant it from seed now into October.

In the lower elevations, groundcovers that don't go winter dormant, such as verbena and dalea, can be planted this month and up to two weeks before first frost.

Gardeners in all elevations can collect seed of ornamental grasses and plant that seed now. Container-grown plants are better planted in the warmer soils of spring.

HERE'S HOW

TO STORE SUMMER-BLOOMING BULBS

In zones 8 and cooler, many summer-blooming bulbs (including corms, tubers, and rhizomes) do not survive the winter outdoors, even with mulching. These bulbs of tropical origin, including amaryllis, begonia, canna, dahlia, etc., should be dug and stored when the leaves on the plants turn yellow.

- Carefully dig bulbs out of the ground and gently brush soil off. Do not divide or separate them. Some instructions say to wash your bulbs, but here in the Southwest we have low enough humidity that leaving soil on the bulbs rarely harms them. Spread the bulbs in a shaded place so any moist soil on them will dry.
- Exception: leave ample soil on achimenes, begonia, canna, caladium, dahlia and ismene bulbs. Store these bulbs in their original clumps on a slightly moistened layer of peat moss or sawdust.
- Store bulbs away from sunlight in a cool, dry basement, cellar, garage or shed at 50 to 65°F. Avoid temperatures below 50°F or above 70°F.

You can easily construct summer bulb storage bags out of window screen and staples. Include some garden twine so you can hang the bags for best air circulation.

- Be sure that air can circulate around your stored bulbs. Store bulbs on trays with screen bottoms, or hung up in old onion sacks. If you just have a few, keep them in paper bags hung by strings from the ceiling. Never store bulbs more than two or three layers deep; they generate heat and can decay.
- To avoid confusion next spring, separate your bulbs by species or variety *before* storing them.

CARE

After a summer of growth, some plants may be leggy and unkempt. If you prune these, go easy. A too-heavy pruning encourages new growth, which can be damaged in the colder months ahead.

Few plants require pruning in September. With so much else to do this month, you can leave the pruners on the shelf unless you are deadheading or wish to harvest some flowers for a bouquet.

ANNUALS & BULBS

Towards the end of their growing season, annuals often show signs of stress. Previously healthy plants may develop powdery mildew or whitefly infestations. Remove and throw away such infested plants.

Warm-season bulbs, such as amaryllis, gladiolus, and rain lily, will be taking energy out of their leaves and transferring it to underground storage. In upper elevations, wait until the leaves are entirely brown before digging these summer bulbs to store in a cool but not freezing area. In zone 8b and warmer, these bulbs can be left in the soil over the winter.

EDIBLES

In the upper elevations, some vegetables can be stored in the soil, rather than harvesting them now. Mulch parsnip, celeriac, turnips, and similar root

HERE'S HOW

TO OVERWINTER FROST-TENDER TROPICALS

In all but the hottest zones of the Southwest, you will have to bring some (or many) plants indoors before frost: adenium, bay, bougainvillea, citrus, crown of thorns, desert rose—the list goes on.

1. Bring the plants into an isolated quarantine area for two weeks. A porch, garage, or sunroom closed off from the house is ideal.
2. Monitor plants for pests, such as scale, spider mites, earwigs, caterpillars, pill bugs, and crickets. Treat pests as needed to eliminate them before you bring plants inside your home.
3. Move plants indoors to a sunny location, such as south- or southwest-facing rooms. If your home doesn't have a good area, consider putting grow bulbs into your lamps and light fixtures for the winter.
4. Monitor water needs through the winter. Water when the top 1 inch of soil is dry.
5. Avoid fertilizer until the plant has shown it is adjusted to its new location by producing new growth. Do not fertilize the succulents even if they do produce new growth.
6. Monitor for pests through the winter months. It is best to deal with any pests before their populations swell.
7. One month before last frost in your area, lightly prune any overgrown plants. Fertilize now if you haven't yet, using fertilizer at half the recommended dose.
8. Two weeks before last frost, transition your plants gradually. Move them to an unheated but protected area, such as a garage or porch. You can place them outdoors after last frost.

crops with a thick, 6-inch layer of straw to protect the roots from a hard freeze. When you harvest them in November and December they'll be sweet and tasty. Autumn kale should be mulched, too, with 4 inches of straw, to keep the plant growing and the leaves harvestable into late October.

In all elevations, harvest winter squash and pumpkins as they mature. This is generally later in the month, but certainly before first frost. The outer skin needs to be firm and too hard to penetrate with a fingernail. Frost will soften the skin and allow decay.

In all elevations, rake up and discard fallen leaves of grape vines. A number of grape pests overwinter in fallen grape leaves.

Harvest basil and other warm-season annual herbs before frost kills the plants. (See August, Here's How to Harvest & Preserve Herbs.) If you are too busy, you can simply cut all plants at their base and invert them into a large paper grocery bag to dry. Later—say in November—gently remove the leaves from the stems and store them in jars. Jars of dried herbs make lovely holiday gifts from your garden.

In the lower elevations, lightly prune any perennial herbs that look bedraggled after the hot summer, such as rosemary or oregano. They'll respond with fresh new growth. In the upper elevations, plan on bringing frost-tender herbs indoors.

LAWNS

In all elevations, if you are not going to overseed your lawn, help prepare it for next summer with a good core aeration now. You should also heavily dethatch and add ½ inch of compost over the entire lawn every other year. In the upper elevations, do this work early in the month before chance of frost.

PERENNIALS

Remove spent flowers, old bloom stalks, and dead leaves from anything that may need it. This helps keep any diseases under control, since many fungi and bacteria overwinter on such dead plant material. Otherwise, wait to prune fall-flowering plants until spring, after blooming and any chance of frost are well past.

In lower elevations, dividing perennials is best done after bloom but before frost. Sharpen your shovel or have a hatchet on hand for this garden chore, because many clumps are very tough to break apart. Divide these perennials at least two weeks before the first frost in your area: iris, daylily, coreopsis, pineapple sage, rain lily (*Zephyranthes*), Angelita daisy (*Hymenoxis*), dwarf ruellia, scarlet monkey flower, and scarlet bugler. Tropicals such as aloe, bulbine, and tuberose (*Manfreda*) should be divided in spring.

ROSES

In the lower elevations, groom roses once temperatures remain below 100°F. In the upper elevations, if you didn't groom in August, do so before mid-month. This is a light pruning, not a major one. Grooming consists of removing dead canes, as well as any diseased or malformed canes. Remove yellowed or diseased leaves and throw them away, but not into the compost.

In all areas, deadhead any spent blooms. If you're growing varieties for rose hips, check for ripeness and harvest when ready.

SHRUBS

In all elevations, lightly prune summer-flowering, frost-tolerant shrubs now and up to two weeks before first frost. Otherwise, wait until spring.

TREES

If at all possible, avoid pruning trees unless you're shaping a young tree or removing water sprouts and sucker growth. Olives especially tend to develop water sprouts over the summer. Both citrus and olives grow with fewer sunscald and water sprout issues if their trunk is shaded from the sun.

In all areas, prune trees for safety issues, such as storm damage, thorny branches near walkways, or branches rubbing on structures. Just don't go overboard.

VINES, GROUNDCOVERS & ORNAMENTAL GRASSES

Evergreen tropical vines, such as bougainvillea, yuca vine, and lilac vine, should be left unpruned as cool weather approaches. Deciduous vines that go dormant for winter, such as queen's wreath, should not be pruned while they translocate their resources.

In the lower elevations, summer-blooming groundcovers such as lantana or creeping dalea may have become leggy and are producing fewer blooms. You can prune them back to be more manageable, as long as you complete the work at least four weeks before first frost in your area. Now is not the time for extreme rejuvenation pruning.

Before you deadhead, look carefully at flower structures. Some plants produce swirls of bloom from the same site for months on end and should not be deadheaded.

In the upper elevations, avoid pruning at all unless the groundcovers are in pathways. In lower elevations, Herculean groundcover herbs originally from the eastern Mediterranean, such as oregano, thyme, and germander, can be divided now, at the start of the rainy season in their native land.

Most ornamental grasses are just starting to bloom now. Enjoy them, but don't prune them. In fact, don't trim them in fall or in any freezing month. They need that tuft of dried foliage to cover their crowns and protect them from the cold ahead.

WATER

Fall calls for less water, but this month is still hot in much of our region. In the upper elevations, watering plants as they prepare for winter helps them move sugars and phytochemicals into storage for next spring. Water also helps because plant roots keep growing even through winter in nonfreezing soils. But have care not to overwater; waterlogged roots can drown and then the plant dies.

Irrigation system maintenance in the lower elevations this month is to check all emitters and sprinklers for proper moisture distribution. If you live in the upper elevations, be sure any irrigation system is properly winterized to avoid costly repairs from frost damage. Drain and store all hoses, including soaker hoses in a place where they will not freeze and crack.

ANNUALS & BULBS

In all elevations, cool-season annuals, as well as any lingering warm-season plants, will need water every 2 to 10 days, while those in containers may still need water daily.

In lower elevations, any seeds of spring annuals or wildflowers will need to be kept evenly moist while establishing, especially if we have a warmer than usual month. This may mean daily watering at first. Be sure you have a watering wand or hose head that delivers water in a gentle, rain-like spray, not an uprooting blast.

Irrigation microtubes are manufactured with drippers every 6 inches. This makes watering a vegetable garden easy.

Irrigate any still-blooming bulbs every three to seven days. You can water less once flowering is done. Most spring bulbs you'll plant and forget about—unless it gets too hot. Ideally the soil should stay lightly moist, not bone-dry. If summer bulbs are not dormant yet, taper off watering to encourage them to go dormant before frost.

EDIBLES

Young transplants of cool-season vegetables need daily watering as they send their baby roots down into the soil. Any seeds also need to be kept evenly moist. September can be windy, so you might need to water tiny plants twice each day.

Gardeners in all elevations should monitor water needs of all plants still in the vegetable garden, especially ripening winter squashes and pumpkins. Water once the soil is dry below 2 inches.

Upper-elevation gardeners who planted a cover crop should plan on daily water until the seeds emerge and have at least five sets of true leaves, then water once the soil is dry below 1 inch.

For other edibles, see their growth form (tree, shrub, vine) for water instructions.

LAWNS

As the season cools, all types of lawns need less water. The lower-elevation lawns now need water every 5 to 10 days, while in the upper elevations, cool-season lawns need water every 6 to 10 days. For warm-season grasses in the upper elevations, however, taper off watering to every 10 to 14 days.

PERENNIALS

Shorter days and slightly cooler temperatures mean less water is needed now. You can water less than in August, but any perennials that have been in the ground less than a month still need extra water to help them get established. Perennials need water once the soil is dry below 1 to 2 inches deep.

Succulents need water if temperatures are above 90°F. Water at least once before mid-month, or more often if they're in containers.

ROSES

Roses survive winter better if they have ample water in September. In the highest elevations, be sure you give them one good soak prior to the first frost. In lower elevations, water now may be rewarded with an extra cycle of bloom next month.

Just a reminder: roses growing in the ground need water once soil is dry 2 to 3 inches below the surface—this generally means every 5 to 12 days. Container roses should be watered once their potting soil is dry 1 inch below the surface.

SHRUBS

In all elevations, fall flowering and any fruiting shrubs produce better if they're not stressed by lack of water. Since it can still be in the triple digits in some areas, monitor water needs carefully. You can let a hose drip slowly near the plant's drip line for several hours to give the soil a good soak. Apply water so it soaks at least 2 feet deep for all shrubs.

TREES

Think of palms as really tall ornamental grasses. Native palms, such as *Washingtonia* and blue sabal, plus palms with Mediterranean genes (date palms, Mediterranean fan palms), are genetically programmed to expect autumn rains and will remain actively growing through the cooler months. They need a soak that goes 3 feet deep once every three weeks in September and in any non-freezing month.

Joshua trees (*Yucca brevifolia*), native to the Mojave Desert, are breaking their summer dormancy now. Be sure to water them as you would palms.

VINES, GROUNDCOVERS & ORNAMENTAL GRASSES

Vines that are going dormant for winter, such as queen's wreath or wisteria, will need water to help the process. Drought-adapted vines and

Looking somewhat like shining bursts of fireworks, the seedheads of ornamental grasses explode with bounty for the birds.

groundcovers need water every 5 to 18 days; non-drought-adapted species, every 5 to 12 days.

Most ornamental grasses need water every week or two depending on how hot it is in your area. Fall blooming ornamental grasses especially need water once per week in September to produce ample seed to feed the goldfinches and other seed eaters.

FERTILIZE

In the lower elevations, Labor Day is the time to fertilize everything to help plants recover from summer stress and get healthy for the winter ahead. This fertilizer application is especially important for plants that have been through summer storms, which may have washed the nutrients down below the root zone. Use a fertilizer that supplies trace minerals, such as those made from seaweed. Avoid fish emulsion and bone meal fertilizers; in the Southwest they attract rodents and even javelina.

In zone 7, September is one of those exception months for you. You can fertilize if you do so at the start of the month, but avoid fertilizing after mid-month.

In zones 6 and cooler, you have little fertilizing to do in September because it's too close to first frost. If you feel like you have to do something to reward plants for bloom, then give them a 2- to 4-inch layer of compost over their roots. It will slowly release nutrients into the soil through winter for a springtime burst of glorious growth.

ANNUALS & BULBS

In zones 7 and warmer, fertilize annuals and any bulbs that are growing.

EDIBLES

In the vegetable garden, you're harvesting warm-season crops and planting cool-season ones now, and in either case, fertilizer is not needed. Enrich garden soil with ample compost for best vegetable growth through winter. The one exception is in the lowest, nearly frost-free elevations: Here, fertilize tomatoes with a bloom fertilizer for a fall crop.

September is the time for the last dose of lawn fertilizer for most lawns this year—make it a complete lawn fertilizer.

For other edibles, follow the fertilizer tips for their growth form.

LAWNS

It's time for a last dose of fertilizer for two types of lawns—upper elevation cool-season grasses, and lower-elevation warm-season grass that will not be overseeded. Use a complete lawn fertilizer that contains micronutrients. Fertilizing will be in addition to such care as aeration or dethatching. If you have an overseeded lawn, you will continue to fertilize in any frost-free month in your area.

PERENNIALS

In lower elevations, boost bloom production of fall-flowering perennials by applying a flowering fertilizer. I have successfully used whatever I had on hand, including rose, citrus, and tomato fertilizers. Caution: Twice as much is not twice as good! Excessive fertilizer can kill the plants you wish to help. Do not fertilize succulents this month.

ROSES

In zones 7 and warmer, fertilize roses to help them recover from the heat of summer. Use a general-purpose fertilizer; even a slow-release fertilizer is fine for roses now. If you have fall-blooming roses, use a bloom fertilizer to encourage a robust fall display.

Fertilize fall-blooming perennials such as this butterfly mist with a bloom fertilizer four weeks before first frost in your area.

SHRUBS

Fall-blooming shrubs in zones 7 and warmer will appreciate a bloom fertilizer at this point. Others, especially fruit-bearing, spring-flowering, shrubs such as quince or Natal plum, can use a general fertilizer or a topdressing of compost.

TREES

Fertilize trees before mid-month in zones 7 and warmer. Spring-flowering trees, especially the nut and fruit producers, such as apples, citrus, or walnuts, will particularly benefit from a good all-around fertilizer now. If you wish, you can skip fertilizer on well-established, non-fruit-bearing trees.

Earlier I mentioned that a 2- to 4-inch layer of compost over roots of plants is helpful to slowly release nutrients into the soil through the winter. For trees, this layer can be as deep as 6 inches. Just be careful to not mound it against the trunk, where it will cause problems rather than helping.

VINES, GROUNDCOVERS & ORNAMENTAL GRASSES

In the lower elevations, fertilize vines. Use a general-purpose fertilizer, especially for summer-blooming vines, such as queen's wreath and all the species called trumpet vine (*Campsis*, *Cobaea*, *Podranea*, *Tecoma*, and *Thunbergia*). General-purpose fertilizer encourages more leaves and fewer flowers, which will help plants store energy for next spring.

In the lower elevations, a number of groundcovers will bloom through winter, especially verbena and mock verbena (*Glandularia*). These can get a bloom fertilizer, while summer-blooming groundcovers, such as lantana, should get a general-purpose fertilizer.

PROBLEM-SOLVE

Wildlife pressures increase in fall. The young are growing up and we all know how hungry teenagers can eat! Worse, they will try to eat anything, even resistant plants. Deer and elk may try to shed their antler velvet by rubbing on your trees and bushes, knocking plants over and rubbing off enough bark to kill plants.

Your garden looks like a lush salad bar to most hungry herbivores.

HERE'S HOW

TO RECOGNIZE & TREAT BIRD-DROPPING CATERPILLAR

In the lower elevations, the bird-dropping caterpillar may appear in citrus trees. Citrus farmers call the caterpillars orange dogs, perhaps because they're such a doggone bother.

These unique-looking caterpillars are the larvae of the giant swallowtail butterfly (*Papilio cresphontes*). The caterpillar resembles bird droppings to deter predators—and if that doesn't work they use their osmeteria, a hornlike structure they unfurl as needed. These horns are coated with a truly foul-smelling oil that clings to your hands for hours, despite repeated washing.

You have three choices in dealing with these pests. You can be generous and let them feed, but this will reduce your citrus crop. You can don disposable gloves, pick each caterpillar off your trees by hand, and drop them into a bucket of soapy water to drown. The third choice is to use Bt to eliminate them.

The bird-dropping caterpillar can be a serious pest on citrus.

A hard winter might bring storms that damage trees. Are there any sick, damaged, or weak-wooded trees that might lose limbs or topple to damage home or auto? A certified arborist can evaluate your trees, make recommendations, and, if necessary, do insured work. Use a certified arborist instead of a landscaping company.

ANNUALS & BULBS

Many warm-season annuals think 70°F is cold, and they promptly die off. To make sure pests don't have a place to snuggle during the cold, pull up dead and dying annuals. If the plants have pests, discard them in the trash. If no pests are evident, you can compost the debris.

EDIBLES

In all elevations, regularly clean up any fruit and nuts fallen from trees. This helps avoid infestations of fruit flies, leaf-footed or stink bugs, wasps, and sour fruit beetles. Another issue may be the rodents and deer attracted to the bounty. Rodents dining on fallen fruit may also draw rattlesnakes, who love to dine on rodents.

LAWNS

If you don't overseed a warm-season lawn, you may wish to consider a preemergent weed control. Apply before the autumn equinox in all areas. Don't apply a preemergent if you have planted bulbs for naturalizing under your lawn. Preemergents are toxic to humans and other animals, so carefully read and follow label directions.

PERENNIALS

In the lower elevations, whiteflies can appear in large numbers as the summer heat is broken. Lantana, justicia, evening primrose, mums, and members of the mint family, including salvia and mint, are often stricken after a long, hot summer. Such infestations are an indicator of plant stress. Wash plants with insecticidal soap, or perhaps cover them with a row cover. Consider removing these species and planting

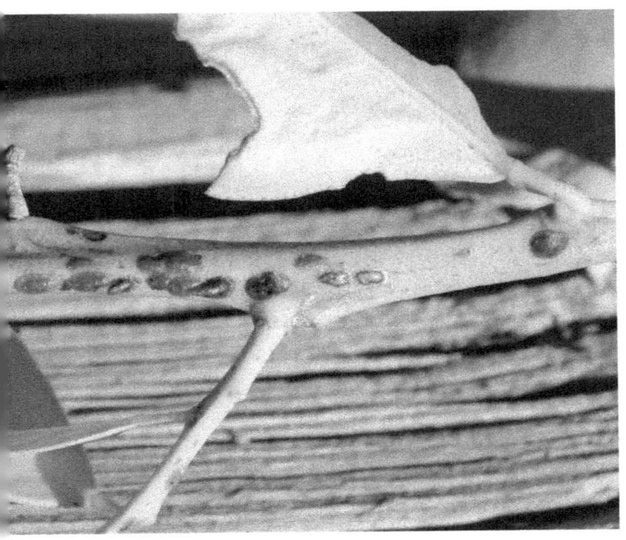

Scale insects cling tightly to the plant as they suck sap. The best treatment is to keep your plants healthy so they can make the phytochemicals that deter these pests.

native plants that will not become so stressed by summer.

ROSES

As you care for your roses, watch for cane borers. Stems infested with this pest will be hollow. Since older canes of some heirloom roses become hollow with age, also look for signs of frass inside the cane. Cut the cane lower, until there's no sign of borer, then coat the cut with carpenter's glue to prevent reentry.

SHRUBS

Pests such as whitefly or aphids appearing on shrubs are often an indicator of plant stress. If the plants are getting enough water, the problem may be a lack of specific nutrients. Commonly, our alkaline soils make it difficult for plants to absorb the iron, zinc, and other micronutrients they need. Acidify the soil with a solution of 1 cup of white vinegar mixed in 4 gallons of water and pour around the roots. Follow this with a topdressing of compost to help further acidify the soil.

TREES

Tree pests are mostly active in spring and summer. But perhaps you just noticed a termite mud tunnel along the trunk of a palm or palo verde. Termites are harmless to the living wood of plants—they only eat dead wood. Those mud tubes are transportation tunnels to their food, as termites prefer to live underground. You can use a broom or your hand to brush away the tunnels.

VINES, GROUNDCOVERS & ORNAMENTAL GRASSES

In the uppermost elevations, rodents may be scouting for cozy winter nests, even now. They love heavily mulched areas. While mulching over the root area of plants is a great idea, avoid mounding mulch against the stems and crowns of vines or ornamental grasses just yet. You should wait until after the ground is frozen to mulch these areas.

In all elevations, anytime is a good time to get rid of weeds, ideally before they go to seed.

Whiteflies often appear at the end of the summer to suck the sap of already stressed plants.

October

October is a great time to add the color and beauty of plants to indoor spaces, and if you can, outdoor spaces as well. In the upper elevations, you may have to bring the garden indoors, and perhaps add houseplants to your indoor spaces. In the lower elevations, add winter flowers outdoors. Which winter flowers? Go to a nursery and simply get what you like. I confess to a weakness for carefree calendula, pretty pansies, and lithesome linarea (and a deplorable weakness for playing with words).

While at the nursery or home-improvement store, be generous with yourself. Spend at least as much money as you would going out to a fancy dinner and a show. Those events last a single evening, while plants and flowers will brighten your life for months, possibly years. Another thing to consider, your purchases can also help independent nurseries or garden centers continue to operate as a viable business, so they will be there for you to use in years to come.

One nice thing about visiting nurseries in October is that many of them have clearance sales. Garden accessories, such as trellises, benches, decorative containers, even pots, will be marked down. Gloves and tools too. If nothing else, new tools will make garden work easier, and thus you'll be less prone to fatigue and injury. But consider a lovely little bench placed in a shady garden nook. After all, you need a place to rest and rehydrate properly, plus it's nice to have a place to relax and enjoy the fruits of your labors. Either way, justification enough to get what you need for your outdoor space. Don't forget to keep an eye out for healthy-looking spring-flowering bulbs.

Fall is a great time in all elevations, a time to relish your garden. Get out and putter. Clean a little, redecorate with fresh flowers, add some herbs for fragrance. Enjoy!

PLAN

Those in the uppermost elevations have likely already experienced a freeze, and most of the rest of us aren't far behind. Most October planning will involve how to deal with this new season, but it's not too soon to think about how you are going to water your garden next summer! Don't have an irrigation system? October is a good time to install one. It is less stressful for plants to have their roots disturbed in the cooler months of autumn than in the searing heat of summer.

Don't forget to note the first frost day in your garden journal. It usually occurs the same week each year, but your yard is a microcosm of its own. You may discover that your yard is cooler or warmer than average. Armed with this knowledge, you can better plan for next year.

ANNUALS & BULBS

In the lower elevations, plan for winter color—beds, containers, or whatever you have. Clean empty containers and purchase new potting soil.

In the upper elevations, you may have had frost already, but if not, consider which annuals you might pot up to bring indoors.

At all elevations, consider forcing bulbs indoors for a cheery note in your home four months from now. Talk about delayed gratification! (See November, Here's How to Force Bulbs to Bloom Indoors.)

EDIBLES

Planting and harvesting continue in the lower elevations. The cool-season vegetable garden should be mostly in the ground, but I find it very hard to yank the last of the squash so long as they're still producing. You can start as many winter vegetables as possible in seed trays for later transplanting.

Upper-elevation gardeners will be planning vegetable gardens for next spring. This may include planting a cover crop, as discussed on page 171. If you're too busy to plant a cover crop, at least add a 2-inch layer of steer manure to age into the soil.

A number of herbs will overwinter indoors on sunny windowsills.

Gardeners in all elevations can plan to add fruit and nut trees and shrubs. Order catalogs or check online now to get your order placed, because some can be planted as early as January. Those in upper elevations may want to dig holes while the ground is still unfrozen. You should add soil amendments to the soil removed from the hole while you are at it.

Those in lower elevations can plant the cool-season annual herbs this month. Decide if these will go into the vegetable garden or into containers right outside the kitchen door for easy harvest and use.

Gardeners in the upper elevations will need to bring cold-tender herbs indoors. Consider bringing in some herbs that will otherwise overwinter underground (as roots), such as mint. Think about a sprig of fresh mint in Christmas cocoa (yum!).

LAWNS

Many lawn owners overseed during this month, but this practice isn't recommended. Overseeding stresses warm-season turfgrasses, especially during the transition periods. In spring the winter grass shades and competes with warm-season grass trying to break dormancy. This battle occurs again in fall when the warm-season grass is trying to store energy for winter and the winter grass starts crowding it. If you still want to overseed, plan to do so before the end of the month. If you're not overseeding, then very little lawn work needs to be done this transition month.

In the upper elevations, if you have an underground lawn irrigation system, plan to winterize it to prevent freeze damage. Use a reputable sprinkler service for this chore, and get a written contract. Frost protection includes the aboveground portions, including the back-flow preventer. Wrap everything with a blanket or insulation, then cover with well-secured plastic to keep it dry.

PERENNIALS

Plan ahead for locations of plant divisions. Why divide at all? Because uncrowded plants flower better and can resist diseases better. In all but the coldest elevations, autumn is a good time to divide many perennials, including rhizomatous iris, if you didn't do it last month.

ROSES

In all elevations, if you really like roses, then make more space for them. Plan to place them where they'll have all the sunlight and air movement they need for health, where you can easily care for them, and where you can enjoy them. (See March, Here's How to Help Your Roses Thrive.) Xeriscape principles advocate placing roses in the oasis zone.

Many native plants, such as this wild cotton, offer vivid autumn color.

SHRUBS

Plan for fall shrub planting in all zones but 5 and 4. By planting in fall, plants will have more than six months to establish a good feeder root system before the heat of summer. Some planning should be done from inside the house. Look out your windows and identify bland and boring views. Autumn color is possible even in the lowest elevations. A number of landscape shrubs, such as clove currant (*Ribes odoratum*) or wild cotton (*Gossypium thurberi*), brighten the autumn landscape and it's not too early to plan where you might add some now or next spring, depending on elevation.

TREES

Those in the lower elevations can plant trees this month, so check your journal to see where you may have noted the need for summer shade.

In all elevations, you will need to stake any 15-gallon-sized trees you plant as part of the planting process. Be sure to have the materials you will need on hand as discussed in Here's How to Stake Trees.

Don't forget about microclimates in your yard. If you want fall color and spring bloom, consider planting Mexican redbud (*Cercis canadensis* var. *mexicana*). This small tree is hardy to zone 6 and grows successfully in zone 9 with afternoon shade in summer. Its cousin, Texas redbud (*Cercis canadensis* var. *texensis*), can survive in zone 10 with summer shade.

VINES, GROUNDCOVERS & ORNAMENTAL GRASSES

In all elevations, colorful fall foliage can come from any number of plants, including the ones in this group. Visit a local botanical garden or arboretum and take notes, or just pay attention as you drive around town. Take photos of interesting plants so experts can help you with identification. If possible, get an overall shot of the plant and how it grows, combined with a closeup of leaves, bark, and any flowers or fruit.

Autumn brings a wealth of compost materials.

Virginia creeper provides vivid fall color, and the plant can be trained as either a groundcover or a climbing vine. Some cultivars, such as the Hacienda Creeper™ (*Parthenocissus* × 'Hacienda Creeper'), which can be grown in lower elevations, are remarkably drought tolerant. Other cultivars are good in upper elevations.

Ornamental grasses really come into their own this month, many with shining seedheads. They are a good addition to any garden, and also look quite charming covered in snow in the upper elevations.

PLANT

October is for planting in all but the coolest zones. Getting plants in the ground now is good because plants have ample time to establish a healthy feeder root system long before the heat of summer arrives.

Fall plant sales at garden centers and local botanical gardens are always so tempting! Before you go wild, remember that you will have to plant all your purchases before frost arrives.

ANNUALS & BULBS

In lower elevations, an entire alphabet of annuals can be planted now as transplants: alyssum, bachelor's buttons, bells of Ireland, blue sage, calendula, corn flower, cosmos, dianthus, dusty miller, firecracker vine, flax, foxglove, gaillardia, geranium, godetia, heliotrope, hollyhock, Johnny-jump-up, linaria, lobelia, mina, monkey flower, nigella, pansy, pinks, poppy, rudbeckia, snapdragon, stock, sweet peas, toadflax, verbena, violets, and wallflower.

In the lower elevations, you have until the first of November to plant spring wildflowers. If you planted earlier and still don't have sprouts, keep watering, or add more seed to bare spots. Perhaps cover the seed a little deeper, ¼- to ⅓-inch deep, to discourage seed-eating birds. Cover with a topdressing of potting soil, which has a darker color than most garden soil and will help warm and nurture the tiny seedlings this late in the season.

Those in the upper elevations can still plant the really cold-tolerant annuals, such as ornamental cabbage and ornamental kale. They could last into December in zone 6 gardens.

Gardeners in all elevations should be planting spring-flowering bulbs now if you haven't already. You can still get them in the ground even in

Ornamental cabbages and kales look good in containers and can survive light frosts.

zone 4. (See Plant, Bulbs, in September for recommended bulbs for your area.)

EDIBLES

Traditionalists insist that Columbus Day is the day to plant garlic bulbs for harvest next year. In all zones except zone 10, anytime around the first frost will work. In zone 10, plant garlic in January.

Planting a winter vegetable garden continues in zones 10 and 9. Resow seed of radish and leaf lettuce every three weeks for a continuous supply. Other winter vegetables to enjoy (if you haven't planted yet) are artichoke, arugula, beets, bok choy, broccoli, brussels sprouts, cabbage, carrots, cauliflower, chives, collard greens, endive, garlic, horseradish, jicima, kale, kohlrabi, leeks, lettuce (head and leaf types), mesclun mix, mizuma, mustard greens, onion, pak choy, parsnip, potato, radish, radiccio, scallion, shallots, spinach, Swiss chard, and turnip.

Fruits and nuts! For almost everyone reading this, from zones 10 to 6, this is the time to plant container-grown fruiting trees and shrubs (except tropicals, such as citrus and dates).

Gardeners in zones 10 and 9 can plant cool-season annual herbs. The list includes calendula, caraway, chamomile, chives, cilantro, cumin, dill, fennel, German feverfew, parsley, and salad burnet. In other parts of the world, some of these are biennial or even perennial, but in the lower elevations in our region they grow all winter and generally flower and die the following spring. Gardeners in the upper elevations will plant these herbs in spring after last frost.

Zone 7 gardeners can plant cover crops in the vegetable garden now. (See Here's How to Use Cover Crops to Help a Dormant Garden.)

LAWNS

In the lower elevations, if you opt to overseed lawns, then do so once daytime highs are below 90°F. Start the process by mowing closely, but not so low that it scalps the lawn. Next, rake the area to remove thatch so seeds can reach the soil's surface. Scatter seeds of annual or perennial ryegrass at a rate of 10 to 15 pounds per 1,000 square feet.

Cover the seed with a lawn topdressing specifically made to help hide seed from birds and to help keep it moist as it starts growing. Water the area well and don't let it dry during seed germination and establishment. Don't fertilize until the warm-season lawn is entirely dormant.

HERE'S HOW

TO USE COVER CROPS TO HELP A DORMANT GARDEN

Cover crops help suppress weed growth, reduce soil erosion, rebuild soil texture, increase water retention, discourage some pests, and aid in loosening the soil. Cover crops such as peas, clover, and vetch add fertilizer in the form of nitrogen.

Cover crops can be seeded as soon as any vegetable crop has reached maturity and has been harvested. In fact, cover crops should be sown while the weather is still warm enough for seeds to germinate. There's no special soil preparation for seeding a cover crop—simply spade or till the soil after harvest, and sow the cover crop seed. If you have late crops in a part of the garden, then simply sow the cover crop in the space between the rows.

A wide variety of seeds can be grown as cover crops. Among the most popular are annual rye (not perennial rye), crimson clover, garden pea, vetch, alfalfa, and buckwheat. These can be planted individually, or they are often mixed and planted as a blend because of the various benefits the different crops offer. Do share some blades of rye with your cat or dog.

In the upper elevations, it's generally too late for planting lawns. You may have heard of dormant-seeding a lawn but if you don't have a reliable snow cover, this is not recommended.

In zone 7b, you could sod a new lawn or replant bare spots with new sod pieces. You could also consider the newer drought-resistant varieties of fescue instead of the older varieties of ryegrass or Kentucky bluegrass. Use 7 to 10 pounds of seed per 1,000 square feet. This could be done next year as early as August.

PERENNIALS

In all elevations, continue to plant perennials anytime the ground is not frozen. This includes perennials you divided. If you splurged at plant sales, try to get the plants out of their containers and into the ground this month. It is far better for them to be in the ground and perhaps moved in spring than it is to spend winter cramped in a chilly plastic pot.

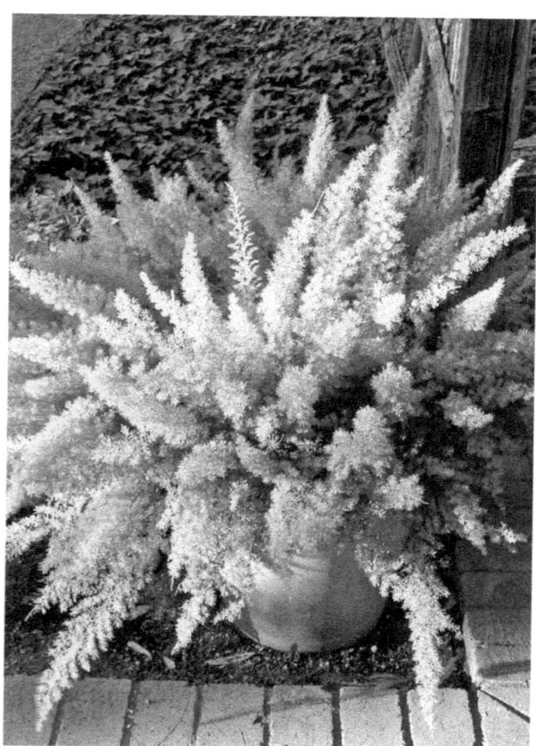

Some perennials can live their lives in containers, moving indoors every winter.

ROSES

For all elevations except the uppermost, gardeners can plant container-grown roses through this month. Ideally, you want them in the ground before first frost.

SHRUBS & TREES

Plant evergreen and deciduous shrubs and trees this month in lower elevations and in zone 7. Those in zones 6 and cooler should have any shrub and tree plantings done by mid-month. The exception to this are the tropicals, such as palm and paloverde, in the lowermost zones: those should be planted in spring.

Trees and even shrubs are not cheap. For best success, plant them in a good hole that will help them become established and thrive in their new home. (See Here's How to Dig a Hundred-Dollar Hole.) Once planted, many tree species need sturdy staking to help them withstand our ample Southwest winds, as discussed in Here's How to Stake Trees.

VINES, GROUNDCOVERS & ORNAMENTAL GRASSES

Did you see some awesome fall color you want? In the lower elevations and zone 7, buy that plant and get it in the ground this month. In zones 6 and cooler, any plantings in this category should be completed by mid-month.

Even though vines and groundcovers are not as expensive as trees, you should still dig a nice, wide hole for their roots to grow into. Amend the soil of the planting space with a half-and-half mix of soil plus compost, peat moss, or even old potting soil out of containers.

CARE

October is clean up time! Clean out beds and pots. Pick up fallen leaves, twigs, and other wind-blown debris. Clean tools, especially if you live in upper elevations and will store them for winter.

Clean your plants. Lack of rainfall is an issue for many landscape plants, and it's not just the roots that need moisture. If you've lived here for a

HERE'S HOW

TO DIG A HUNDRED-DOLLAR HOLE

Years ago, my Grandpa taught me, "For a twenty dollar tree, dig a twenty-dollar hole." Well, inflation has set in since then. Now you need a hundred-dollar hole. When you factor in what it costs to get a tree or shrub growing—labor, soil amendments, water costs, irrigation lines, the plant itself, plus the time waiting for the plant to become established and thrive, the reality is closer to a five-hundred-dollar hole.

Add a raised berm of soil at the edges of the planting hole to help hold in the water when you irrigate your tree.

Dig big. This refers to width, not depth. A planting hole shouldn't be deeper than the pot the plant came in but it should be wider, at least three times the width of the pot. A plant in a 1-foot-diameter pot needs a hole 3 to 5 feet in diameter.

Amend your soil. Your new plant is a pampered darling sitting in nice, moist, and nutritious nursery soil. You need to introduce it gently to our not-so-ideal soils. Plan on filling the planting hole with a fifty-fifty mixture of compost and the soil from the hole you dug. If you have clay soils, add sand and coarse pea gravel to promote better drainage.

Water immediately. Water immediately after planting to help settle the soil and drive any air pockets out. If part of the rootball ends up above ground, or if the whole plant settles a few inches deeper, you'll need to replant (but not right away). Ideally, give it one day to dry out before you replant, because a soggy rootball easily falls apart, which generally kills the plant.

Stake your trees. If your tree came in anything larger than a five-gallon pot, it will need to be staked. In the nursery, the tree stood in a grove of similar trees and was thus somewhat protected from wind. Now that it's standing all alone in your yard, it'll need sturdy staking. (See Here's How to Stake Trees.)

Water to establishment. In the nursery, plants are watered at least once daily. You'll need to do the same at first, even if it's a low-water plant. Water the area well out from the rootball to make sure the soil where you want the plant to extend its roots into is amply moist. After the first two weeks, cut back to every other day, then every third day. Plants will need supplemental water until they're fully established—generally, one year for shrubs, three years for trees.

while, you know how dusty it is in the Southwest. Plants can tolerate being dusty, but dust blocks sunlight from reaching their photosynthetic tissue. Less light isn't altogether bad if there's no rain to trigger growth, but with irrigation, dusty leaves can become troublesome. While it is not critical, evergreen plants do appreciate a nice rinse. I spray water up over all my plants once a month or so. Do this early in the day in all elevations, and don't do it if your area is already freezing.

Most zones will have frost this month. Be ready to protect tender plants from freezing. (See Here's How to Protect Plants from Freezes.)

ANNUALS & BULBS

Care for annuals includes getting rid of all worn-out summer annuals. If they're disease free, add them to the compost. Gardeners in the lower elevations can plant new annuals, but those in upper elevations can't. If you're not replanting,

HERE'S HOW

TO STAKE TREES

Container-grown trees come from the nursery with a tiny nursery stake, but most species need something better to help them become established in their new home. That said, some species, such as ironwood and pine, don't need staking unless you have an especially windy site.

Supplies: You will need plastic-coated wire, nails or screws, and two sturdy stakes, generally called poles. These poles are available in 2- and 3-inch diameters. For 15-gallon trees, select poles 8 feet tall.

Site the two poles, one on either side of the tree, perpendicular to the major wind direction. Our winds mostly come out of the west, so the poles will be on the south and north sides of the tree. Site the poles well away from the trunk of the tree, at least 6 inches beyond the tree's current canopy. This space gives the tree room to grow and ensures that branches will not rub on the poles and become scarred.

Pound the poles into the ground so they stand on their own—this will have to be down into undisturbed soil, generally 2 to 3 feet deep.

Loop the plastic-coated wire from one pole and loosely around the tree's trunk. Nail or screw the wire to the pole so it won't slip down. Now, loop a second wire from the other pole. Nail or screw it to its pole. The wire must be loose enough so the tree can sway slightly in the daily breezes and grow the strengthening cells needed to stand strong on its own.

Staking helps a tree stand up to storms while it's in its first establishment phase of growth. The degree of sway should be 10 to 15 degrees from perpendicular in all directions. Floppy trees such as desert willow require the lesser amount of sway space, while rigid trees such as hackberry barely need staking at all.

Remove the small nursery stake as soon as you're done planting and staking. Within one year, remove the stake system. If the tree falls down or flops over, dig it up and start over with a brand new tree. You will not win with that plant.

cover any bare spots in the landscape with mulch, such as cedar bark or pine needles. This will shade the soil and prevent weeds from sprouting. Mulch also reduces frost heaves and helps protect soil creatures such as worms from excessive cold.

EDIBLES

In all elevations, harvest winter squash and pumpkins as they mature and before the first frost. The outer skin should be firm and too hard to penetrate with your fingernail. Frost will soften the skin and allow decay.

In the lower elevations, very lightly prune any perennial herbs that are looking bedraggled after our hot summer. Since they'll respond with new growth, avoid excessive pruning that may be harmed by freezing.

In the upper elevations, it's time to clean up the garden and eliminate potential pest problems before they haunt you next summer. Both squash-vine borer and cucumber beetles overwinter in debris from squash-family plants. Even if you didn't see these pests, if a neighbor had them, you need to discard all plant debris in the trash. Winter cover crops such as buckwheat or crimson clover appear to help reduce the incidence of these pests. (See Here's How to Use Cover Crops to Help a Dormant Garden.)

LAWNS

For gardeners in the lower elevations, if you've not overseeded your lawn you'll note it's beginning to turn brown and go dormant this month. Continue to water, but don't fertilize.

HERE'S HOW

TO PROTECT PLANTS FROM FREEZES

If you are willing to fuss over your plants, then you can grow plants that are marginally cold-hardy for your area. But you will have to protect them when temperatures dip below their hardiness rating. Often the dip is just a few degrees for a few hours, and it generally occurs in the few hours prior to sunrise. In all cases, you will need to cover both the plant and the ground under the plant. To avoid cold burn, try to ensure that the foliage itself does not come in contact with the cover.

- **Temporary covers.** Household blankets, bed sheets, plastic tarps, cardboard boxes, and layers of newspaper for shorter annuals or groundcovers will all work for one night. Do weight them down at the edges if it's a windy night. Do take the cover off once the sun rises.
- **Constructed covers.** Construct a framework of PVC pipe or wire, depending on the size of the plant. Cover this with clear plastic or row cover fabric, also sold as frost cloth. These can stay in place for several days but should be removed as soon as frost is no longer a threat. Plastic covering can heat excessively in the sunshine and burn the plants you just saved from frost.
- **Heat the protected space.** By covering the ground as well as the plant, the latent heat of the soil helps protect the plant. You can increase area warmth with low-wattage incandescent light, such as a 25-watt bulb or a string of Christmas lights. Avoid accidental fires—keep even low-wattage lights from contact with the cover. Make sure electrical connections and lights are away from dry grass or mulch.

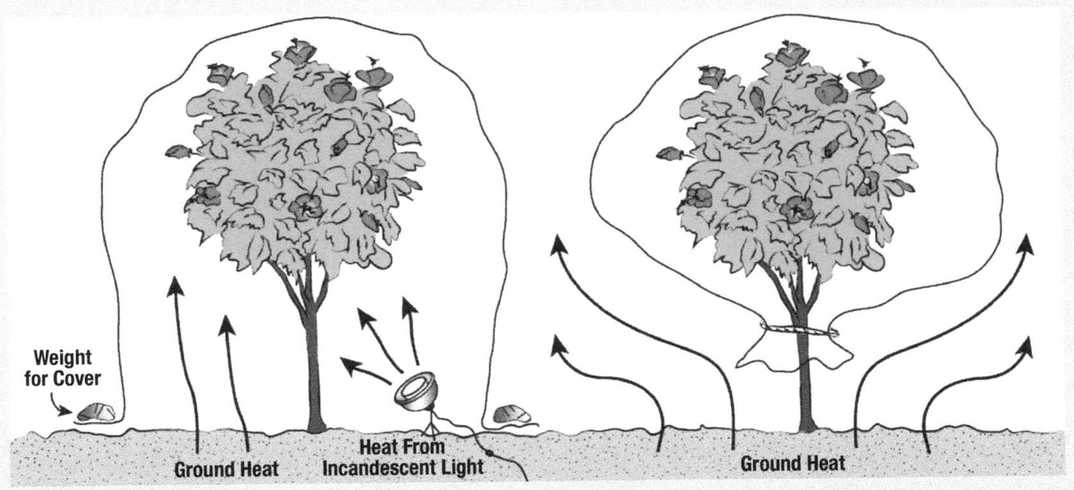

In the upper elevations, it's critical that you rake autumn leaves off your lawn. Rain and snowfall combine with fallen leaves to form mats that will smother grass.

PERENNIALS

Gardeners in the lower elevations can prune semiwoody summer-flowering perennials such as gaillardia or gaura. Lightly prune back up to one-third of the plant, especially if they're getting leggy.

Lower-elevation gardeners should avoid October pruning of winter-blooming perennials, such as damianita (*Chrysactinia mexicana*) or our native marigolds, Palmer's marigold (*Tagetes palmeri*), and Mt. Lemmon marigold (*T. lemmoni*).

If you are growing succulents in containers, be aware of the date for first frost in your area, and be ready to move them to a protected area. Some succulents, such as desert rose (*Adenium*) and elephant bush (*Portulacaria afra*) are harmed with lows of only 45°F.

Upper-elevation gardeners should wait for the first hard killing frost before clean up. The perennial's roots will still be alive underground, while the stems and leaves turn into a blackened mess. Prune off all aboveground material. If the plant had powdery mildew or pest problems, throw the clippings in the trash; otherwise, compost them.

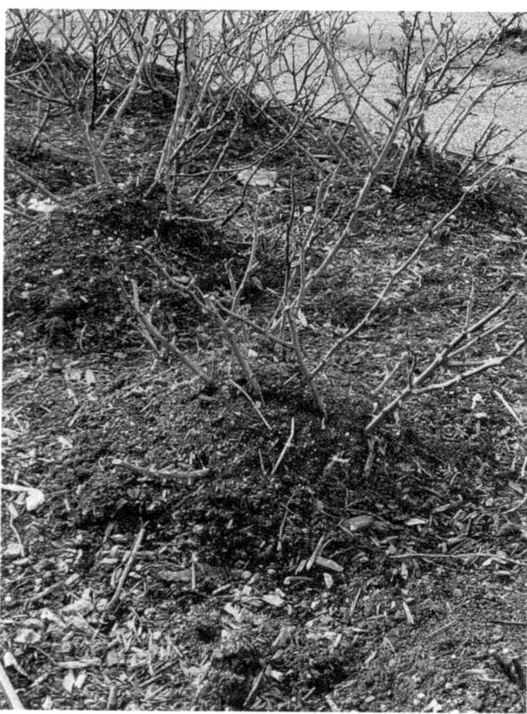

Mulch for roses in winter will eventually be piled over the crown. Wait until after a hard freeze to do this.

Once the ground is frozen, you should add a heavy layer of mulch over the crown of your perennials. Don't do this too soon, as it is an invitation to rodents to move in and nest in the crowns of the plants. In most areas, you will mulch over your perennials in November or even December, but in zones 5 and 4 you need to do it now.

If you brought plants inside, give their containers a ¼ turn each week, so all leaves get ample light and plants do not grow unevenly.

ROSES

Roses growing in the zones 9 and 10 may put on a second flush of bloom now that the weather has cooled. To help them rebloom, lightly prune the canes, up to one-third. With water and a sidedressing of fertilizer they may bloom again before Christmas. While you're out there, check for water sprouts and remove any you find.

In the upper elevations, after the first hard freeze, prepare roses for winter. Prune plants back by two-thirds and mulch the top completely. Some gardeners place a tomato cage over a plant and fill it with dry leaves or pine needles. You can also wrap the plant in burlap.

SHRUBS

Lower-elevation gardeners should avoid October pruning of winter-blooming shrubs, including woolly butterfly bush (*Buddleja marrubiifolia*), Baja fairy duster (*Calliandra californica*), pink fairy duster (*C. eriophylla*), bush dalea (*Dalea pulchra*), 'Valentine' emu bush (*Eremophila maculata* 'Valentine'), red justicia (*Justicia californica*), and Mexican honeysuckle (*J. spicigera*). Incidentally, if you want some winter color, it's not too late to plant any of these in the lower elevations.

Upper elevations should limit pruning of shrubs this month to the removal of the three Ds—diseased, damaged, or dead branches and stems.

TREES

In all elevations, deciduous trees will be shedding their leaves. Rake these up and recycle them into mulch or compost. Leaves make wonderful organic mulch in beds or under shrubs and trees (but not trees in the lawn). Or add leaves to your compost.

There is little autumn pruning that needs to be done, but removing dead wood can be done at any time.

If you don't have a composting area, leaves are an excellent and easy way to start. (See January, Here's How to Compost in the Southwest.) Start now and you will have nice, rich compost to add to your garden next spring.

VINES, GROUNDCOVERS & ORNAMENTAL GRASSES

Those in the lower elevations should avoid October pruning of winter-blooming vines such as lilac vine (*Hardenbergia*). Do not prune tropical vines such as bougainvillea or yuca vine, either.

Despite all this talk of raking leaves elsewhere, don't bother raking leaves *under* groundcovers. The beauty of having them in the first place is that they hide fallen leaves. If groundcovers have fallen leaves on top of them, remove those leaves.

Gardeners in the lower elevations should avoid October pruning of winter-blooming groundcovers, such as mock verbena (*Glandularia gooddingii*) or rock verbena (*Glandularia pulchella*).

WATER

Depending on where you are in the Southwest, early rains off the Pacific or a late squall from the Gulf of Mexico may provide precipitation this month. Or record highs may persist and provide no precipitation at all. Either way, gardeners in all elevations will have to pay attention to the weather during this transitional month.

If you don't have an irrigation system, October is a good time to install one. Plants tolerate root disturbance better now than in the dead of summer. You may be able to get a good deal on installation because companies may reduce their prices just to have the work in this otherwise slow month.

Gardeners in the lower elevations should give the irrigation system a good going over. Replace clogged or missing emitters, and repair any leaks. Replace the backup battery in your timer if you haven't done so in more than a year. Adjust the controller to the fall schedule. Changing the water application schedule with the seasons can reduce landscape water use by 30 to 50 percent. In upper elevations, winterize your irrigation system now if you didn't last month.

ANNUALS & BULBS

As long as soils aren't frozen, you'll need to do some watering. (See April, Here's How Often to Water Your Landscape.)

Irrigate any bulbs still blooming, such as naked ladies or rain lilies, every three to seven days. You can water less once they're done flowering, but as long as bulbs still have green leaves, do keep watering them.

This month, you won't need the pruners for winter bloomers, such as this sandpaper verbena.

Soaker hoses can withstand mild freezes, but plan on putting them away before temperatures dip into the mid-20s.

With most spring bulbs you plant and forget about them—unless it gets too hot. Ideally their soil cover should stay lightly moist, not bone-dry, for the 18 weeks or so it takes for them to emerge from underground. Water bulb beds at least once this month if your soil isn't frozen.

EDIBLES

Any seeds or seedlings, including cool-season crops and cover crops, need to be kept evenly moist. This may mean daily until plants become larger; then you should only need to water every three to five days.

For other edibles, see their sections based on growth form (trees, shrubs) for water tips.

LAWNS

Water a newly seeded or overseeded lawn two to four times per day until the seeds sprout. Water two hours after sunrise and two hours before sundown to lessen the chances of fungal growth. As seedlings grow, apply water to a depth twice as deep as they are tall. Taper off to daily watering, and eventually to once every two to three days, watering more deeply each time to at least 6 inches deep. (See March, Here's How to Gauge How Deep Irrigation Goes.)

Irrigate warm-season lawns that are going dormant at least twice this month to help them go into dormancy unstressed. Cool-season lawns of perennial ryegrass or fescue will be emerging from summer dormancy. Be sure to irrigate them.

PERENNIALS

In all elevations, water any new transplants more than you would established plants. In upper elevations, continue to water as long as the ground remains unfrozen. If you live in an area of little persistent snow cover, soil moisture is important to maintain the root system.

In lower elevations, succulents still need water when highs are above 80°F. Water them at least once before mid-month.

ROSES

Monitor the soil moisture for your roses, especially any newly planted ones. Unstressed roses produce a robust root system that helps them through the upcoming dormant period. If there are no autumn rains in your area, get out the soaker hose or turn on the irrigation. In upper elevations, be sure you drain and put away the hose in event of a freeze.

SHRUBS

Gardeners in zones 5 and 4 should deeply water all shrubs early in the month before the

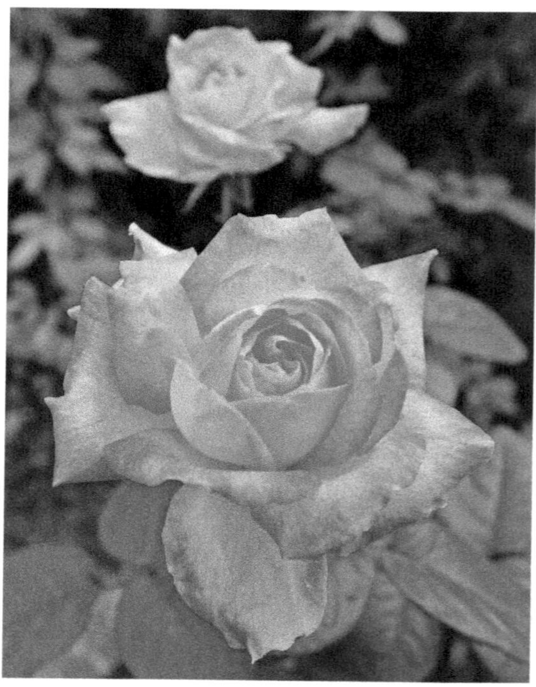

With water and care, roses often rebloom in October in lower elevations.

ground freezes solid. Shrubs can suffer severe desiccation during the winter, causing the roots to die. Such damage will not be apparent until next spring. Evergreen shrubs lose moisture from their leaves all year long, thus water for them is especially necessary. In zones 7 and 6, you will need to water your shrubs at least twice this month.

In lower elevations, shrubs flowering and fruiting now, such as abelia, quince, or turpentine bush (*Ericameria laricifolia*), will produce better if they're not stressed by lack of water; plan to water every 7 to 10 days.

TREES

Gardeners in the upper elevations should check the soil under the drip line of any trees that are still leafed out—this includes evergreens such as pines and junipers. Water if the soil is dry below 3 inches. Plan on at least one good soak around mid-month as trees go into winter dormancy. You may have to water again if it is especially windy after mid-month.

Water Joshua trees by mid-month if you don't get rain in your area.

In all elevations, don't forget to water any newly planted trees if weather remains dry for longer than two weeks, or if it is especially windy.

VINES, GROUNDCOVERS & ORNAMENTAL GRASSES

Be sure to water any new plantings in this category, especially if the weather is windy and dry. Vines that are going dormant for winter need water to help that process.

In lower elevations, summer-dormant groundcovers, such as the daleas and native verbenas, will begin to grow again as temperatures drop. These will need some extra water as they break summer dormancy. Other groundcovers, such as lantana, are becoming winter dormant and can use some extra water as they translocate their resources.

In all elevations, water ornamental grasses every 10 to 18 days if the soil is not frozen solid.

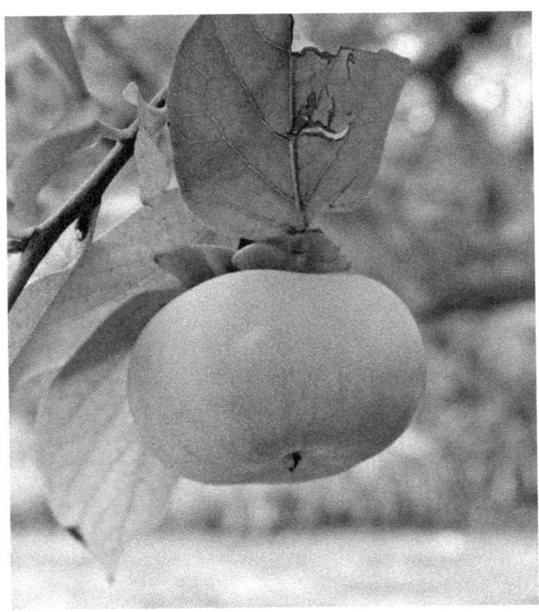

If any fruit is still developing on trees, monitor soil water carefully so you will reap a luscious harvest, not a mealy one.

FERTILIZE

Fertilizer is not required for most plants in any elevation. Avoid encouraging growth, because frost has either happened or is on its way. There are two exceptions: edibles and lawns.

EDIBLES

In the lower elevations, the winter vegetable garden benefits from a slow-release fertilizer mixed into the soil around young transplants. Sidedressing is an option.

LAWNS

Don't fertilize lawns in any elevations in any month that includes the chance of frost.

In the lowest elevations, if you overseeded, fertilize two weeks after overseeding with a lawn starter formula that nourishes roots and leaves, generally sold in a 3-1-2 ratio. You can follow this with a general-purpose lawn fertilizer once a month in any frost-free month in your area.

If you have a St. Augustine or zoysia lawn, fertilize for the last time this year.

PROBLEM-SOLVE

As temperatures drop across our region, the primary problems this month are weeds and wildlife. They're not the only problems—just the primary ones.

Get rid of summer weeds. If they've already gone to seed, try to remove gently without shaking the seed around. Carry a bucket around the yard with you to put their corpses into just as soon as they are pulled. Get rid of cool-season weeds that are sprouting this month.

Is that tiny seedling in your wildflower patch a weed or a wildflower? Sometimes your only recourse is to give them little numbered tags (using Popsicle sticks) and take photos. Check back every few weeks to see if they are weeds or wildflowers. Keep these photos in your journal to refer to next year.

ANNUALS & BULBS

If you planted wildflowers, keep the birds out. Chicken wire laid flat on the ground over your wildflower bed seems to deter them. The growing plants will eventually hide it from view.

EDIBLES

In lower elevations, aphids and whiteflies are still around. Hose them off with water, or use a soapy spray.

If you have bird feeders, clean up spills to avoid attracting rodents into the garden.

Caterpillars may still visit. If you still have tomato family crops in your garden and it has not dropped below 50°F yet, keep watch for hornworms (see July). Watch your citrus for bird-dropping caterpillars (see September). In some years both can show up as late in the year as December.

In all elevations, eliminate potential pest problems before they haunt you next summer. Clean up debris that can shelter overwintering pests, including squash-vine borer and cucumber beetles. Sowing winter cover crops such as clover and buckwheat also help reduce the incidence of these pests.

Clean up any fallen fruits and nuts to avoid inviting rodents and larger herbivores into your garden.

LAWNS

Overseeding a lawn attracts countless seed-eating native birds, and keeping them away is a real chore. Inflatable snakes and owl statues will work but need to be moved daily. Glittering strips of shiny silver foil fluttering in the breeze will work somewhat, and inflated beach balls with giant eyes painted on them swinging in the breeze are fairly effective.

If four-footed wildlife, such as skunk or javelina, are digging up your lawn, this is a sure sign you have grubs. If the soil temperature is below 50°F, it's too late to treat now, but consider ordering milky spore (an IPM bacteria) to eliminate these pests early next year as the soils warm.

PERENNIALS

In all elevations, eliminate weeds early and often.

In the lower elevations wildlife issues are mostly javelina and rabbits. Storms may have loosened your fence, or the persistent creatures will slowly dig under it. Take a stroll around your property and seal any holes before critters get in and dig up your bulbs.

In the upper elevations, wildlife that bother perennials are mostly smaller mammals, such as mice, voles, chipmunks, and the like. They're looking for a winter nesting site, and the solution is in your garden culture. Although mulch over the roots is fine now, avoid spreading protective

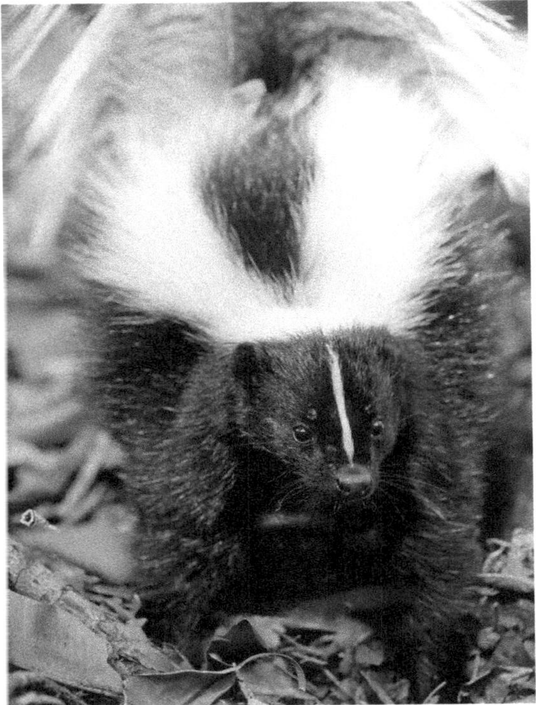

Skunks digging in your lawn is a sure sign of a grub infestation. Order milky spore next spring and apply it once soils start to warm.

mulch against the crown of plants until the ground is fully frozen. By then, the rodents will have nested elsewhere.

ROSES

Gardeners in the lower elevations need to keep out hungry wildlife, such as javelina. They eat prickly pear in the wild, so a few rose thorns don't bother them. Most repellent coatings simply aren't repellent to javelina. Dried granular coyote urine is commercially available and works for two to three weeks as a deterrent.

Deer in upper-elevation gardens tend to avoid roses, but if they're hungry enough they will munch. A number of repellent coatings work but need to be reapplied after precipitation.

SHRUBS

Other than weeds and wildlife, in the lower elevations shrub problems are negligible this month.

In the upper elevations, a type of damage called snow spread can occur in the months ahead. A number of evergreens and other weak-wooded shrubs can have their branches pulled downward and distorted by heavy snowfall. Before the first snow, bind these shrubs with heavy garden twine. Start at the bottom and pull the twine tight around the shrub in a spiral. Remove this twine after chance of heavy snow is past. Never cover your shrub in plastic; a sunny day can cook a shrub.

TREES

In all elevations, leaf drop is not confined to deciduous trees. Evergreens may ever be green, but that doesn't mean they don't drop litter at some point. Some litter a little bit, all the time, while others litter all at once. A number of evergreen oaks, as well as various species of pine and spruce, shed their three- to four-year-old foliage all at once, often in October.

VINES, GROUNDCOVERS & ORNAMENTAL GRASSES

Weeds steal water and nutrients. Try to catch the cool-season ones while they're little.

In the upper elevations wildlife that bother plants in this category are all those tiny ones that also bother perennials. See that category for treatment.

Deer are now appearing in urban gardens across the Southwest.

November

When is the last time you simply sat in your garden? In most of the Southwest, now is a pleasant time to use your outdoor space. It will be even more useful if you include seating throughout the garden. Not just seating for entertaining, but also spots to rest. Rest is an important part of working in the garden. One needs to stop every so often and check progress. A garden seat is also a place to stop and metaphorically smell the roses—enjoy the plant and animal life around us.

Garden seating can take many forms. Concrete benches are simple, weatherproof . . . and hard on the backside. Wood is nice, but can be a maintenance issue in our arid climate. Metal chairs can get uncomfortably toasty in the summer. Plastic garden chairs decay and break unexpectedly, depositing Aunt Fanny on her fanny. Since there are no ideal solutions, why not have some of each? Garden center clearance sales are worth a look, especially as they clear the aisles now for the onslaught of Christmas items.

This cooler month is ideal for the heavier tasks, such as digging tree-planting holes, turning compost, digging new beds for spring planting, digging amendments into the vegetable garden—unless you have the vegetable garden full of cool-season vegetables or cover crops.

November is a good time to tidy the garden and get everything looking great for the holiday season ahead. Time spent now also eliminates problems later. If you can't work outdoors, now is a good time to organize all your seed packages, plant tags, and garden photos and enter data into your garden journal.

Meanwhile, if you do add some seating to your garden, take some time to use it. Sit, enjoy the fruits of your labor, and just plain enjoy life in this wonderful corner of the globe.

PLAN

A good task for this month is to take care of your garden tools. This is especially good in cooler areas where you are not going to use them for several months. (See Here's How to Clean Your Garden Tools.)

ANNUALS & BULBS

If nights will remain mostly above freezing in your area, you can plan to plant annuals in containers as seasonal decoration.

If it's too cold outdoors, plan on forcing some indoor bulbs. Paperwhites (*Narcissus papyraceus*) are one easy option for bright flowers as part of your indoor holiday decor. Unlike most bulbs, these don't require a chilling period before they bloom. Flowers appear in three to four weeks, so purchase paperwhite bulbs now. If you run across other bulbs on your shopping trip, add some to your cart. Most of the other types take 18 weeks to force, but start them now to ensure indoor blooms for the spring holidays, such as Passover or Easter. (See Here's How to Force to Bulbs to Bloom Indoors.)

EDIBLES

A winter fallow period is an important stage of a vegetable garden's year. If you're not going to plant a winter garden, then plan to help the garden soil during this fallow season. This includes cover cropping or adding manure, compost, and mixing in chopped leaves.

Even when not in bloom, hellebores are attractive in the garden.

LAWNS

Consider reducing your lawn care chores by reducing your lawn area. Look at your lawn objectively and identify areas that are a constant issue, such as shady spots. Shade is a good spot to add a seating area! Flagstone or other hardscape helps make the seating area easy to maintain.

As water restrictions increase throughout the region, some gardeners opt to reduce lawn space with seating areas. Freed from lawn tasks, you will have more time to enjoy the rest of your garden.

PERENNIALS

Even the coldest locations can have a colorful winter garden with the right plantings. Upper-elevation gardeners can start their dream design now by planning where to site plants for the best viewing pleasure. You lucky folks also can grow hellebores (Lenten rose); it's too hot for them in the lowest elevations.

ROSES

Roses don't need to live in a rose bed—they can live virtually anywhere in the landscape. Rose producers offer landscape roses, also called shrub roses, and heirloom or old garden varieties that require little special care and can bloom for months. Now is a good time to order catalogs from rose growers and plan where to add some colorful and fragrant roses, such as 'Carding Mill' or 'Skylark'.

Ornamental grasses really shine in the autumn garden, and you can harvest the seed heads now for dried arrangements.

SHRUBS

Shorter than trees but taller than perennials, shrubs are essential in a landscape. Now that leaves are off many trees, plan where you might add some evergreen shrubs to tie your landscape together—or possibly to block that unobstructed view of your neighbor's hulking RV.

TREES

Gardeners in all elevations should decide now if they want living Christmas trees. You may have to order it from a local nursery, and this can take time. Those in the upper elevations need to dig a planting hole before the ground freezes. No matter where you live, remember to consider mature height and spread of any species you select. (See December, Here's How to Select a Living Holiday Tree.)

VINES, GROUNDCOVERS & ORNAMENTAL GRASSES

Mature trees lose leaves earlier than understory plants such as vines and groundcovers. Now is the chance to plan if you wish to expand the presence of this category of plants in your yard.

PLANT

Gardeners in lower elevations can plant up until mid-month, but it's risky with first frost so near. November is late to plant in all but zone 10.

If upper-elevation gardeners have plants that did not get into the ground, you should store the container out of the elements in an unheated garage. Wrap pots with household blankets to help prevent root damage. You will need to water these stored plants every few weeks, once their soil is dry down 1 inch or so.

ANNUALS & BULBS

Gardeners in the lower elevations can sow seeds of cool-season annuals, including nasturtium, clarkia, and sweet pea. Set out transplants of ageratum, calendula, candytuft, coreopsis, dianthus, English daisy, foxglove, larkspur, lobelia, pansy, scabiosa, snapdragon, and stock. In zone 10, add petunia to the list.

EDIBLES

Those in lower elevations can continue to plant transplants of cool-season vegetables and herbs listed in October. Soils are too cool for most seeds, although if it's been a warm autumn, you can try.

If you're doing a great deal of vegetable gardening, a lighted seed starter rack is a useful alternative to having flats of plants scattered about the house.

HERE'S HOW

TO FORCE BULBS TO BLOOM INDOORS

Encouraging bulbs to flower early is termed forcing, but it requires very little force. The process is more like coaxing, or maybe hoaxing. You have to fool the bulb into thinking it's spring, a surprisingly easy thing to do. There are just four key factors: the right variety, good drainage, planting, and good culture or care while growing.

- **Get the right stuff.** From the list below, select individual bulbs that are large for their species. Larger bulbs will have more stored energy to put into flowers.
- **Good drainage.** Drainage is essential for bulbs, and container selection is key for drainage. If using soil, be sure that drainage holes are adequate. Use a potting soil mixed with one third perlite and one third sand. Succulent mix is ideal.

  You can also force bulbs in water. You will need a container that will hold the bulbs above water and allow only the roots to submerge, such as a dish with pebbles or colorful marbles.
- **Planting time.** Count back from when you want the floral display. Different species take differing amounts of time.
- **Planting depth.** Forced bulbs are planted shallower than normal bulbs. Place so that ¾ of the bulb shows above the soil.
- **Proper watering.** Part of good drainage is proper watering. Allow the soil to dry fairly well between waterings, but not bone-dry. Once bulbs show green leaves, keep the soil a little more moist.
- **Temperature and light.** If you purchase a bulb prepared for forcing, it has received any chilling required. Hyacinth and narcissus are two exceptions: they don't require chilling and should be planted as soon as you buy them.
- **Chill the planted, moistened, bulbs** in a dark, unheated garage or the shady north side of the house under a roomy cardboard box. The time to chill is roughly ⅓ of the total time to bloom—thus about three weeks for a nine-week bulb. After the ⅓ chilling time, uncover the pot and expose to filtered or low light for another ⅓ of the total time. Finally, expose to warmer temperatures inside the house. Don't forget to water them during this process.

- **Care of bulbs that are showing growth.** Keep the soil moist. For longer lasting blooms, avoid direct sunlight. You may need to stake taller flowers.
- **Great kid project.** If you don't want to try it with costly flowering bulbs, why not try forcing a supermarket onion or garlic? A small pot with garlic or onion can easily grow in the kitchen windowsill.
- **Bulb safety.** Many bulbs have toxic defensive compounds. Toxic bulbs are extremely bitter tasting, so ingestion is rare; but if ingestion does occur, induce vomiting. Seek medical care if pet or child becomes lethargic or displays abnormal symptoms.

RECOMMENDED BULBS FOR FORCING	TIME FROM PLANTING TO FLOWERING
Amaryllis	7 to 8 weeks
Crocus	12 weeks
Daffodil	5 to 6 weeks
Gladiolus	8 to 12 weeks
Grape hyacinth (*Muscari*)	4 weeks
Hyacinth	10 weeks
Lily-of-the-valley	3 to 4 weeks
Narcissus	4 weeks
Ornithogalum	5 weeks
Squill (*Scilla*)	4 to 6 weeks

Cover seed with dark-colored seed-starting mix or potting soil to help warm the soil around them.

Those in the lower elevations can plant container-grown deciduous fruit and nut shrubs. Southwest natives Mexican elderberry (*Sambucus mexicana*) and western sand cherry (*Prunus besseyi*) tolerate planting this late.

LAWNS

In the warmest areas, you can continue to overseed lawns as described in October.

PERENNIALS

In the lower elevations, plant container-grown, winter-blooming native perennials, such as desert marigold and Angelita daisy.

ROSES

Lower-elevation gardeners can plant the hardier heirloom and old garden roses this month, such as the cultivars 'Paul Shirville' or 'Joseph's Coat'.

SHRUBS

Lower-elevation gardeners can plant some of the more cold-tolerant native shrubs, such as squaw bush (*Rhus trilobata*) or Mojave Desert sage (*Salvia dorii* var. *dorii*).

TREES

Avoid planting trees this month in all but zone 10.

VINES, GROUNDCOVERS & ORNAMENTAL GRASSES

It's too late to plant vines and groundcovers in all but zone 10. Avoid planting ornamental grasses this month in any zone.

CARE

In areas of occasional freezes, be sure you have frost-protection materials on hand. (See October, Here's How to Protect From Freezes.)

ANNUALS & BULBS

Lower-elevation care for annuals includes removing the last of warm-season annuals and weeding the flower beds. Deadhead spent flowers of cool-season annuals to promote new blooms.

Upper-elevation garden care is to get rid of frost-killed annuals before they rot. Ornamental cabbages can smell particularly foul.

Gardeners who dug up and stored summer bulbs (such as amaryllis or dahlia) should check on them. Inspect the bulbs and discard any diseased ones before the disease can spread. (See September, Here's How to Store Summer-Blooming Bulbs.)

EDIBLES

Lower-elevation gardeners should be ready to protect recently planted seedlings from frost.

Harvest fruits and nuts that are ripening now, such as pecans, persimmon, pomegranates, and tangerines. You have five to six weeks in late autumn to enjoy tangerines, while most other types of citrus ripen later. Pecans right off the tree taste delightful—far better than store bought.

HERE'S HOW

TO KNOW IF FRUIT IS RIPE

When fruits and nuts are fully ripe, the parent plant will take steps to metaphorically "cut the apron strings." They do this by forming a layer of barrier tissue, called an abscission layer, somewhere between themselves and the fruit.

To determine if the fruit is fully ripe, give it a gentle tug. It will easily drop into your hand if ready. Don't yank fruits or cut them off the plant; they will not be fully ripe. Fully ripe fruit will leave the tree without tearing the flesh of the fruit or the stem of the parent plant.

LAWNS

Begin mowing an overseeded lawn once leaf blades are 2 inches tall. With this first mowing, reduce height only slightly, to 1½ inches. After that, you will mow to the heights recommended in Here's How to Select the Mowing Height for Your Lawn (in June).

PERENNIALS

In upper elevations clean up perennials after there has been a hard freeze. The roots are still alive underground, but stems and leaves have turned into a blackened mess. Prune off all aboveground material. If the plant had powdery mildew, throw the clippings in the trash; otherwise, compost them. Once the ground is frozen, add a heavy layer of mulch over the crowns of perennials. You have already mulched the roots; this is an additional layer of protection. Don't do this too soon, because it is an invitation to rodents to move in and nest in the crowns of the plants.

Gardeners in the lower elevations have little perennial care this month, except to maintain mulch to deter weeds, especially in areas of winter rains.

ROSES

Hybrid tea roses are the most sensitive to cold, followed by the floribunda and grandiflora types. Climbers, miniatures, heirlooms, and shrub and old garden varieties are more cold tolerant. If you live in an area of occasional freezes or light freezes, the more highly bred varieties need attention.

In the upper elevations, protect the crowns of roses once the ground is frozen. Add a heavy layer of mulch over the lower 4 to 6 inches of the plants. You mulched the roots in October; this is protection for the crowns.

If you brought containers of roses inside or onto a protected porch, give them a ¼ turn each week so all leaves get ample light and plants do not grow unevenly.

In the lower elevations, you can deadhead spent flowers to promote more bloom. Other than deadheading, don't prune roses this month in any elevation.

Climbing roses are not cut to the ground, so they need other protection in the upper elevations. A wrapping of landscape fabric or burlap helps protect them against deep winter cold.

TREES, SHRUBS, VINES, GROUNDCOVERS & ORNAMENTAL GRASSES

In all elevations, limit any pruning to the three Ds—diseased, damaged, or dead branches and stems.

You can harvest the seed stalks of your ornamental grasses for indoor floral displays, but avoid trimming off any leaves. Grasses need them to protect their crowns and roots from freeze damage.

In all elevations, mulch is used with the plants in this category to protect roots. Avoid mounding it up against trunks or crowns.

HERE'S HOW

TO CARE FOR GARDEN TOOLS

- Start by removing any clinging soil and debris. Soak the tools in a bucket of water and scrub with a wire brush if necessary.
- If tools are badly rusted, use coarse steel wool or 60- to 100-grit sandpaper to remove the rust. Don't obsess over this. A light coating of rust is easily removed when you oil the tools.
- Sharpen the edges of spades, shovels, hoes, and trowels to make digging easier. Use a bench grinder or a mill file.
- Check all your wooden handles for rough spots and splinters. Use 80- to 120-grit sandpaper to smooth them as needed. Don't forget to check wooden wheelbarrow handles.
- Oil everything metal and wood. I do this last, using an old towel soaked in olive oil. Grandpa saved and used the oil from his cars, but I prefer vegetable oil instead of mineral oil for my hands and garden soil.
- Grease your wheelbarrow axle. Grease lasts longer and clings better than oil.
- Treat fiberglass handles with a fiberglass protective coating. Our Southwestern sun and aridity quickly cause fiberglass decay.

Treat your garden tools with some TLC to help protect yourself from injury and to help them last longer.

WATER

For parts of Nevada and Arizona, November means Pacific precipitation will arrive; snow in the upper elevations, rain in the lower. Meanwhile, New Mexico will receive little to no rain this month. Even dormant plants will need some moisture this month, because prolonged dry periods can damage plant roots.

In the lower elevations, the irrigation system maintenance this month is to check emitters and sprinklers. Replace clogged emitters as needed.

ANNUALS & BULBS

Lower-elevation gardeners will need to water cool-season annuals on a regular basis. Wildflower seed should be kept evenly moist until the seedlings emerge; once they have 8 to 12 true leaves, you can taper off. Water is especially needed if we have a warmer than usual fall.

Irrigate any bulbs with leaves every 5 to 10 days. You can water less once leaves die back. In the upper elevations, but especially zone 7, water your spring bulb beds twice this month (if the soil is not frozen).

Gardeners who have dug and stored summer bulbs need to monitor moisture of bulbs stored in media, such as canna and dahlia. Check once each month, and moisten the peat moss or sawdust as needed. Avoid pouring water on the bulb clumps themselves.

EDIBLES

Recently planted seedlings of cool-season vegetables need daily watering. Any seeds, including cover crops, also need to be kept evenly moist. Once the vegetable garden is better established you can water every three to five days. For other edibles, see the section for their growth form (shrubs, groundcovers) for water tips.

In the upper elevations, if you have asparagus or rhubarb beds, check their soil. Water once this month if there's little or no rain. If the ground is frozen, don't water.

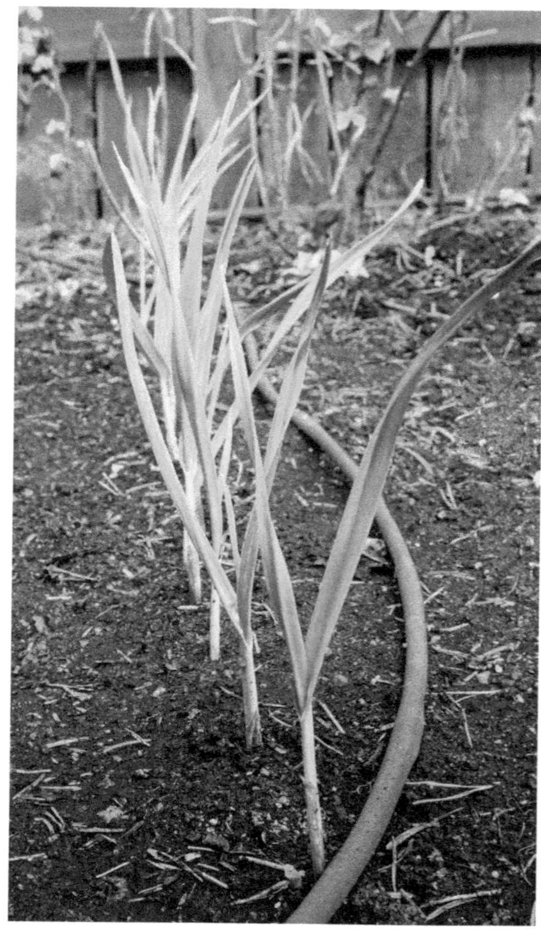

In a winter garden in the lower elevations, a soaker hose or drip tube is better for water than a hose because it keeps water off foliage in these colder months.

LAWNS

In lower elevations, you should water warm-season lawns that are going dormant at least once this month to help them go into dormancy unstressed. Cool-season and overseeded lawns need water every 5 to 10 days, depending on temperatures in your area.

In the upper elevations, if the ground is not frozen, water lawns that were seeded or sodded in the last year. This is especially important for fall-seeded lawns early in the month, because then the lawn will better withstand freezing weather.

PERENNIALS

It's important that any recently planted perennials do not dry out. Dry soil at this point can kill them, so pay particular attention to any perennials you divided this fall. Check their soil and apply water, even if this means hauling out hoses in the upper elevations. Water early in the day, so any splashes onto foliage can dry. Once soil is frozen, you no longer need to check them.

Succulents from the Mojave and Sonoran Deserts of Nevada and Arizona are genetically programmed to respond to the winter rains off the Pacific. Water these at least once this month. Succulents from the Chihuahuan Desert of eastern Arizona and New Mexico grow with summer rains off the Gulf of Mexico, and thus are mainly winter dormant. These will not need water this month. Don't know where your succulents are from? No worries! As long as they are growing in well-drained soil, dormant succulents will not be harmed by winter irrigation.

ROSES

In all elevations, the transitional seasons, both spring and fall, can be very hard on roses. One day, freezing winds; next day it's sunny and warm. Use your soil probe to check the soil every 5 to 14 days as long as it is still above 45°F in your area. Upper elevations should water at least twice this month if the soil remains unfrozen. Lower elevations may need to irrigate roses four to six times this month.

SHRUBS

Smaller shrubs and any recently planted ones will have an especially tough time if it is windy or unseasonably warm. Check recently planted shrubs every four to seven days; established ones every 7 to 14 days. Water shrubs whose soil is dry below 3 inches. Try to water early in the day and when highs are expected to be above 45°F.

In all elevations, evergreens do not shed their leaves or needles and thus need more water than deciduous plants. In upper elevations, give them at least one good watering this month before the ground freezes solid. In zone 7 and warmer, this might be twice this month, especially if it's windy.

TREES

If you live in an area of autumn rain, that rainfall may be enough for established trees, but it won't be sufficient for any trees still establishing themselves. Be sure you pamper young trees with enough irrigation so that they have sufficient resources to survive the winter.

Evergreens lose moisture from their foliage all winter long. Irrigate as necessary to avoid winter stress. This is especially important in upper elevations. Provide a deep watering before the ground freezes, so plants will survive into spring without permanent damage.

VINES, GROUNDCOVERS & ORNAMENTAL GRASSES

Vines in upper elevations are primarily deciduous. To help them into winter dormancy, water them deeply early in the month.

Many vines in lower elevations are evergreen and require irrigation through the winter. Some vines, such as Cape honeysuckle (*Tecoma capensis*), are cold deciduous, losing leaves only if it gets too cold for them. In a mild winter they may not lose any leaves at all. Gardeners in the warmer zones should continue to monitor moisture levels for all vines right through the winter.

In the upper elevations, evergreen groundcovers such as junipers need water every 14 to 21 days if soil is not frozen. Lower-elevation groundcovers will still need regular irrigation, especially any in bloom, such as the native verbenas.

Ornamental grasses will need water during prolonged dry periods. Their leaves may be brown but the central crown is still living and can be killed by excessive drying. Ornamental grasses need water every 10 to 21 days if it has not yet frosted in your area.

As winter approaches, the sun's angle shifts. Some areas of the garden may get more sun, and thus those plants will need more water.

FERTILIZER

It's best to skip fertilizer this month in all areas in the Southwest. If you're gardening indoors, fertilize minimally this month.

PROBLEM-SOLVE

ANNUALS & BULBS

In the lower elevations, remove weeds in annuals and especially in wildflower beds. Aphids can gain a foothold in weeds and move to other plants in your garden.

In the upper elevations, check annuals you brought indoors. If they have pests such as spider mites or whiteflies, decide if you want to fuss with treating them with insecticidal soap. It might be a better option to discard infested annuals before pests spread to other indoor plants.

EDIBLES

Weeds and wildlife are the two main issues facing edibles this month.

In the lower elevations, many birds, including quail, seem to be hungry for a dose of green tonic in the form of newly planted vegetables. You may have to install bird netting over a winter garden.

In the warmest areas, watch for harlequin cabbage bugs and cabbage looper caterpillars on cabbage family plants. The best control for the home gardener is to simply remove these pests by hand and toss them in a bucket of soapy water. Incidentally, don't throw this soapy water away once the pests are killed; tip it onto compost or under shrubs. Used in moderation, the soap will not harm plants, and can help the water-holding capacity of our alkaline soil (which is why greywater systems work so well in the Southwest).

Be ready to protect frost-tender fruits such as citrus. Some of the other tropicals, such as pineapple guava (*Acca sellowiana*, formerly *Feijoa sellowiana*), are hardy into the mid-teens.

In all elevations, fruit trees and shrubs, especially young ones in the rose family, may be visited by hungry herbivores, including deer, elk, rabbits, javelina, and the occasional porcupine; plus the small ones, including mice, pack rats, and rabbits. All of these gnaw on bark. If they *girdle* a plant (gnaw bark off completely around the trunk), this will kill it.

There are many home remedies against herbivores, including bars of scented soap, mothballs, and mesh bags of human hair. A number of commercial deterrents, such as garlic spray and granular coyote urine, are effective, but they need frequent reapplication. The most reliable deterrent is a wire mesh cage made of hardware cloth, wrapped around the trunk and staked to the ground so it can't be knocked over.

LAWNS

Eliminate weeds in lawns while they are small. If you wait too long, your lawn will bear the scars of winter weeds when it regreens in spring. Weeding

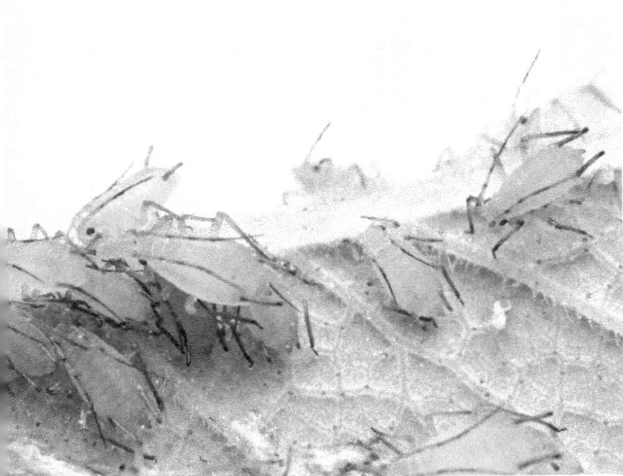

Aphids can still be a problem on roses and other plants this month in the lower elevations.

now will save you the effort, not to mention the cost, of sodding or seeding later.

PERENNIALS

If you grow succulents, be ready to protect them from frost. Some people place Styrofoam cups over growing tips of frost-tender cacti such as organ pipe. This is fine for the short term, but don't leave them in place all winter. If your succulents are in containers, move them to the porch or a similar well-protected and brightly lit area for winter.

In all elevations, drying winds can be problematic, especially for newly planted or transplanted perennials. A protective layer of mulch can help them survive. Select mulch that will mat down, such as pine needles, that will be less likely to blow away. Renew as needed. In the upper elevations, you may wish to construct a low windscreen made from landscape fabric or burlap. Fasten it to stakes at the windward side of the beds (generally the west).

ROSES

Aphids and spider mites may still appear in the lower elevations. Use a blast of water from the hose or a soapy spray to treat them. Do this early in the day when roses have ample time to dry before a cold night.

In the upper elevations, check roses you brought indoors for aphids and spider mites. Remove by hand, use insecticidal soap, or give the plants a rinse in the sink. Use cool (60 to 70°F) water, not ice-cold water.

SHRUBS & TREES

Protect tender bark from hungry herbivores as discussed in Edibles.

In upper elevations, trees can suffer winter sunscald. We think of summer sun intensity and its ability to burn, but winter sun can be equally as injurious, even to healthy trees. During warm winter days, the sun warms the exposed bark of the trunk and main branches on the southwest side. At night, temperatures fall rapidly below freezing, and this alternate cooling and warming injures the bark tissues. The bark can tear microscopically at first, opening the door to pests and diseases. If you pruned a young tree late in the season, exposing trunk that had been shaded, wrap these tender trunks with burlap or shadecloth.

VINES, GROUNDCOVERS & ORNAMENTAL GRASSES

In all elevations, hungry herbivores may visit your garden to dine on almost all your plants. A stout fence or wall may be the only deterrent.

Protect young tree trunks from gnawing rodents and other hungry herbivores by using wire mesh cages.

December

December, the darkest month of the year, need not darken your spirits. Many people stress out now, wanting everything to be perfect. Many overspend. One way to save your nerves and your budget is to do some decorating using your garden.

Evergreens are great. The Southwest abounds with evergreens, such as juniper, pine, arborvitae and cypress. Prune some—yours or those of a neighbor (with their permission of course). Don't like the idea of pruning your trees, or are they too tall? Virtually every Christmas tree retailer will let you salvage leftover cut branches; it saves them from hauling them off to the dumpster. You can tie boughs to a wire wreath form or simply place branches in decorative vases. Want some red berries? Nandina, mountain ash, and pyracantha all offer some at this time of year.

Miss getting out in the garden? You can still play with plants if you give them as gifts. Many plants can live for years in containers, making great gifts for people with small gardens. For the cook, consider a potted herb such as bay laurel or rosemary. For others, roses make a wonderful gift, especially the miniature and heirloom varieties. Succulents are durable gifts for everyone. Many species pup readily so check your own collection before you run to the nursery.

There are advantages to plants as gifts. First, you get to use them as home decorations right up until gift time, and no one expects them to be gift wrapped. Get some extras to have on hand in case you forgot someone. (Or at least this is the story you can give your spouse.) It is thoughtful to include plant saucers when you give plants as gifts.

The main thing to remember is to relax and enjoy the season. There's very little to do in the garden this month, except perhaps to sit in it. Rest your eyes and spirit with the beauty of nature.

PLAN

In all elevations, winter is a good time to get ahead of tasks such as cleaning old pots, oiling wooden handles of garden tools, and greasing your wheelbarrow. (See November, Here's How to Care for Garden Tools.)

Catching up on your garden journal during long winter nights is a good idea too. It will make planning under the onslaught of gardening catalogs easier.

ANNUALS & BULBS

One way to envision spring is to leaf through garden catalogs, be they from last year or newly arrived. If your family is stumped on what gifts to get you, add a gift certificate for bulbs from your favorite plant supplier to your wish list.

EDIBLES

Plan to add sweet potatoes in your vegetable garden next spring, but meanwhile grow them as a lush indoor plant. (See Here's How to Grow Sweet Potato Slips.)

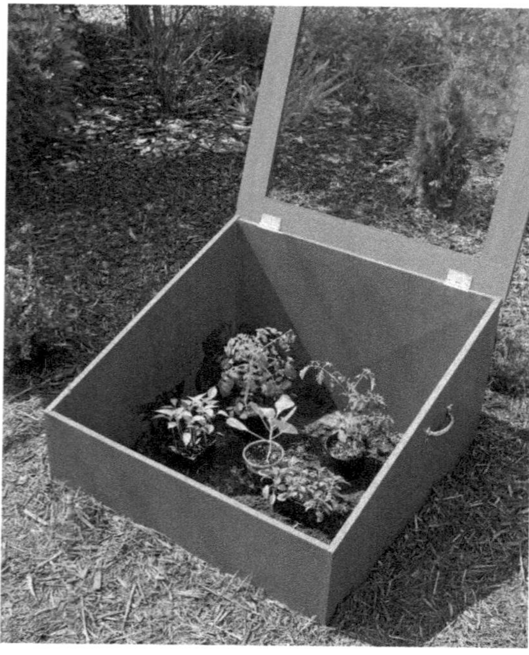

Plan for setting out transplants next spring by constructing a cold frame now.

If you wish to add an unusual or hard-to-find fruiting plant to your garden, it's not too soon to place your order. You may have to hunt for a supplier, and often stocks are limited.

Consider adding rosemary to your garden repertoire. It lives in containers indoors in winter or quite well outdoors in our Southwest soils in the lower elevations. Some stores offer them now—sheared into Christmas tree form, but they will revert to a more natural shrub form in a few months. Note that these plants are generally treated with systemic biocides and are not safe to cook with for 12 to 16 weeks after purchase.

LAWNS

Continuing the theme of reducing lawn care chores by reducing lawn size, consider replacing lawn with a shade structure such as a gazebo or ramada. With a solid surface beneath them, these make lovely spots to add table and chairs for garden dining or entertaining. In addition, consider an outdoor kitchen. Anytime you can cook outdoors in summer, you'll save money cooling the house.

PERENNIALS

Although this isn't a good month to plant perennials, there's no reason why you can't plan to add some once the weather warms. Look for good spots.

ROSES

Start looking for locations to put bare-root roses when they become available. This could be as soon as January in the lower elevations, but not until April in the upper elevations. Consider adding roses outside of a rose bed. There are so many types to select from.

SHRUBS

Shrubs not only tie together the landscape and block unsightly views, but they also help define property lines. As you plan, just make sure they don't interfere with the use of your driveway.

Instead of a living holiday tree, how about a living holiday *shrub*? One friend charmingly used a sugar sumac (*Rhus ovata*), which looked quite nice decked out with holiday ornaments. A decade later,

HERE'S HOW

TO SELECT A LIVING HOLIDAY TREE

- Check the mature size of the plant before you buy it, making sure it will fit in your yard. Many of these trees get quite large.
- Choose a species that will thrive in your elevation and overall environment. Afghan pine is an excellent choice for smog-ridden areas, whereas bristlecone tolerates very little smog.
- At the nursery, avoid plants showing poor vigor or evidence of mishandling. Discoloration (yellowing or browning) or needle shedding may indicate serious damage that may kill the tree or require years to overcome.

Living Christmas trees make a nice addition to the landscape. Ideally, plan where you will plant one before you buy it.

- Nevada and New Mexico can consider using your official state tree for your holiday tree (see below). The Arizona state tree, palo verde, is evergreen but not very festive.

BELOW 5,000 FEET:

Afghan or Eldarica (*Pinus eldarica*), 70' × 30'

Aleppo pine (*Pinus halepensis*), 60' × 30'

Canary Island pine (*Pinus canariensis*), 60' × 30'

Italian stone pine (*Pinus pinea*), 60' × 30', source of pine nuts

BETWEEN 4,000 AND 7,500 FEET:

Pinyon pine (New Mexico state tree; *Pinus edulis*), 20' × 20', source of pinyon nuts

Single-leaf pinyon pine (Nevada state tree; *Pinus monophylla*), 20' × 25', source of pinyon nuts

Longleaf pine or chir pine (*Pinus roxburghii*), 60' × 30'

Southwestern white pine (*Pinus strobiformis*) 100' × 40'

Austrian pine (*Pinus nigra*), 100' × 30'

Scots pine (*Pinus sylvestris*) 50' × 30'

ABOVE 6,500 FEET:

Blue spruce, Colorado spruce (*Picea pungens*), 100' × 40'

Bristlecone pine (*Pinus aristata*), 30' × 15'

Douglas fir (*Pseudotsuga menziesii*), 80' × 25'

White fir (*Abies concolor*), 60' × 30'

it lives on in her garden, ornamented only with berries in season. Mahonia or pyracantha, although somewhat prickly, could also be used.

TREES

If you like the idea of a living holiday tree, plan for where you will put it before you head to the nursery to buy it. Some species are quite massive when mature, offering both good and bad news. The good news—large trees are nice if you want shade, and trees add to home resale value. The bad news—too much shade means less sun for flowers and vegetables, plus a massive tree can dwarf your home, making it look smaller and less desirable when sale time comes.

VINES, GROUNDCOVERS & ORNAMENTAL GRASSES

If you have ornamental grasses, keep your bird book and binoculars handy! A wide variety of winter birds visit the grasses.

PLANT

ANNUALS & BULBS

In all but zone 10, it's too cool to plant annuals this month. Lower-elevation gardeners should get spring-flowering bulbs into the ground now if you forgot to earlier.

EDIBLES

All elevations can start sweet potatoes indoors for spring planting.

Those in zones 8 and colder will not plant a vegetable garden now, but gardeners in lower zones can be busy in the winter vegetable garden. While it's too late to start vegetables from seed, you can use sets from the nursery. Plant onion sets, broccoli, arugula, and autumn kale. Instead of a garden plot, vegetable planting can be containers in a protected area, such as a south-facing porch that gets at least five hours of sunlight on the shortest day of the year (usually December 21). Use containers 8 inches deep for lettuce and other greens 14 to 18 inches deep for bigger crops, such as broccoli. You can also plant cool-season annual herb seedlings, including cilantro, parsley, dill, fennel, and calendula.

If your patio gets an average of six hours of winter sun a day, consider a miniature winter garden of cut-and-come-again greens.

LAWNS

There is no lawn planting in December.

PERENNIALS

Those in the lower elevations can plant spring-flowering native perennials now. Consider penstemons, desert zinnia, paperflower, and the globe mallows.

ROSES

In zone 10, you can plant bare-root roses this month, as soon as they appear in reputable nurseries. Bargain prices often mean inferior plants and future problems. Look for thriving canes—ones where the bark is intact and the stem firm and pliable. There should be ample tiny buds but no leaves showing yet. Root systems should include three to five sturdy anchor roots that have a number of secondary and feeder roots. Avoid roses whose canes have been dipped in wax.

When you get them home, keep plants cool and in the shade. The roots should remain moist but not soaking wet until you're ready to plant. Wrap them in a wet cloth; don't set them into a bucket full of water. Plant within one week of purchase.

HERE'S HOW

TO GROW SWEET POTATO SLIPS

Both the "sweet potatoes" and "yams" we eat are the same species (*Ipomea batata*). There are hundreds of varieties to choose from.

Select a firm sweet potato and find a container that will hold the tuber upright without tipping over as the foliage grows. Avoid a narrow-necked container, since you want a plant have ample space to develop many slips. Similar to forcing bulbs, you don't want to overly submerge the tuber. Don't damage the tuber with toothpicks, either—this all too often leads to rot.

Prop the tuber so the bottom of it is off the bottom of the container. Use smooth stones or decorative marbles to prop it up. Add water until the tuber is halfway covered, and place it in a brightly lit, warm location. These are tropical plants, so avoid chilly windowsills.

Add water as needed to keep the tuber partially submerged. Although not required, you can carefully change the water every two to three weeks being cautious to not disturb the tender roots. Sprouts will develop in two to four weeks (photo, left).

In spring (or earlier if the plant is getting too big), slip the shoots off the parent tuber plant. They will readily pull off, roots and all, after 6 to 10 weeks. Transplant the slips into containers with potting soil (photo, right) for planting outdoors once soil temperatures are above 55°F.

SHRUBS

In lower elevations, you can plant heat- and cold-tolerant native shrubs, such as quail bush (*Atriplex lentiformis*) and fourwing saltbush (*A. canescens*). If you don't like the silvery foliage, drought-adapted, nonnative nandina or heavenly bamboo (*Nandina domestica*) comes in a wide selection of foliage tints. Despite the common name, the plant is an entirely different plant family from bamboo and will stay stay small and shrublike.

TREES, VINES, GROUNDCOVERS & ORNAMENTAL GRASSES

It is not ideal to plant any of these this month in the Southwest.

CARE

Little care is needed this month, except protection from freezing and any tidying up work you have

Plant breeders are constantly at work to create new cultivars with enticing new colors, such as this 'Lemon Lime' nandina.

not already completed. If you haven't yet, rake up autumn leaves from deciduous trees. If the trees had no pests or diseases, use this wonderful free mulch under trees and shrubs, but don't mound it right against the trunks where it can cause problems.

ANNUALS & BULBS

In the lower elevations, protect recently planted annuals if freeze is predicted. Plants that have been in the ground for less than two weeks are more susceptible to frost damage than those with well-established root systems. Little annuals can be covered with a thick layer of newspaper tented over them—but not if rain is predicted. Cardboard boxes work well. Anchor the protection with rocks or bricks so it doesn't blow away, but don't forget to take this protection off first thing in the morning so plants can get the sunlight they need.

HERE'S HOW

TO MAKE MULCH THE THRIFTY GARDENER'S WAY

Virtually the entire garden benefits from mulch, yet the cost of purchasing it can be a drawback. Fortunately, you can easily make free mulch. Collect cut branches from Christmas tree retailers. These branches are too bulky to use intact as mulch, so instead, cut them into 4- to 6-inch pieces. These smaller pieces are now ready to be used as mulch.

Some cut evergreens, such as Douglas fir (not a true fir), shed their needles. Others, such as spruce, hold onto their needles. This is the reason to cut the pieces small. I mix species together so that even if the needles drop, I'll still have protective mulch. Note—these evergreens are flammable due to their natural oils. Avoid using this mulch in areas of forest fires or careless cigarette smokers.

This mulch is doubly thrifty. First, you save money by not having to purchase mulch. Second, you save money as a taxpayer by keeping these evergreens out of your area landfills.

Mulch made of evergreens adds green to the winter landscape, at least for a few weeks.

If you have unused annual beds, you can bury raked leaves there. Don't bury leaves in the same beds where you're actively growing bulbs or other plants, because the busy little compost bacteria rob the soil of nitrogen while they work. The bacteria ultimately release nitrogen when they are all done, but meanwhile living plants can suffer.

EDIBLES

Lower-elevation gardeners shouldn't worry about frost in the vegetable garden once plants are established. The warm-season crops are gone and most cold-season crops tolerate mild freezes. But be ready to protect citrus and other tender fruits from frost.

In the upper elevations, mulch perennial vegetables, such as rhubarb and asparagus, once the ground is frozen. You also need to mulch root crops stored in the soil, such as parsnip and rutabaga. Wheat or sorghum straw work well as mulch in the vegetable garden, but don't use hay, even if it's advertised as mulch hay—it often contains weed seeds. This winter mulch layer should be 4 to 6 inches thick to help insulate plants from the cycles of freezing and thawing that can heave them out of the ground. Cut fall-bearing raspberry canes to the ground now, and mulch them as well.

Harvest fruits and nuts as they ripen. (See November, Here's How to Know if Fruit is Ripe.)

The lower-elevation herb garden should be free of annual warm-season herbs at this point. Other lower-elevation landscape herbs discussed through this book are frost tolerant.

In the upper elevations, mulch any herbs you didn't mulch yet or bring them inside, including sage, mint, catnip, and chives. If you did bring herbs inside, give them a ¼ turn each week, so all leaves get ample light and plants grow evenly.

LAWNS

If you have a winter lawn, continue mowing at the recommended height. (See June, Here's How to Select the Mowing Height for Your Lawn.) To maintain a healthy lawn, remove winter weeds and fallen leaves.

PERENNIALS

Protect both recently planted perennials, as well as those growing in containers, from freezes. Just like annuals, perennials that have been in the ground for less than two weeks are more susceptible to frost than those with well-established roots. Cover perennials with cardboard boxes, household blankets, or frost cloth. Anchor the protection with rocks or bricks so it doesn't blow away, but don't forget to take this protection off first thing in the morning. Have the materials on hand to protect cold-tender succulents from frost.

In the upper elevations, once the ground is frozen you will add a heavy layer of mulch over the crown of your perennials. Keep watch on this protective layer, as wind may blow it away. You can anchor the mulch down with chicken wire or landscape cloth held in place with landscape staples.

ROSES

No rose pruning is required this month at any elevation.

In the upper elevations, if you haven't yet, protect roses from winter as discussed in October.

SHRUBS & TREES

The only pruning required this month in all elevations is pruning the three Ds—diseased, damaged, or dead branches and stems. If you are pruning for holiday display, prune carefully to maintain the overall form of your plant.

To avoid future problems, such as fungus or bare patches, rake leaves off your lawn.

Ornamental grass seedheads can be striking. Harvest some for indoor use or leave them for winter interest in the garden.

In the lower elevations, don't worry if some desert plants lose their leaves. Many are what is termed "cold deciduous." In a warm winter they may not lose any leaves at all, but if it gets cold enough, start raking.

VINES, GROUNDCOVERS & ORNAMENTAL GRASSES

No pruning is required this month by plants in this category, although you can harvest seed stalks from your ornamental grasses for indoor floral displays.

In the upper elevations, if you haven't yet, add a 3- to 4-inch layer of mulch over the roots of plants in this category, especially if they are newly planted. Mulch will help protect them from temperature fluctuations and help hold in soil moisture.

WATER

Many Southwest cities base your annual sewer rate on the amount of water used during December. If this is the case in your area, consider landscape watering in moderation during this slow growth month. You can also recycle household water as described in Here's How to Collect Water Inside the House (in July). Unless it rains, you'll need to water some, because even dormant plants need water.

In the lower elevations, the irrigation system maintenance this month is to switch the controller to the winter schedule.

ANNUALS & BULBS

Ecologists have determined that our native winter wildflowers, such as gold poppy and desert bluebells, grow best with rain every 10 to 14 days. If the weather doesn't cooperate, it will be up to you to irrigate these tiny plants.

Water bulb beds at least once this month if the soil isn't frozen.

EDIBLES

In the upper elevations, if you have asparagus or rhubarb beds, check their soil. Water once this month if there's little or no rain, but if the ground is frozen, don't water.

Active fruit trees and shrubs (citrus, loquat) need water once the soil around their feeder roots is dry lower than 3 inches. This may be as often as every two weeks in warm locations. Dormant deciduous fruit and nut trees need water once this month if the soil remains unfrozen. Date palms will need water once this month, as well.

LAWNS

In all elevations, if the ground isn't frozen, monitor the moisture level of any lawn you installed in the past year. Irrigate early on a sunny day if the soil

Even in the cooler areas, cold may not kill plant foliage. Sunshine plus leaves equals photosynthesis, and thus plants will need water.

is dry below 2 inches. Winter drying can lead to a failure to thrive next spring. Be extra vigilant if you live in a windy area.

PERENNIALS

In the lower elevations, any winter-blooming perennials, such as Europs daisy or justicia, will need more water than any nonblooming perennials.

South African succulents, including aloe, bulbine, gasteria, and haworthia, are gearing up for winter flowering—some may even start this month. Be sure they get irrigated, but allow the soil to dry before you water again.

In upper elevations, until there is a major freeze and winter truly sets in, perennials need water during prolonged dry periods. Use a trowel to check the soil under the mulch and water early on a sunny day if the soil is dry below 2 inches deep.

ROSES

In all elevations, roses will need water; exactly how much depends on local conditions. Pull back some mulch and use a cultivator or hand trowel to check the soil. If it is dry 2 to 3 inches below the surface, water early on a sunny day. Be sure to also check after a period of wind or prolonged drought. Water container roses, indoors or out, once their potting soil is dry 1 inch below the surface.

SHRUBS

Sonoran and Mojave Desert succulents should be watered once this month. Chihuahuan Desert succulents are winter dormant and need no water this month.

There is recent evidence that winter water helps saguaros in their juvenile growth phase. If you have a young saguaro you want to help get bigger faster, water the soil around its roots once or twice every winter month on a warm, sunny day.

TREES

In all areas with unfrozen soil, irrigate all your trees—drought adapted or not, evergreen or not—once this month. Any recently planted trees still becoming established, including palms, should be watered once the soil around their feeder roots is dry lower than 3 inches.

Don't forget to provide water for our fine-feathered friends, especially if you have gone to the trouble to establish a wildlife-friendly garden. You may need a birdbath with a built-in heater to keep the water from freezing.

VINES, GROUNDCOVERS & ORNAMENTAL GRASSES

If you water on a regular basis, don't stop cold turkey. Evergreen groundcovers and vines especially will suffer. Indeed, in lower elevations some plants, such as the lilac vine and black dahlia groundcover, will bloom next month, so be sure they receive ample water now.

Ornamental grasses in nonfrozen soils should be watered once this month. Don't water if the soil is frozen, because the water will simply run off.

FERTILIZE

Don't fertilize in any elevation this month. Even indoor plants don't need the encouragement of fertilizer this month of long, dark nights. Winter lawns also do not need fertilizer in December.

PROBLEM-SOLVE

Mammalian herbivores that move about easily in this cold month are the primary problem in all elevations. Few insect pests or microscopic disease organisms are troublesome outdoors in this cold, dark month.

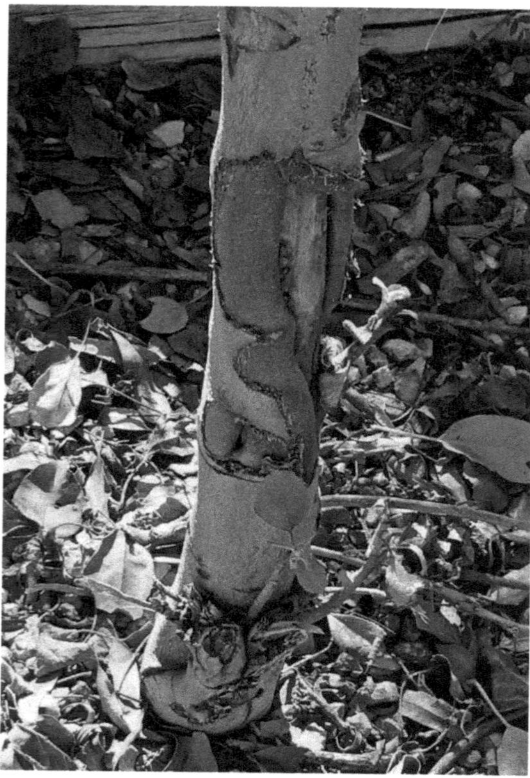

Rabbits and rodents gnaw the bark off a number of species, often killing the plant.

The bark, tender twigs, and roots of virtually all landscape plants are susceptible to all manner of hungry herbivores, including (depending on your location) voles, mice, chipmunks, packrats, ground squirrels, rabbits, javelina, deer, or elk. Confirm that any barriers remain intact after wind, heavy rains, snow, or freezing and thawing cycles and repair as needed.

ANNUALS & BULBS

If you're overwintering annuals indoors, give them a ¼ turn once a week to prevent uneven growth, and while you are at it, check for insect infestations. Meanwhile, aphids may appear on outdoor annuals in the warmest areas. In both these cases, insecticidal soap is a good treatment option.

EDIBLES

In zone 10, aphid and whitefly may appear on cool-season vegetables. On a warm, sunny day you can spray them off with water from a hose. Insecticidal soap is also an option.

Indoor edibles, such as herbs and microgreens, can suffer from some of the same insect pests as

HERE'S HOW

TO RECOGNIZE COMMON PLANT PEST SYMPTOMS

It takes time to get to know your plants and what they are trying to tell you. Being a gardener means you are going to lose plants, but to minimize your losses in the future, learn to recognize these symptoms of pest infestation.

- Tiny beads of sticky sap on stems, leaves, and skin of succulents indicate some sort of sap sucker. It may be aphids, flea beetles, or leaf-footed plant bugs (stink bugs). Look for the cause, and treat as needed.
- Randomly scattered fine webs generally very close to leaves and stems equals spider mites. Another sign is a salt-and-pepper look to the leaves. You need to treat both tops and bottoms of leaves to get rid of this pest.
- Wilting or drooping that doesn't go away after sundown means something is interfering with the roots—generally grubs, but perhaps mice. It could also be overwatering. Be sure you give soil a chance to dry before you water again.
- Leaves become twisted and shriveled, often turning yellow or brown, all within a day or two. Most commonly this is due to herbicide injury. Most virus or fungal issues take longer to develop.

houseplants (spider mites, mealy bug, fungus gnats). Prevention is best, so provide ample light, avoid overwatering, avoid overcrowding, provide some (but not excessive) air movement. Treatment with insecticidal soap may be necessary.

Gardeners in all elevations need to verify that fruit and nut trees and shrubs remain protected. Their bark and tender twigs are especially appealing to deer and elk. In the upper elevations, frost heaves may dislodge anti-mouse collars around the trunks. Resecure the collars to the ground with landscape staples or tent pegs.

LAWNS

In upper elevations, deicing salts can be a real problem for lawns. Ideally use nonsalt deicing products, such as coarse sand, cinders, unused kitty litter, or even alkaline wood ash on your sidewalks and driveways. While these alternatives can cause issues if used excessively, the problems they cause are far easier to correct than the problems caused by sodium salts.

PERENNIALS

In upper elevations, verify that your perennials remain under their protective mulch, because our Southwest winds can be incredible. You may have to lay some chicken wire over the bed to hold the mulch down. Hold the chicken wire in place with landscape staples, tent pegs, or rocks.

ROSES

Aphids may still appear in the lower elevations. Remove by hand or use strong jets of plain or soapy water. Use water early in the day when roses will have ample time to dry before a cold night.

In the upper elevations, this is a good time to check rose winterization. Mice may have moved into the mulch right after you applied it. Disturbing their nest is often enough to send them packing, but you may need to use traps. Mechanical traps work in freezing weather but a number of sticky traps will not. Next year, apply winter mulch only after the ground is frozen.

SHRUBS

In the lower elevations, a hard freeze may damage the top growth on tropical plants, such as red bird of paradise, bougainvillea, and lantana. Leave this frosted material on plants until all future chance of frost is past (last frost day for your area). The dead branches provide an insulating layer over the soil and protect the roots from freezing.

TREES

Winter winds can whip around and threaten the stability of young and newly planted trees (and shrubs). Stake them as described in Here's How to Stake a Tree (in October). You may also want to construct a windscreen of burlap. For trees, make sure it's as wide as your tree is tall. Burlap typically comes in 30-, 45-, and 60-inch widths, so you may have to sew two pieces together. Do not use plastic; it acts like a sail and tends to blow away.

VINES, GROUNDCOVERS & ORNAMENTAL GRASSES

Meadow mice can be an issue under the snow in upper elevations, because they view ornamental grasses as an especially choice home. They rarely kill the grasses, but if they bother you, mechanical traps do work. If you live in an area with coyotes and foxes, it is a delight to watch these predators hunt and pounce in the snow.

Decorate for the holidays using plants from your garden.

Resources

This list offers some resources to help your gardening in the Southwest. Many of these companies have websites that offer valuable growing tips.

Beneficial Insectary
IPM supplies
9664 Tanqueray Ct.
Redding, CA 96003
800-477-3715
www.insectary.com

BioWorks
IPM supplies, plant nutrients
100 Rawson Rd. Ste. 205
Victor, NY 14564
800-877-9443
www.bioworksinc.com

Bountiful Gardens
Herbs and fruit plants
1712-D South Main St.
Willits, CA 95490-4400
707-459-6410
www.bountifulgardens.org

Burnt Ridge Nursery & Orchards
Fruit plants
432 Burnt Ridge Rd.
Onalaska, WA 98570
360-985-2873
www.burntridgenursery.com

DripWorks, Inc.
Irrigation and landscape supplies
190 Sanhedrin Cr.
Willits, CA 95490
(800) 522-3747
www.dripworks.com

High Country Gardens
Fruits, bulbs, lawn alternatives
223 Ave. D, Ste. 30
Williston, VT 05495
800-925-9387
www.highcountrygardens.com

Gardens Alive
IPM supplies, soil inoculants
5100 Schenley Pl.
Lawrenceburg, Indiana 47025
513-354-1482
www.gardensalive.com

Mountain Valley Growers
Organic herbs and perennials
38325 Pepperweed Rd.
Squaw Valley, CA 93675
559-338-2775
www.mountainvalleygrowers.com

Native Seeds/SEARCH
SW landraces and heirloom seed
3584 E. River Rd.
Tucson, AZ 85718
520-622-0830
www.nativeseeds.org

One Green World
Fruit trees and shrubs
6469 SE 134th Ave.
Portland, OR 97236-4540
877-353-4028
www.onegreenworld.com

Old House Gardens
Heirloom bulbs
536 Third St.
Ann Arbor, MI 48103
(734) 995-1486
www.oldhousegardens.com

Peaceful Valley Supply
Fruit nursery, IPM supplies
P. O. Box 2209
Grass Valley, CA 95945
888-784-1722
www.groworganic.com

Plants of the Southwest
Seeds, herbs, fruits and nursery
3095 Aqua Fria Rd.
Santa Fe, NM 87507
800-788-7333 (seed only orders)
505-438-8888 (Santa Fe store)

Albequerque location:
6680 Fourth St. NW
Albequerque, NM 87107
505-344-8830
www.plantsofthesouthwest.com

Raintree Nursery
Fruit trees and shrubs
391 Butts Rd.
Morton, WA 98356
800-391-8892
www.raintreenursery.com

Supreme Growers
IPM supplies, soil inoculants
4543 Turntable Rd.
Chattanooga, TN 37421
844-398-2810
supremegrowers.us

Terrior Seeds
Heirloom vegetable and herb seed
P. O. Box 4995
Chino Valley, AZ 86323
888-878-5247
www.underwoodgardens.com

LOCAL BOTANICAL GARDENS, ARBORETA & ZOOLOGICAL PARKS

Don't forget these nearby places that grow plants. They have a wealth of knowledge to share, including mature examples of any number of the plants mentioned in this book. Don't forget zoological parks—most of them have trained horticulturists on staff, and *their* garden pests come in all sizes.

COOPERATIVE EXTENSION SERVICE

The Cooperative Extension Service websites now offer many easy to read publications on our regional growing conditions. Their office in your county has resources to help you deal with your local growing conditions.

Arizona
www.extension.arizona.edu/pubs

Colorado (useful for upper elevations)
extension.colostate.edu/publications-2

Nevada (search both "Agriculture" and "Horticulture" publications)
www.unce.unr.edu/publications

New Mexico
www.aces.nmsu.edu/pubs

IPM for California (useful throughout our region)
www.UCIPM.ucdavis.edu

Index

Photo Credits

Heather Claus: 89 (bottom)

Corona Tools: 89 (top)

Don Davis: 64

Katie Elzer-Peters: 20 (all), 22 (both), 24 (both), 25 (top left, both), 28 (left), 33 (top), 34 (all), 40 (bottom), 45 (top), 52, 53, 54 (top), 56, 70 (top), 78 (bottom), 93, 100 (bottom), 102, 105 (top), 109, 119, 120 (top), 123 (top), 138 (top), 171, 177 (top), 178 (top)

Eliza Evans: 29 (bottom), 147

Bill Kersey: 38, 55 (top), 70 (bottom), 72, 106, 108 (bottom), 152

Charles Mann: cover, 67

Jerry Pavia: 184 (top)

Plant Development Services, Inc.: 200 (top)

Skip Richter: 173, 175 (both)

Shutterstock: 6, 21, 26, 28 (right), 29 (top), 30, 33 (bottom), 39, 44, 45 (bottom), 46, 48, 50 (both), 51, 59, 60 (top), 65, 77 (top), 79 (top), 80, 83 (bottom), 87 (left, middle), 88 (both), 94 (left, middle), 96 (left, top right), 97 (left, both, and bottom right), 98, 101 (top), 103 (top), 105 (bottom), 108 (top), 111 (bottom), 112 (both), 114, 117 (bottom), 128 (top), 129, 130 (bottom), 131, 135 (bottom), 141 (top), 145 (bottom), 146, 148, 150, 155 (both), 158, 163 (bottom), 164, 165 (bottom), 168, 170 (both), 181 (top), 185 (top), 186, 189 (both), 190, 193 (top), 194, 197, 199 (all), 202 (top), 203

Neil Soderstrom: 68, 176

Jacqueline Soule: 9, 10 (bottom), 11, 12, 13 (both), 16, 18 (bottom), 19, 25 (bottom right), 27, 35, 36 (bottom), 37 (both), 40 (top, all), 41, 43, 49, 54 (bottom), 55 (bottom, all), 57, 60 (bottom), 61, 62, 66, 69 (both), 71, 73, 75, 76, 77 (bottom), 79 (bottom), 83 (top), 87 (right), 90, 91, 96 (middle and bottom right), 97 (top right), 100 (top), 103 (bottom), 107, 111 (top), 113, 116, 117 (top), 120 (bottom), 121 (both), 122 (both), 123 (bottom), 125, 127, 128 (bottom), 130 (top), 132, 134, 138 (bottom), 140, 145 (top), 149, 153 (both), 157, 159, 160, 161, 163 (top), 165 (top), 166, 169, 172, 177 (bottom), 178 (bottom), 179, 180, 181 (bottom), 182, 184, 192, 198, 200 (bottom), 202 (bottom), 204, 205

Mark Turner: 216

US Department of Agriculture: 14–15

Barbara Wise: 84

Meet Jacqueline A. Soule

Jacqueline Soule is a longtime Southwestern gardener and award-winning garden writer. Of her eleven published books, nine are on gardening in our unique climate, including *Southwest Fruit & Vegetable Gardening* for Cool Springs Press. She has been a popular columnist for many years with weekly and monthly *Gardening With Soule* and other regular columns in a number of national, regional, and local publications, including *Arizona/Nevada Lovin' Life News*, *Southwest Trees and Turf*, *Explorer* newspaper, and *Angie's List* magazine.

Dr. Soule grew up in Tucson, and obtained a B.S. in Horticulture and a B.S. in Ecology, Evolutionary Biology from the University of Arizona both with Honors and *cum laude*, then left Tucson to experience life "back East." Academically she acquired an M.S. in Botany from Michigan State University, and a Ph.D. in Botany from the University of Texas, while she discovered gardening in various climates. Included in Dr. Soule's "back East" sourjorns were positions in botanical gardens and arboreta, including the Morris Arboretum in Philadelphia, Chicago Botanic Garden, and the Frederik Meijer Gardens and Sculpture Park in Grand Rapids.

Jacqueline returned to the Southwest in 1997, and has been active in the plant and gardening community ever since, serving in various offices in writing groups and plant societies, clubs, and organizations both locally and beyond, including chairing the board of the international Desert Legume Program. Jacqueline is a popular public speaker and offers numerous lectures, presentations, and classes on plants and gardening for all ages and in various venues around the region.

Jacqueline's garden is the entire landscape around her home, filled with herbs, fruiting plants, raised beds, and containers. There is something to harvest virtually every day of the year from the garden or yard. Jacqueline prefers plants that need as little care as possible, because there is just so much! Her husband Paul appreciates this low-care approach, since he often gets called on to water and help weed. Many of the plants and garden techniques discussed in this book have been tested in Jacqueline's garden.